Advances in

COMPUTERS

VOLUME 82

Advances in
COMPUTERS

EDITED BY

MARVIN V. ZELKOWITZ

Department of Computer Science
University of Maryland
College Park, Maryland
USA

VOLUME 82

AMSTERDAM • BOSTON • HEIDELBERG • LONDON • NEW YORK • OXFORD
PARIS • SAN DIEGO • SAN FRANCISCO • SINGAPORE • SYDNEY • TOKYO
Academic Press is an imprint of Elsevier

ELSEVIER

ACADEMIC
PRESS

Academic Press is an imprint of Elsevier

32 Jamestown Road, London, NW1 7BY, UK
Radarweg 29, PO Box 211, 1000 AE Amsterdam, The Netherlands
30 Corporate Drive, Suite 400, Burlington, MA 01803, USA
525 B Street, Suite 1900, San Diego, CA 92101-4495, USA

First edition 2011

Library of Congress Cataloging-in-Publication Data
A catalog record for this book is available from the Library of Congress

British Library Cataloguing-in-Publication Data
A catalogue record for this book is available from the British Library

ISBN: 978-0-12-385512-1

ISSN: 0065-2458

For information on all Academic Press publications
visit our web site at elsevierdirect.com

Printed and bound in USA

11 12 13 14   10 9 8 7 6 5 4 3 2 1

Working together to grow
libraries in developing countries

www.elsevier.com | www.bookaid.org | www.sabre.org

ELSEVIER   BOOK AID
International   Sabre Foundation

Contents

The Hows and Whys of Information Markets

Areej Yassin and Alan R. Hevner

Measuring and Monitoring Technical Debt

Carolyn Seaman and Yuepu Guo

A Taxonomy and Survey of Energy-Efficient Data Centers and Cloud Computing Systems

Anton Beloglazov, Rajkumar Buyya, Young Choon Lee, and Albert Zomaya

Applications of Mobile Agents in Wireless Networks and Mobile Computing

Sergio González-Valenzuela, Min Chen, and Victor C.M. Leung

Virtual Graphics for Broadcast Production

Graham Thomas

Advanced Applications of Virtual Reality

Jürgen P. Schulze, Han Suk Kim, Philip Weber, Andrew Prudhomme, Roger E. Bohn, Maurizio Seracini, and Thomas A. DeFanti

Contributors

Anton Beloglazov is a Ph.D. candidate at the Cloud Computing and Distributed Systems (CLOUDS) Laboratory within the Department of Computer Science and Software Engineering at the University of Melbourne, Australia. He has completed his Bachelor's and Master's degrees in Informatics and Computer Science at the faculty of Automation and Computer Engineering of Novosibirsk State Technical University, Russian Federation. In his Ph.D. studies, Anton is actively involved in research on energy- and performance-efficient resource management in virtualized data centers for Cloud computing. He has been contributing to the development of the CloudSim toolkit, a modern open-source framework for modeling and simulation of Cloud computing infrastructures and services. Anton has publications in internationally recognized conferences and journals. He is a frequent reviewer for research conferences and journals.

Roger Bohn, Ph.D., is a professor at the School of International Relations and Pacific Studies, University of California San Diego (UCSD), with research on management of technology. He studies engineering and manufacturing in a variety of high-tech industries, including semiconductors (expert witness work), hard disk drives, and information technology. A current project examines the transition from art to science in manufacturing, flying, and medicine. He heads the Global Information Industry Center, which recently completed analyses of information consumption in households and industry. In addition to UCSD, he taught at the Harvard Business School and MIT. He has degrees from Harvard in Applied Mathematics, and from MIT in Management.

Rajkumar Buyya is professor of Computer Science and Software Engineering and director of the Cloud Computing and Distributed Systems (CLOUDS) Laboratory at the University of Melbourne, Australia. He is also serving as the founding CEO of Manjrasoft Pty Ltd., a spin-off company of the university, commercializing its innovations in Grid and Cloud Computing. He has authored and published over 300 research papers and four text books. The books on emerging topics that Dr. Buyya edited include High Performance Cluster Computing (Prentice Hall, USA, 1999), Content Delivery

ix

Networks (Springer, Germany, 2008), Market-Oriented Grid and Utility Computing (Wiley, USA, 2009), and Cloud Computing (Wiley, USA, 2019). He is one of the highly cited authors in computer science and software engineering worldwide. Software technologies for Grid and Cloud computing developed under Dr. Buyya's leadership have gained rapid acceptance and are in use at several academic institutions and commercial enterprises in 40 countries around the world. Dr. Buyya has led the establishment and development of key community activities, including serving as foundation Chair of the IEEE Technical Committee on Scalable Computing and four IEEE Conferences (CCGrid, Cluster, Grid, and e-Science). He has presented over 250 invited talks on his vision on IT Futures and advanced computing technologies at international conferences and institutions in Asia, Australia, Europe, North America, and South America. These contributions and international research leadership of Dr. Buyya are recognized through the award of "2009 IEEE Medal for Excellence in Scalable Computing" from the IEEE Computer Society, USA. Manjrasoft's Aneka Technology for Cloud computing developed under his leadership has received "2010 Asia Pacific Frost & Sullivan New Product Innovation Award."

Min Chen is an assistant professor in School of Computer Science and Engineering at Seoul National University. He received the Best Paper Runner-up Award from QShine 2008. He is TPC cochair for BodyNets 2010. He is managing editor of *International Journal of Autonomous and Adaptive Communications Systems* and an editor/associate editor of *KSII Transactions on Internet and Information Systems*, *Wiley International Journal of Security and Communication Networks*, *Journal of Internet Technology*, and the *International Journal of Sensor Networks (IJSNet)*. He is an IEEE senior member. He can be reached at minchen@ieee.org.

Thomas A. DeFanti, Ph.D., is a research scientist at the California Institute for Telecommunications and Information Technology, University of California, San Diego, and a distinguished professor emeritus of Computer Science at the University of Illinois at Chicago. He is principal investigator of the NSF International Research Network Connections Program Trans-Light/StarLight project, the NSF Green Light Instrument project, and the KAUST Calit2 OptIPresence project. He is recipient of the 1988 ACM Outstanding Contribution Award and was appointed as an ACM Fellow in 1994. He shares recognition along with EVL director Daniel J. Sandin for conceiving the CAVE virtual reality theater in 1991. He can be reached at tdefanti@ucsd.edu.

Sergio González-Valenzuela received the B.E. in electronics (special mention) at Instituto Tecnológico de Sonora in Ciudad Obregón, Sonora, Mexico, in 1995, and the M.A.Sc. and Ph.D. degrees in electrical and computer engineering from the

University of British Columbia (UBC), Vancouver, BC, Canada, in 2002 and 2008, respectively. From 1995 to 1999, he held diverse engineering positions in the Mexican industry. From 2001 to 2002, he worked as a research engineer at the Department of Electrical and Computer Engineering, also in UBC. At present, he is a postdoctoral fellow in the same department. His research interests lie in the areas of wireless sensor networks, body area networks, and ad hoc networks. Dr. González-Valenzuela served in a Technical Program Committee of BodyNets 2010 and Adhocnets 2010, and he continues to participate as guest reviewer of diverse journals and conferences sponsored by IEEE and ACM. He can be reached at sergiog@ece.ubc.ca.

Yuepu Guo received the BS degree in industrial economics from Tianjin University, Tianjin, PR China, in 1996, and the MS degree in information systems from University of Maryland Baltimore County, Baltimore, USA, in 2009. He is a Ph.D. student in the Department of Information Systems at University of Maryland Baltimore County (UMBC). His research interests include software process, maintenance, and evolution. In particular, he is interested in and currently investigating issues of technical debt in software lifecycle, part of which forms his doctoral dissertation. His research on technical debt is funded through an NSF grant by his advisor, Dr. Carolyn Seaman. He can be reached at yuepu.guo@umbc.edu.

Alan R. Hevner is an eminent scholar and professor in the Information Systems and Decision Sciences Department in the College of Business at the University of South Florida. He holds the Citigroup/Hidden River Chair of Distributed Technology. Dr. Hevner's areas of research expertise include information systems development, software engineering, distributed database systems, health care information systems, and service-oriented systems. He has published more than 150 research papers on these topics and has consulted for several Fortune 500 companies. Dr. Hevner has a Ph.D. in computer science from Purdue University. He has held faculty positions at the University of Maryland and the University of Minnesota. Dr. Hevner is a member of ACM, IEEE, AIS, and INFORMS. He recently completed an assignment as a program manager in the computer and information science and engineering directorate at the U.S. National Science Foundation.

Han Suk Kim is a Ph.D. candidate in the Department of Computer Science and Engineering at the University of California, San Diego. His research interests include large-scale scientific visualization, multi-dimensional transfer function in volume rendering, and immersive virtual reality. Dr. Kim received his BS in computer science and engineering from Seoul National University in 2005. His advisor is Dr. Jürgen Schulze. He can be reached at hskim@cs.ucsd.edu.

Young Choon Lee received the Ph.D. degree in problem-centric scheduling in heterogeneous computing systems from the University of Sydney in 2008. He received Best Paper Award from the 10th IEEE/ACM International Symposium on Cluster, Cloud, and Grid Computing (CCGrid 2010). He is a member of the IEEE. His current research interests include scheduling strategies for heterogeneous computing systems, nature-inspired techniques, and parallel and distributed algorithms.

Victor C.M. Leung is a professor and holder of the TELUS Mobility Research Chair in the Department of Electrical and Computer Engineering at the University of British Columbia (UBC). Victor's current research focuses on wireless networks and mobile systems, and he has coauthored more than 500 journal/conference papers and book chapters in these areas. He is a fellow of IEEE, fellow of the Engineering Institute of Canada, and fellow of the Canadian Academy of Engineering. He serves on the editorial board of the IEEE Transactions on Computers, and is a distinguished lecturer of the IEEE Communications Society. He can be reached at vleung@ece.ubc.ca.

Andrew Prudhomme is a virtual reality software developer at the California Institute for Telecommunications and Information Technology (Calit2). He received his B.Sc. degree from the University of California, San Diego, in 2008. The focus of his work is on the research and development of software applications for immersive virtual reality systems. He can be reached at aprudhomme@ucsd.edu.

Jürgen Schulze, Ph.D., at the University of California, San Diego, is a research scientist at the California Institute for Telecommunications and Information Technology, and a lecturer in the Department of Computer Science. His research interests include scientific visualization in virtual environments, human–computer interaction, real-time volume rendering, and graphics algorithms on programmable graphics hardware. He holds an MS degree from the University of Massachusetts and a Ph.D. from the University of Stuttgart, Germany. After his graduation, he spent two years as a postdoctoral researcher in the Computer Science Department at Brown University. He can be reached at jschulze@ucsd.edu.

Carolyn Seaman is an associate professor at University of Maryland Baltimore Country (UMBC) in Baltimore and a scientist at the Fraunhofer Center, Maryland. Her research emphasizes software measurement, maintenance, communication, and qualitative research methods. She holds degrees in computer science and mathematics from the University of Maryland, Georgia Tech, and the College of Wooster (Ohio). She has worked in the software industry as a software engineer and consultant, and has conducted most of her research in industrial and governmental settings. She can be reached at cseaman@umbc.edu.

Maurizio Seracini is the director of the Center for Interdisciplinary Science for Art, Architecture, and Archaeology (CISA3) at the University of California San Diego's California Institute for Telecommunications and Information Technology (Calit2). He is a pioneer in the use of multispectral imaging and other diagnostic tools as well as analytical technologies as applied to works of art and structures. He has studied more than 2500 works of art and historic buildings. He can be reached at mseracini@soe.ucsd.edu.

Graham Thomas joined the BBC Research Department at Kingswood Warren in 1983 after graduating from the University of Oxford with a degree in Physics. His Ph.D. included the development of motion estimation methods for standards conversion, which led to an Emmy award and a Queen's Award. Since 1995 he has been leading a team of engineers developing 3D image processing and graphics techniques for TV production and is currently the Section Lead for Production Magic. His work has led to many commercial products including the *free-d* camera tracking system, Chromatte retroreflective chroma-key cloth, and the Piero sports graphics system. Graham has led or worked in various United Kingdom and European collaborative projects, has written many papers, and holds over 20 patents. He is a chartered engineer and member of the IET. He can be reached at graham. thomas@bbc.co.uk.

Philip Weber is a virtual reality software developer at the California Institute for Telecommunications and Information Technology (Calit2). He received his B.Sc. degree from the University of California, San Diego, in 2007. The focus of his work is on the research and development of software applications for immersive virtual reality systems. He can be reached at pweber@ucsd.edu.

Areej Yassin received her doctoral degree in Information Systems and Decision Sciences from the University of South Florida. Her research specialties are software project management, decision support systems, information markets, and enterprise systems.

Albert Zomaya is currently the chair professor of High Performance Computing and Networking in the School of Information Technologies, The University of Sydney. He is the author/coauthor of seven books, more than 350 publications in technical journals and conferences, and the editor of eight books and eight conference volumes. He is currently an associate editor for 16 journals such as the *IEEE Transactions on Computers, IEEE Transactions on Parallel and Distributed Systems*, and the *Journal of Parallel and Distributed Computing*. He is also the founding editor of the Wiley Book Series on Parallel and Distributed Computing and was the chair of the IEEE

Technical Committee on Parallel Processing (1999–2003) and currently serves on its executive committee. He also serves on the Advisory Board of the IEEE Technical Committee on Scalable Computing and IEEE Systems, Man, and Cybernetics Society Technical Committee on Self-Organization and Cybernetics for Informatics and is a scientific council member of the Institute for Computer Sciences, Social-Informatics, and Telecommunications Engineering (in Brussels). Professor Zomaya is also the recipient of the Meritorious Service Award (in 2000) and the Golden Core Recognition (in 2006), both from the IEEE Computer Society. He is a chartered engineer, a fellow of the American Association for the Advancement of Science, the IEEE, the Institution of Engineering and Technology (UK), and a distinguished engineer of the ACM. His research interests are in the areas of distributed computing, parallel algorithms, and mobile computing.

Preface

This is Volume 82 of the *Advances in Computers*. Since 1960, the *Advances* series has been chronicling the ever-changing landscape of computer technology. The series is now entering its sixth decade of publication, and it is the oldest series covering the development of the computer industry. In this volume, we present six chapters that discuss a variety of topics, including economic models applied to information technology problems, the evolution of the Internet, as well as using the computer to simulate reality. All these represent an evolution of the computer from simply a tool to solve a specific problem to a device that interacts with users in a "semi-intelligent" way.

The first two chapters use economic theory to solve specific information technology problems. In the first chapter, "The Hows and Whys of Information Markets," authors Areej Yassin and Alan R. Hevner discuss the use of information markets to arrive at decisions. It is well known that asking a specific expert to make a prediction is highly imprecise. Techniques such as the Delphi method require a feedback cycle among a small set of experts to arrive at a consensus. This method, while better than single experts, still permits a wide margin of error. In the first chapter, the authors discuss the use of information markets as a business intelligence tool, where an unlimited number of players make their own predictions about future events. The result is that the group produces a highly accurate model of what is likely to happen. This chapter explains this process and gives several examples of its application.

The second chapter, "Measuring and Monitoring Technical Debt" by Carolyn Seaman and Yuepu Guo, discusses a monitoring system for software development that is based upon an economic model that monitors the predicted problems in a software development by the amount that a given artifact is deficient. "Technical debt is a metaphor for immature, incomplete, or inadequate artifacts in the software development lifecycle that cause higher costs and lower quality in the long run," say the authors. In this chapter, the authors discuss the trade-offs of delaying software development decisions (e.g., increasing the technical debt) with the expected rise in problems later in the development. They give several examples of technical debt and provide mechanisms for measuring and addressing issues that later arise using this technology.

In the third chapter, "A Taxonomy and Survey of Energy-Efficient Data Centers and Cloud Computing Systems" by Anton Beloglazov, Rajkumar Buyya, Young Choon Lee, and Albert Zomaya, the authors discuss a rapidly growing model for computing today—Cloud computing. With this model, users access information somewhere on the Internet (i.e., "the Cloud"). This means that they are not tied down to accessing their information on a specific computer. In addition, they can access their data from numerous other locations, potentially from any other computer connected to the Web. In this chapter, the authors focus on one specific aspect of using "the Cloud." They discuss energy efficiency (i.e., "green computing") of hardware, operating system, virtualization, and data center designs.

The forth chapter is concerned with perhaps the opposite problem of the previous chapter on Cloud computing. With Cloud computing, the user is unconcerned about where in the network a particular piece of information resides as long as the user can retrieve the information reliably and that the system has sufficient integrity and security to protect that information. In "Applications of Mobile Agents in Wireless Networks and Mobile Computing" by Sergio González-Valenzuela, Min Chen, and Victor C.M. Leung, the problem is how to best use mobile agents. A mobile agent is a software program that can sense its own environment and best adapt its operations to that environment. Thus, a mobile agent can reside on a cellular telephone, portable device, or fixed-location computer and best adapt its operations to that environment. In this chapter, the authors present the general problem with mobile agents and then discuss their *Wiseman* approach toward solving that problem.

The fifth chapter is entitled "Virtual Graphics for Broadcast Production" and is authored by Graham Thomas. Anyone who has watched television recently or seen many feature films has probably marveled at the seamless integration of animation with live action film. How is that accomplished? In particular, in live television, the merging of what a camera sees and what is broadcast to the viewer at home has to be accomplished in real time in a fraction of a second. In this chapter, Dr. Graham reviews the history of virtual graphics in television production and presents an overview of television graphics today.

In the sixth chapter, the last chapter of this volume, Jürgen P. Schulze, Han Suk Kim, Philip Weber, Andrew Prudhomme, Roger E. Bohn, Maurizio Seracini, and Thomas A. DeFanti in "Advanced Applications of Virtual Reality" presents an evolution in graphics over the television graphics of the fifth chapter. In this case, they discuss "virtual reality" where the user is embedded in an environment that simulates an aspect of the real world. By virtual reality they mean a system that includes devices for rendering high-quality graphics, 3D stereo display units for presenting that information, and a tracking system to serve as the interface between the user and the system. They discuss the problems of virtual reality and then present their systems, StarCAVE and NextCAVE, as research examples of where this technology is heading.

I hope that these topics provide you with needed insights in your work. I also want to say that I have enjoyed producing these volumes. I have been series editor of the *Advances in Computers* since 1993, and Volume 82 is the 42nd volume I have worked on in 19 years. The 2011 volumes will be my last; however, the series will continue under new competent leadership. I hope that you will continue to find this series of use to you in your work.

Marvin Zelkowitz
College Park, Maryland

The Hows and Whys of Information Markets

AREEJ YASSIN

*Information Systems and Decision Sciences,
University of South Florida, Tampa, Florida, USA*

ALAN R. HEVNER

*Information Systems and Decision Sciences,
University of South Florida, Tampa, Florida, USA*

Abstract

The use of information markets as a business intelligence (BI) technique for collecting dispersed intelligence and forming knowledge to support decision making is growing rapidly in many application fields. The objective of this chapter is to present a focused survey of how information markets work and why they produce accurate and actionable knowledge upon which effective decisions can be based. Numerous exemplars from the literature are described and key future research directions in information markets are highlighted.

ADVANCES IN COMPUTERS, VOL. 82
ISSN: 0065-2458/DOI: 10.1016/B978-0-12-385512-1.00001-3

1

1.   Business Intelligence and Information Markets

The key to any business intelligence (BI) tool is the ability to aggregate information from many disparate sources, summarize it into meaningful measures, and display it appropriately in forms usable by decision makers. The capabilities of BI tools have changed dramatically since the term was first coined by Luhn [1], but the main objective of BI tools is, and will always be, to inform decisions. BI tools can uncover trends or patterns that were previously unknown and improve the quality of inputs to the decision-making process [2]. They can also forecast future events such as product sales, market trends, and project delivery dates. Project managers can be provided with a realistic view of existing conditions to improve management understanding of current situations to help managers form more realistic expectations of performance.

The spirit of BI lies at the heart of *information markets*. Much of the enthusiasm for using information markets as a method for eliciting forecasts and aggregating information held by individual members of an organization comes from the strong-held belief in the power of collective intelligence (i.e., wisdom of the crowds) to overcome the limitations of the various other methods of forecasting and information aggregation. Teams and individuals of an organization oftentimes feel they do not have enough information or insight to inform business decisions, such as those related to demand forecasting, market assessment, and production planning, thus, the need for an effective technique like information markets.

Information markets can be used to transfer information and intelligence from those who have it, to those who need it to make decisions [3]. Drawing from fundamental notions of rational self-interest, free markets of trade in materials, services, and ideas, and collective wisdom/intelligence of the crowd, we survey in this chapter the hows and whys of information markets. Exemplars from real use provide convincing evidence of the power and usefulness of information markets in many fields. We end with a call for future research directions in a number of promising areas.

2. Information Markets Theory Base

To begin, it is important to appreciate the broad base of theory from economics and other sociotechnical disciplines that ground current research and application of information markets.

2.1 Hayek Hypothesis

Information markets are a distinct form of futures markets whose main purpose is to aggregate information about uncertain future events. The ability of markets to aggregate information dispersed among individuals can be traced back to Smith [4] and his invisible hand theory. The invisible hand process works via free markets and division of labor where outcomes are produced in a decentralized way with no explicit agreement between thousands of independent, utility-maximizing agents, whose aims are neither coordinated nor identical with the actual outcome, yet bringing wealth to their nations. This vision of decentralized planning of economies that secures the best use of knowledge in society is what Hayek [5] believed can only be maintained through the free markets price system.

Thus, according to the Hayek hypothesis, a society is composed of individuals, each spatially separated from others or decentralized, who have only partial local knowledge of a phenomenon. Each individual's thoughts and beliefs are diverse and independent. It does not matter if only few know about a certain circumstance, as long as they all act and think independently seeking their own self-interest. Under these conditions, free markets can collect, coordinate, and ensure cooperation where the whole act as one bringing about, in form of prices, a collective wisdom purified from cognitive problems of those few [6].

2.2 Rational Expectations Theory

The information aggregation property of prices is what gives rise to information markets. This property is formalized by Muth [7] in the theory of rational expectations and price movement. According to rational expectations theory, individuals take all available information into account in forming expectations about future events.

In a perfectly competitive market, the rational expectation equilibrium is the intersection point of supply and demand curves. Buyers and sellers make sequential trades at discrete points in time with imperfect information bringing about the price observed in the market. The process of acquiring information in the market advances traders through different states ranging from no information to perfect information. As traders discover and learn, they adjust their expectations, and the observed price consequently evolves in a series of disequilibrium price adjustments to an expected price which theoretically should soon become the equilibrium [8].

2.3   Random Walk Theory

Understanding prices' behaviors and their formation process in order to predict future prices has attracted economists, market analysts, and investors' attention for many years. It is a fascinating area of study and a great way of making money. There are three major schools of thought with regard to how prices form: technical, fundamental value, and random walk. While all agree that market prices form through series of successive price adjustments, it is why these adjustments take place and how independent they are, that make them disagree.

Technical analysts, also known as chartists, assume that the series of past price changes has memory and the past tends to repeat itself. They carefully analyze historical price changes to identify patterns to help them predict future prices and eventually increase their chances of making profit. On contrary to this implied dependency assumption, random walk theorists assume independence. In other words, patterns identified cannot be used to predict future changes and any profit made using technical analysis cannot exceed those made by chance, or by using a buy and hold trading strategy [9]. *A Random Walk Down Wall Street* [10] argues that a buy and hold strategy is best, as attempts to outperform the market based on technical, fundamental, or any other forms of analysis are vain.

Fundamental value analysis is consistent with the random walk independence assumption. Fundamental value analysts believe that each security has an intrinsic value. They evaluate the company's earnings, dividend policy, the riskiness of their investments, and the political and economic factors affecting them to estimate securities value and expected return. Changes in market prices can be caused by disagreement between traders on how valuable securities are, new information arriving at different points in time, or by the mere accumulation of random noise due to individuals' impulsive betting behavior [11]. The arrival of new information or the noise created by irrational behavior can cause prices to change in a dependent way to levels above or below their intrinsic values. However, experienced intrinsic value analysts will shortly notice that activity and act quickly by selling or buying, thus, driving price levels back toward their intrinsic values and eliminating any dependence in successive price changes [11].

2.4   Efficient Market Hypothesis

The efficient market hypothesis (EMH) [12], which requires traders to have rational expectations, is connected to random walk theory. The EMH asserts that markets are informationally efficient, and thus are impossible to beat. In other words, prices of traded assets reflect all available information about future prospects of the asset. Since prospects are analogous to events, prices in efficient information markets reflect all available information about the likelihood of the events. Thus, information markets utilize market efficiency to harness the collective knowledge of participants to predict the likelihood of future events.

Modern behavioral finance has shown that people make systematic errors when predicting the future. This irrational behavior could also arise due to emotional errors [13], wishful thinking, or making mistakes, biased or not [14]. These behaviors create market inefficiencies and anomalies in prices that may be inexplicable via any available hypothesis [15,16].

However, information markets' effectiveness seems to be immune to irrationality. Forsythe et al. [17] analyzed Iowa political stock market data to test the market ability to aggregate information about political events. Trader level analysis showed that some traders appeared rational, while others exhibited substantial cognitive and judgmental biases, such as assimilation-contrast and false-consensus effects. In spite of that, the market forecasts were notably accurate.

2.5   Marginal Trader Hypothesis

In efficient information markets, it does not really matter if all traders are rational or not, as long as the marginal trader is rational and motivated by profit; the market generated forecast will be fairly accurate [17,18]. The marginal trader hypothesis claims that "marginal traders who are influential in setting market prices are all that is needed for the Hayek hypothesis to succeed" [14, p. 84]. The marginal traders are those who submit limit orders close to the market price. While those who are inactive, make only market orders, or make limit orders at prices far away from market prices are not considered marginal [14].

Each market trade is determined by two separate acts or two trader roles: a market maker submitting a limit order and a price taker accepting it (submitting a market order). Traders self-select into these two roles. Violations of the law of one price, the no-arbitrage assumption, and those of individual rationality, can be classified into price taking and market making violations [19]. Even though average traders might exhibit judgment biases, marginal traders, or market makers, are who determine whether markets are efficient or not [19].

Studies have found that marginal traders appear to behave more rationally, exhibit less biased trades, and are more experienced and knowledgeable [14,17,19]. It is worth noting, though, that a market maker cannot exist without a price taker, otherwise the no-trade theorem will bind and traders will not agree to disagree [20,21]. It is still an important open question in the information markets literature on how to attract those price takers, despite their possible irrational behavior, to participate in trading due to their critical role in executing trades [22].

3. How Information Markets Work

Information markets, often known variously as prediction markets, decision markets, event markets, and idea futures, are an emerging form of futures markets created to aggregate information, rather than to hedge risks.

3.1 Types of Information Markets

Information markets can be organized into two main categories as shown in Fig. 1 based on the market objective for which the information is aggregated [23]. Verifiable outcomes information markets seek to predict the likelihood of future states of either a discrete or a continuous variable. Unverifiable outcomes information markets allow participants to either create or choose among alternative courses of action.

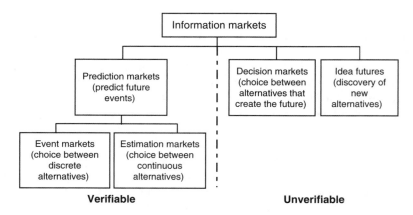

FIG. 1. Information markets typology (from Ref. [23]).

Information markets can be used to aggregate information about a wide range of events, such as sporting outcomes, interest rates, marketing campaigns, and research ideas. Although markets differ in many respects, such as market design and incentive structure, they generally consist of one or more events for which you would like a reliable forecast.

The standard contract in the market is the binary contract, a.k.a. winner-take-all. It costs a certain amount and pays off, for instance, $1 if and only if the event occurs, and nothing otherwise. Traders buy and sell contracts of future events based on their beliefs in the event's likelihood of occurrence. For example, if a trader believes the event is going to happen, he/she will buy contracts in the event. But if a trader has information to the contrary, he/she will sell contracts in the event. Contract prices and events probabilities are positively correlated. The higher the likelihood of the event, the higher its contract price, and vice versa. The result is a trading price that tracks the consensus opinion [24], and can be interpreted as a market-aggregated forecast of the event probability [18]. For example, if a contract price is selling for $70 with a $100 payoff, that means there is a 70% chance of the event happening.

3.2 Virtual Market Design

Based on research results in the fields of experimental economics, financial markets, and political stock markets, Spann and Skiera [25] grouped main aspects of information markets design into three categories, outlined in Fig. 2.

3.2.1 Forecasting Goal

The choice of a forecasting goal is concerned with the types of questions asked about future events. In other words, what is specifically being predicted? Predicted events must be easy to verify and future outcomes must be easy to measure.

Questions can be formulated to predict the occurrence/nonoccurrence of an event, such as whether a project will be delivered on a specific date or not. Other questions can predict numbers such as units sold, or sales in dollars or percentages such as market share, or election vote share. Questions must be clear and easy to understand. They must be interesting enough to attract traders, and controversial enough to sustain trading.

3.2.2 Portfolio Composition

The designer of the market must decide on the composition of traders' initial portfolios and on whether traders will use their own money to buy shares or will be given an initial endowment of shares. Another related design issue is the use of real

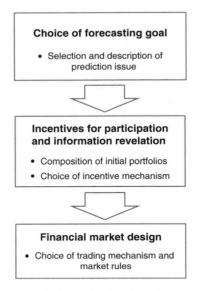

FIG. 2. Steps for designing a virtual stock market (from Ref. [25]).

or play money. Real money might motivate traders to collect more information about the events. On the other hand, it might deter informed, but risk adverse, traders from participating. Additionally, gambling laws might restrict the use of real-money markets, making the play money alternative the only one feasible. In terms of predictive accuracy, studies have shown that real and play money markets result in equally accurate predictions [26].

3.2.3 Incentive Structure

Designers must also decide on an incentive structure to motivate traders to participate, and to truthfully reveal what they know about an event. After all, a trade requires a trader to put his/her money where his/her mouth is. The incentive structure, and the type of contracts used, can elicit the collective expectations of a range of different parameters, such as the probability, mean, or median value of an outcome [18]. For example, when the outcomes of an event are mutually exclusive, such as yes/no or occur/not occur, the binary contract, described in the previous section, can be used to elicit the event's probability of occurrence.

The same applies to events with more than two mutually exclusive outcomes. State-contingent or winner-take-all contracts can be used, and their prices can be interpreted as the collective or the market forecast of the event probability. This is only true as long as the no-arbitrage condition is satisfied, though. In other words, the sum of prices of the traded state-contingent contracts should be exactly equal to the payoff of the winning contract [27]. For example, in case of binary contracts, if the winning contract pays off $100, the sum of prices of the two traded contracts must be equal to 100 (e.g., Yes → $40, No → $60).

The Iowa Electronic Markets (IEMs), a well-known real-money prediction market, used winner-take-all contracts to predict the outcomes of the 2008 U.S. presidential elections (Table I). IEM's winner-take-all prediction market opened in June 2006. The founder of the IEM, Professor Tom Rietz, said "the IEM traders saw Obama's win even before anyone knew who the two parties' nominees would be." At midnight the day before the election, prices indicated a 90% probability that the Democratic candidate would win the popular vote (IEM press release, November 5, 2008).

In support of Professor Rietz's statement, Fig. 3 shows that for more than 2 years the democratic contract price never once dropped below the republican. Prices were exceptionally responsive to unfolding events on the campaign trail, and fluctuated around primary, caucus, and major party convention dates.

When forecasted outcomes are numbers or percentages, such as sales in dollars, vote count, or percentage of vote share, index contracts can be used that pay off proportionately to the outcomes [18]. IEM vote share contracts (Table II) are examples of index contract.

Prices on the IEM's Vote Share Market (Fig. 4) predicted the percentages received of the two-party presidential popular vote to within half percentage point: the market predicted 53.55% for Barack Obama and 46.45% for John McCain. After the ballots were counted, Obama received 53.2% of the vote and McCain received 46.8% (IEM press release, November 24, 2008).

The price of an index contract represents the market mean expectation of the outcome. On the other hand, a spread contract with even money bet represents the market's expectation of median outcome and is used to forecast whether outcomes

TABLE I
IEM 2008 U.S. PRESIDENTIAL ELECTION WINNER TAKES ALL CONTRACTS

Code	Contract description
DEM08_WTA	$1 if the Democratic Party nominee receives the majority of popular votes cast for the two major parties in the 2008 U.S. Presidential election, $0 otherwise
REP08_WTA	$1 if the Republican Party nominee receives the majority of popular votes cast for the two major parties in the 2008 U.S. Presidential election, $0 otherwise

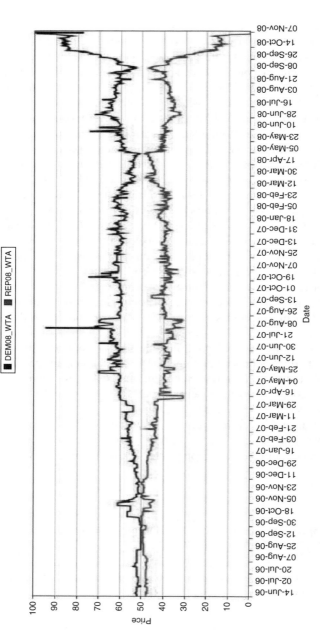

Fig. 3. IEM 2008 U.S. Presidential Election Winner Takes All Market (source: http://iemweb.biz.uiowa.edu/graphs/graph_PRES08_WTA. cfm).

TABLE II
IEM 2008 U.S. PRESIDENTIAL ELECTION VOTE SHARE CONTRACTS

Code	Contract description
UDEM08_VS	$1.00 times two-party vote share of unnamed Democratic nominee in 2008 election
UREP08_VS	$1.00 times two-party vote share of unnamed Republican nominee in 2008 election

will exceed a certain cutoff point, such as a candidate receiving more than a certain vote share [18]. Table III summarizes the discussed contract types.

3.2.4 Market Trading Mechanism and Trading Rules

The choice of market trading mechanism is another important aspect of market design. The dominant market trading mechanism is the continuous double auction (CDA), where *bids*, submitted by buyers, and *asks*, submitted by sellers, wait in queues to be executed. Bids are sorted by prices in descending order and then by posting time in ascending order; while asks are sorted by prices then by time, both in ascending order to facilitate matching with pending bids. The CDA mechanism poses no risk on the market institution, provides incentives for continuous incorporation of information, and offers the option of cashing out by selling shares at the currently offered bid price. However, CDA might suffer from illiquidity due to market thinness, or wide bid–ask spread [28].

Continuous double auction with market maker (CDAwMM) is the bookie mechanism used for sports betting. This trading mechanism guarantees liquidity by transferring the risk involved to the market institution. Pari-mutuel mechanisms also guarantee liquidity without posing any risks on the market institution; however, unlike CDAwMM, it does not continuously incorporate information into the price, but rather waits until the event can be identified with certainty [28].

Market scoring rule (MSR), invented by Hanson [29,30], can elicit forecasts over many combinations of outcomes and from both individuals and groups. MSR combines the advantages of information markets and scoring rules while solving the thin market and irrational betting problems of standard information markets as well as the information pooling problems of simple scoring rules. MSR is currently used at Inkling Markets, the Washington Stock Exchange, BizPredict, and several other active markets.

Pennock [28] developed a novel market mechanism called dynamic pari-mutuel market (DPM) that is used at Yahoo! Tech Buzz Game. DPM combines some of the

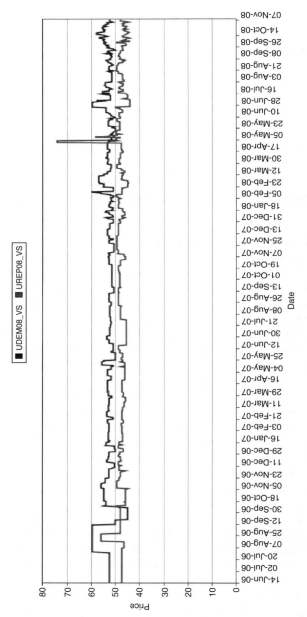

Fig. 4. IEM 2008 U.S. Presidential Election Vote Share Market (source: http://iemweb.biz.uiowa.edu/graphs/graph_PRES08_VS.cfm).

TABLE III
INFORMATION MARKETS CONTRACT TYPES

Contract type	Payoff	Parameter
Winner-take-all	Pays $1, $0 otherwise	Probability
Index	Proportionate to outcome	Mean
Spread	Double money if outcome exceeds cutoff point; $0 otherwise	Median

TABLE IV
MARKET MECHANISMS PROS AND CONS

Market mechanisms	Advantages	Disadvantages
Continuous double auction (CDA)	2, 3, 4	Fails 1
Continuous double auction with market maker (CDAwMM)	1, 3, 4	Fails 2
Pari-mutuel (PM)	1, 2	Fails 3 and 4
Dynamic pari-mutuel (DPM)	1–4	5, 6
Market scoring rule (MSR)	1, 3, 4	Fails 2, but risk is bounded
Bookie (Bookmaker)	1, 3, 4	Fails 2

1. Guaranteed liquidity.
2. No risk for the market institution.
3. Continuous incorporation of information.
4. Ability to cash out by selling before the market closes.
5. Payoff depends on the price at the time, and final payoff per share.
6. One-sided nature (only accept buy order).

advantages of both pari-mutuel and CDA markets, yet like all other mechanisms, has its own limitations. Table IV summarizes the pros and cons for the various available market mechanisms as discussed by Pennock [28].

4. Information Markets Applications

While research on information markets has witnessed an exponential growth in the number of published articles in the past 10 years [31], prediction markets have been around for a long time. Betting on political outcomes has a long tradition in the United States, with large and formal markets, such as the New York betting market, operating for over three-quarters of a century [32]. These markets have had a very large volume of activity and a notable predictive accuracy [32].

Today, the IEM, the most well-known application of information markets, offers markets in which traders can bet on a wide variety of events ranging from the outcomes of presidential elections to the periodic interest rate decisions of the Federal Reserve's Open Market Committee [33]. Since 1988, prices on the IEM have proved more accurate than traditional polls in forecasting elections more than 75% of the time, with an average absolute error of only 1.5% points, compared to 2.1% points for polls [17,33,34].

Market forecasts can be used to inform decisions made by political parties, such as nominating presidential candidates that are likely to win, as well as decisions made by the candidates themselves regarding their campaign strategies such as what issues to focus on. The idea of using markets for decision support was first introduced by Hanson [35] when he used the concept of decision markets, or conditional markets, to illustrate how market forecasts can be used to inform decisions about an event given market predictions of another. Berg and Rietz [36] provided an elaborate analysis of the 1996 presidential election market and described how market prices can be used to support decisions; for example, market forecasts suggested that Dole was not the strongest candidate in the set; concluding that the Republican Party could have used market prediction to select a stronger candidate with a better chance of beating President Clinton [36].

The Hollywood Stock Exchange (HSX) is another successful application of information markets where predictions are made on which movies will succeed or fail in the market. Traders in the HSX buy and sell shares of their favorite actors or movies causing securities' prices to rise or fall. Traders evaluate movies by collecting information from movie Web sites, reading critics' reviews and blogs, and interacting with fan communities to form beliefs about movies' potential prospects. Prices of securities are used to predict Oscar, Emmy, and Grammy award winners and movie box-office returns. The predictions have proved to be highly correlated with actual outcomes. In 2009, players correctly predicted 29 of 37 Oscar nominees for the 81st Annual Academy Awards, a 78.4% success rate, bringing HSX's 11-year average to an impressive 82.1% (HSX press release, January 22, 2009).

The HSX is being used as a market research instrument where movies' box-office prerelease forecasts are used to determine marketing budget, the number of movie screens, and related promotional activities [37]. Spann and Skiera [25] analyzed the HSX forecasting accuracy for 152 movies and compared market predictions to two renowned experts' predictions. They also analyzed the market performance in many other areas, such as predicting the number of movie visitors, the chart position of pop music singles in Germany, and predicting the usage of different mobile phone services of a large German mobile phone operator. Market predictions were fairly accurate. Results showed that markets work well under different incentives structures and with even a small number of participants.

There are many other successful Web-based implementation of information markets designed to aggregate information and forecast events in many areas such sports, politics, finance, law, entertainment, and even the weather. Some examples of real-money information markets include Intrade, TradeSports, Nadex, and BetFair. Other examples of play money markets are NewsFutures, Inkling Markets, and the Foresight Exchange.

By 2006, over 25 companies in the United States had started to experiment with information markets to forecast business objectives [38]. Today, the number has at least doubled and companies have moved beyond the experimentation stage. Examples include many well-respected companies in their industries. Microsoft is using the market to predict software quality issues, such as the number of bugs in new software applications; Google is using it to predict dates of product launches and General Electric is using it to choose the best new research ideas to pursue [39]. AT&T, Yahoo, Corning, and Best Buy are just a few examples of the many Fortune 500 companies that have begun to seriously use information market in various areas of business.

In a series of experiments at Hewlett-Packard laboratories, markets outperformed official HP forecasts 75% of the time in predicting printer sales and DRAM microchip prices [39,40]. Ortner [41,42] conducted an experiment using information markets at Siemens Austria to forecast delays and reveal information about software project progress. Results showed that market prices anticipated delays long before the official release of information, proving the usefulness of using markets in the software project management arena.

Intel integrated an information market designed to forecast demand into the company's standard forecasting processes. The results of early experiments showed that market forecasts are stable, responded well to demand fluctuations, and were at least as accurate as the official forecasts, with 75% of market forecasts falling within 2.7% of actual sales [3].

In addition to aggregating information, and forecasting events, markets can be used to study how organizations process information [43]. The Cowgill et al. [43] analysis of Google's internal prediction market showed how markets can be used to track information flow within the organization and how it responds to external events.

5. Information Aggregation Methods in Information Markets

Organizations employ various methods to elicit forecasts and aggregate information held by members of a group. When the issues at hand are purely factual, statistical groups can be generated by asking a large group of individuals and calculating the statistical mean or median of their answers [44]. However, when the group is anchored by a misleading value for the statistic in question or the group members are ignorant of the issue at hand, the likelihood that the group will decide correctly decreases as the size of the group increases [44].

Alternatively, deliberation can be used to improve group decision making through discussions and debates, especially when the issues are normative rather than factual [44]. Armstrong [45] presented the case against face-to-face meetings, demonstrating how ineffective and inefficient traditional group meetings are at aggregating information. Groups often produce inaccurate outcomes because of informational and social influences. Sunstein [44] argued that informational influence occurs when group members announce their information by conduct, conclusions, or reason-giving, influencing other group members not to disclose any information to the contrary. On the other hand, social influence leads individuals to conform to higher status group members fearing disapproval or social sanctions of various sorts. These influences impair group judgment by emphasizing shared information, creating hidden profiles, cascade effects, and group polarization.

Additionally, individual group members have limited information processing capabilities and therefore rely on heuristics such as representativeness, availability, framing, anchoring, and adjustment to reduce the cognitive load of predicting values or assessing probabilities [46]. The use of heuristics reduces complex tasks to much simpler judgmental tasks, creating biases and errors in individual judgments that are propagated, and often amplified, in group settings.

The Delphi method is utilized to diminish the informational and social influences of deliberative groups. The Delphi technique uses a self-administered questionnaire and a system of controlled feedback wherein a group of experts participate in anonymous rounds of estimates and feedback until the degree of convergence reaches a desired threshold. Members are allowed to communicate their judgments and conclusions anonymously in the form of summary statistics along with their justification and reasoning behind them. Experts can then respond to the forecasts and justifications of others and revise their own based on the feedback they receive. Finally, individual judgments are statistically aggregated [47].

Rowe and Wright [48] reviewed 25 empirical studies that evaluated the effectiveness of the Delphi method in terms of forecast accuracy and quality. Their review showed that Delphi outperformed both statistical and interactive groups roughly over 80% of the time. Although the Delphi technique improved forecasting and decision making, it has its own limitations. In addition to the possible difficultly of recruiting experts in any area of interest, Delphi does not have an incentive structure to motivate experts to reveal their true beliefs. Also, Delphi does not allow incorporation of additional information into the forecasts because it offers results only at a certain point in time [49].

6.   The Advantages of Information Markets

Much of the enthusiasm for using information markets as a method of forecasting and information aggregation comes from the inadequacy of existing methods to accomplish this task. Information markets are being used to overcome the limitations of the various aforementioned methods. Green et al. [49] discussed how information markets can avoid the drawbacks of Delphi. First of all, markets are not restricted by experts' availability; instead, traders self-select to participate in the market if they believe their private information is not yet incorporated into the market price. Second, markets offer incentives for true revelation of beliefs. Monetary incentives eliminate group pressure to conform, where traders can only benefit by trading according to their own beliefs. Third, unlike Delphi, markets are dynamic and responsive to changing circumstances. Prices in information markets incorporate new information almost instantly, providing continuous and up to date forecasts of events.

Information markets offer many other advantages over existing methods as shown in Table V. First, Web-based implementations of information markets are not restricted by location or time. Traders can participate from around the globe, 24×7. Second, markets are more cost effective and time efficient than other information aggregation methods. The process of price formation and discovery collects disparate information scattered around the organization or around the world in a matter of hours, and at relatively little to no cost. Third, market trading is anonymous. Anonymity plays a pivotal role in reducing social and informational influences that prevail in group settings. Fourth, trading dynamics in a market setting cancel out individual biases and errors preventing cascading effects from impacting forecasts [14,17,19].

The substantial body of experimental research on information aggregation (e.g., [17,50–55]) suggests that markets seem to work fairly well in a wide variety of

TABLE V
INFORMATION MARKETS' ADVANTAGES

Why information markets?	
Web-based	Robust to attempts to manipulate
No time or place restrictions	Anonymous
No experts required	Saves time and money
Offers continuous up to date forecasts	Bias and error proof
Versatile	Dynamic and responsive to unfolding events
Offers incentives for honesty	High forecasting accuracy

settings. Empirical studies on information markets prove the feasibility of using the market in a wide range of business settings to forecast a variety of events [40–42]. Further, research has shown that markets are robust to manipulation and insider trading [56,57], and produce forecasts that are at least as accurate as existing alternatives, such as opinion polls and experts' predictions [17,26,58,64].

7. Research Directions for Information Markets

The many advantages of information markets and their impressive performance in many current applications support great potentials for wide use across many business and technical fields. Studies that test the usefulness of information markets in various application domains and processes are greatly needed. Our extensive literature survey found that research on how information markets are used inside organizations is still in its infancy. Little is known about the impact of the business environment on information market design, incentive structures, and the types of questions that can be investigated via such markets. To put it more simply, we need research on what works and what does not work. Little is also known about the impact of the market on work processes, corporate culture, and formal and informal reporting mechanisms in the organization.

7.1 Information Markets as IT Artifacts

From a design view of an information market as an IT artifact, research on designing an information market to meet the requirements of an interesting business problem holds great promise. The information systems research framework (Fig. 5) and the design research guidelines suggested by Hevner et al. [59] can be used to structure the methods and activities performed by researchers designing/studying organizational information markets.

Information markets are fundamentally IT artifacts designed to provide more effective and efficient solutions to identified business problems such as information aggregation, forecasting, and decision making under uncertainty. However, the build and evaluate loops used to produce the information market are informed by foundational theories and methodologies rooted in reference disciplines such as economics (experimental and behavioral), computer science and engineering, finance, psychology, and political science. As a result, current studies tend to view information markets through reference disciplines lens: as a financial market or an economic entity (e.g., Ref. [17]).

Research studies that investigate the design and use processes of *organizational* information markets and their interactions with the business environment are greatly

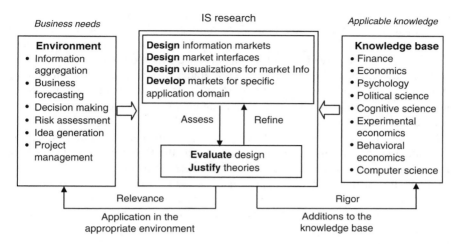

FIG. 5. Research framework for information markets (adapted from Ref. [59]).

needed. However, existing literature on information markets and its current knowledge base might tempt researchers to black box the market, thus, undermining the importance of its interaction with the environment and downplaying the impacts of its technological and structural aspects on the effectiveness and efficiency of organizations adopting information markets [60,61].

Thus, the first step in studying organizational information markets is to reconceptualize markets as technology-enabled information systems. Technology is limited to the hardware and the software components of the market, and the information system encompasses the design, development, implementation, and use processes of the market, as well as the dynamic interaction between the market, people, and its environment to accomplish a certain task. This conceptualization "white boxes" the market, in the sense that it clears some of the doubts surrounding information markets that are mainly due to the black box nature of markets and organization's lack of general understanding of its internal workings. It also serves as grounds for theorizing about information markets from a systems perspective.

7.2   Experimentation on Information Markets

Future research should investigate the impact of different incentives structures and the type of market mechanism used (e.g., pari-mutuel, CDA, MSRs) on the market's forecasting accuracy. Studies should also investigate the impact of incentive structures and market design on organizations' decisions to adopt the market and traders' motivations to participate in it. For example, different trading mechanisms have different associated learning curves which may affect the market perceived ease of use, and consequently, organizations' decisions to adopt the market. It may also require traders to employ different trading strategies that involve a greater cognitive effort to analyze information and to participate in market trading; thus discouraging them from participating in the market.

Moreover, future research should empirically compare information markets to other methods of information aggregation, such as the Delphi method, not only in terms of forecasting accuracy but also on multiple other dimensions, such as the nature of forecasting problems appropriate for each method, sources of relevant information (e.g., external, internal, or a mix of both), the availability of public information to attract participants, the availability of experts in certain areas, and the costs involved in recruiting experts, acquiring the market, training, trading time, incentives, etc.

Comparative studies seek to fill in gaps in the literature, satisfy researchers' curiosity, and help put everything in perspective. One might argue that the value of new innovations can be better appreciated relatively rather than in absolute terms. However, we caution against using forecasting accuracy as the sole basis for comparison between markets and other existing methods. It is important to keep in mind when evaluating the effectiveness of information markets what made them attractive in the first place. Available methods of forecasting and information aggregation such as polls, surveys, and the Delphi method have their own limitations, and produce inaccurate forecasts all the time. So are we really doing markets justice by comparing them to error-prone benchmarks?

Further, unintended uses of markets might emerge that bring additional benefits to organizations, rendering them incomparable to other methods. Markets bring about a unique mix of involvement and enjoyment that other methods do not provide. By promoting democratic participation in decision making and idea generation, organizations might be able to increase employees' loyalty, job satisfaction, and retention rates. Research is needed to study such questions.

Information markets impact on organizations' hierarchy and control structures and on their relationships with employees, customers, partners, and strategic allies might change the way business is done forever. These unanticipated benefits might create a stronger motivation to adopt information markets than their predictive accuracy. Information markets are innovative tools to harness the collective intelligence buried in organizations. They hold great promises for business that are only limited by our own innovation to realize them.

7.3   Information Markets for Policy Making

Information markets have significant potential to support long-term policy making by government and nongovernmental agencies. Abramowicz [62] argues that the objective nature of information markets can be used to effectively predict future normative assessments of policy alternatives. A predictive cost–benefit analysis using information markets can help to overcome the risks of cognitive errors and thwart interest group manipulation. Abramowicz points to the abortive attempt to use information markets to predict terrorist attacks in the aftermath of 9/11 as a failed experiment due to the sensitive nature of variables such as terrorism deaths [63]. There is a compelling need for research to understand how information markets can be used effectively to inform policy-making activities.

References

[1] H.P. Luhn, A business intelligence system, IBM J. Res. Dev. 2 (4) (1958) 314–319.

[2] S. Negash, Business intelligence, Commun. Assoc. Inf. Syst. 13 (2004) 177–195.

[3] J.W. Hopman, Using forecast markets to manage demand risks, Intel Technol. J. 11 (2) (2007) 127–135.

[4] A. Smith, The Wealth of Nations, Oxford, Clarendon, 1776.

[5] F.A. Hayek, The use of knowledge in society, Am. Econ. Rev. 35 (1945) 519–530.

[6] J. Surowiecki, The Wisdom of Crowds, Random House, Inc., New York, 2004.

[7] J. Muth, Rational expectations and the theory of price movements, Econometrica 29 (6) (1961) 315–335.

[8] A.C. Hess, Experimental evidence on price formation in competitive markets, J. Polit. Econ. 80 (2) (1972) 375–385.

[9] E. Fama, Random walks in stock market prices, Financial Analysts J. 21 (5) (1965) 55–59.

[10] B.G. Malkiel, A Random Walk Down Wall Street, W.W. Norton and Company, New York, NY, 1996.

[11] E. Fama, The behavior of stock market prices, J. Bus. 38 (1) (1965) 34–105.

[12] E. Fama, Efficient capital markets: a review of theory and empirical work, J. Finance 25 (2) (1970) 383–417.

[13] J. Clark, Emotional errors, J. Personal Finance 5 (4) (2007) 12.

[14] R. Forsythe, T.A. Rietz, T.W. Ross, Wishes, expectations and actions: price formation in election stock markets, J. Econ. Behav. Organ. 39 (1999) 83–110.

[15] J. Fox, Is the market rational? No, say the experts. But neither are you—so don't go thinking you can outsmart it, Fortune 2002.

[16] B. Rosenberg, K. Reid, R. Lanstein, Persuasive evidence of market inefficiency, J. Portf. Manag. 13 (1985) 9–17.

[17] R. Forsythe, F.D. Nelson, G.R. Neumann, J. Wright, Anatomy of an experimental political stock market, Am. Econ. Rev. 82 (1992) 1142–1161.

[18] J. Wolfers, E. Zitzewitz, Prediction markets, J. Econ. Perspect. 18 (2004) 107–126.

[19] K. Oliven, T.A. Rietz, Suckers are born but markets are made: individual rationality, arbitrage, and market efficiency on an electronic futures market, Manage. Sci. 50 (3) (2004) 336–351.

[20] R.J. Aumann, Agreeing to disagree, Ann. Stat. 4 (6) (1976) 1236–1239.

[21] P. Milgrom, N. Stokey, Information, trade and common knowledge, J. Econ. Theory 26 (1) (1982) 17–27.
[22] J. Wolfers, E. Zitzewitz, Five open questions about prediction markets, in: R. Hahn, P. Tetlock (Eds.), Information Markets: A New Way of Making Decisions in the Private and Public Sectors, AEI-Brookings Press, Washington, DC, 2006.
[23] J.L. Jones, R.W. Collins, D.J. Berndt, Information markets: a research landscape, Commun. Assoc. Inf. Syst. 25 (2009) 289–304.
[24] R. Hanson, Idea futures: encouraging an honest consensus, Extropy 3 (2) (1992) 7–17.
[25] M. Spann, B. Skiera, Internet-based virtual stock markets for business forecasting, Manage. Sci. 49 (2003) 1310–1326.
[26] E. Servan-Schreiber, J. Wolfers, D.M. Pennock, B. Galebach, Prediction markets: does money matter? Electron. Markets 14 (3) (2004) 243–251.
[27] K.-Y. Chen, L.R. Fine, B.A. Huberman, Forecasting uncertain events with small groups, Proceedings of 3rd ACM Conference on Electronic Commerce, October 14–17, 2001, pp. 58–64, Tampa, FL, USA.
[28] D.M. Pennock, A dynamic pari-mutuel market for hedging, wagering, and information aggregation, Proceedings of the 5th ACM Conference on Electronic Commerce, May 17–20, 2004, pp. 170–179, New York, NY, USA.
[29] R. Hanson, Combinatorial information market design, Inf. Syst. Frontiers 5 (1) (2003) 107–119.
[30] R. Hanson, Logarithmic market scoring rules for modular combinatorial information aggregation, J. Prediction Markets 1 (1) (2007) 1–15.
[31] G. Tziralis, I. Tatsiopoulos, Prediction markets: an extended literature review, J. Prediction Markets 1 (2007) 75–91.
[32] P.W. Rhode, K.S. Strumpf, Historical presidential betting markets, J. Econ. Perspect. 18 (2004) 127–141.
[33] R.W. Hahn, P.C. Tetlock, Introduction to information markets, in: P. Tetlock, R. Litan (Eds.), Information Markets: A New Way of Making Decisions in the Public and Private Sectors, AEI-Brookings Joint Center, Washington, DC, 2006.
[34] J.E. Berg, R. Forsythe, F.D. Nelson, T.A. Rietz, Results from a dozen years of election futures markets research, in: C.R. Plott, V. Smith (Eds.), Handbook of Experimental Economic Results, North Holland, Amsterdam, 2003.
[35] R. Hanson, Decision markets, IEEE Intell. Syst. 14 (1999) 16–19.
[36] J.E. Berg, T.A. Rietz, Prediction markets as decision support systems, Inf. Syst. Front. 5 (1) (2003) 79–93.
[37] J. Eliashberg, M.S. Sawhney, A parsimonious model for forecasting gross box-office revenues of motion pictures, Marketing Sci. 15 (2) (1996) 113–131.
[38] R. King, Workers, place your bets, Bus. Week 2006.
[39] E. Schonfeld, Why gambling at the office pays, Business 2.0 Magazine 7 (8) 2006.
[40] K.-Y. Chen, C.R. Plott, Information aggregation mechanisms: concept, design and implementation for a sales forecasting problem, 2002, Social Science Working Paper No. 1131, California Institute of Technology, Pasadena.
[41] G. Ortner, Forecasting markets: an industrial application I, 1997, Mimeo, Technical University of Vienna.
[42] G. Ortner, Forecasting markets: an industrial application II, 1998, Mimeo, Technical University of Vienna.
[43] B. Cowgill, J. Wolfers, E. Zitzewitz, Using prediction markets to track information flows: evidence from Google, 2008.

[44] C.R. Sunstein, Group judgments: statistical means, deliberation, and information markets, N. Y. Univ. Law Rev. 80 (3) (2005) 962–1049.

[45] J.S. Armstrong, How to make better forecasts and decisions: avoid face-to-face meetings, Foresight 5 (2006) 3–8.

[46] A. Tversky, D. Kahneman, Judgment under uncertainty: heuristics and biases, Science 185 (1974) 1124–1131.

[47] J.S. Armstrong, Principles of Forecasting: A Handbook for Researchers and Practitioners, Kluwer Academic Publisher, Amsterdam, 2001.

[48] G. Rowe, G. Wright, The Delphi technique as a forecasting tool: issues and analysis, Int. J. Forecasting 15 (4) (1999) 353–375.

[49] K. Green, J.S. Armstrong, A. Graefe, Methods to elicit forecasts from groups: Delphi and prediction markets compared, Foresight 8 (2007) 17–20.

[50] R. Forsythe, F. Lundholm, Information aggregation in an experimental market, Econometrica 58 (1990) 309–347.

[51] C.R. Plott, S. Sunder, Efficiency of experimental security markets with insider information: an application of rational expectations models, J. Polit. Econ. 90 (1982) 663–698.

[52] C.R. Plott, S. Sunder, Rational expectations and the aggregation of diverse information in laboratory security markets, Econometrica 56 (1988) 1085–1118.

[53] C.R. Plott, Markets as information gathering tools, Southern Econ. J. 67 (2000) 2–15.

[54] S. Sunder, Market for information: experimental evidence, Econometrica 60 (1992) 667–695.

[55] S. Sunder, Experimental asset markets: a survey, in: J.H. Kagel, A.E. Roth (Eds.), Handbook of Experimental Economics, Princeton University Press, Princeton, NJ, 1995, pp. 445–500.

[56] R. Hanson, R. Oprea, Manipulators increase information market accuracy, 2004, George Mason University, Working Paper.

[57] R. Hanson, R. Oprea, D. Porter, Information aggregation and manipulation in an experimental market, J. Econ. Behav. Organ. 60 (2006) 449–459.

[58] K.-Y. Chen, D.M. Pennock, Information markets vs. opinion pools: an empirical comparison, Proceedings of the 6th ACM Conference on Electronic Commerce (EC'05), 2005, June 5–8, Vancouver, British Columbia, Canada.

[59] A.R. Hevner, S.T. March, J. Park, S. Ram, Design science in information systems research, MIS Quart. 28 (2004) 1.

[60] I. Benbasat, R.W. Zmud, The identity crisis within the IS discipline defining and communicating the discipline's core properties, MIS Quart. 27 (2) (2003) 183–194.

[61] W. Orlikowski, S. Iacono, Desperately seeking the 'IT' in IT research—a call to theorizing the IT artifact, Inf. Syst. Res. 12 (2) (2001) 121–134.

[62] M. Abramowicz, Information markets, administrative decisionmaking, and predictive cost-benefit analysis, Univ. Chic. Law Rev. 73 (3) (2004) 933–1020, Summer.

[63] C. Hulse, Swiftly, plan for terrorism futures market slips into dustbin of ideas without a future, New York. Times July 30 (2003) A1.

[64] J. Berg, F. Nelson, T. Rietz, Prediction market accuracy in the long run, Int. J. Forecasting 24 (2008) 283–298.

Measuring and Monitoring Technical Debt

CAROLYN SEAMAN

Department of Information Systems, University of Maryland Baltimore County, Baltimore, Maryland, USA

YUEPU GUO

Department of Information Systems, University of Maryland Baltimore County, Baltimore, Maryland, USA

Abstract

Technical debt is a metaphor for immature, incomplete, or inadequate artifacts in the software development lifecycle that cause higher costs and lower quality in the long run. These artifacts remaining in a system affect subsequent development and maintenance activities, and so can be seen as a type of debt that the system developers owe the system. Incurring technical debt may speed up software development in the short run, but such benefit is achieved at the cost of extra work in the future, as if paying interest on the debt. In this sense, the technical debt metaphor characterizes the relationship between the short-term benefits of delaying certain software maintenance tasks or doing them quickly and less carefully, and the long-term cost of those delays. However, managing technical debt is more complicated than managing financial debt because of the uncertainty involved. In this chapter, the authors review the main issues associated with technical debt, and propose a technical debt management framework and a research plan for validation. The objective of our research agenda is to develop and validate a comprehensive technical debt theory that formalizes the relationship between the cost and benefit sides of the concept. Further, we propose to use the theory to propose mechanisms (processes and tools) for measuring and managing technical debt in software product maintenance. The theory and management mechanisms are intended ultimately to contribute to the improved quality of software and facilitate decision making in software maintenance.

ADVANCES IN COMPUTERS, VOL. 82
ISSN: 0065-2458/DOI: 10.1016/B978-0-12-385512-1.00002-5

25

1. Introduction

A major obstacle to fulfilling society's demand for increasingly complex software systems is the resources that many organizations must devote to maintaining existing systems that cannot, for business reasons, be abandoned. The quality of maintained software often diminishes over time, with respect to its internal system structure, adherence to standards, documentation, understandability, and so on. This eventually impacts maintenance productivity, as modification of low-quality software is generally harder than of high-quality software. The magnitude of the maintenance burden is well documented [1–3] and not likely to decrease. Therefore, advances that address maintenance productivity have a twofold benefit: cost savings in the maintenance of existing systems and newly available resources for development of systems to address emerging problems.

A common reason for the quality decline is that maintenance is often performed under tight time and resource constraints, with the minimal amount of effort and time required. Typically, there is a gap between this minimal required amount of work and the amount required to make the modification while also maintaining the level of software quality. For business reasons, it does not always make sense to completely close this gap, as much of it may not pay off in the end. For example, if a certain portion of the system in fact has no defects, then no harm is done in saving some time by not testing it. Similarly, if a particular module is never going to be modified in the future, then failing to update its related documentation will save some time during modification of the module, without any adverse consequences. The difficulty, of course, is that it is rarely known if a particular portion of the system has defects or not, or if a particular module is ever going to need modification. So the problem is really one of managing risk, and of making informed decisions about which delayed tasks need to be accomplished, and when.

Currently, managers and leaders of software maintenance efforts carry out this risk analysis implicitly, if at all. However, on large systems, it is too easy to lose track of delayed tasks or to misunderstand their impact. The result is often unexpected delays in completing required modifications and compromised quality. Articulating this issue in terms of "technical debt" has helped some practitioners to discuss this issue. This metaphor frames the problem of delayed maintenance tasks as a type of "debt," which brings a short-term benefit (usually in terms of higher productivity or shorter release time) but which might have to be paid back, with "interest," later. The "principal" on the debt is the amount of effort required to "pay off" the debt (i.e., complete the task), while the "interest" is the potential penalty (in terms of increased effort and decreased productivity) that will have to be paid in the future as a result of not completing these tasks in the present. Many practitioners find this metaphor intuitively appealing and helpful in thinking about the issues. What is missing, however, is an underlying theoretical basis upon which management mechanisms can be built to support decision making.

The technical debt metaphor [4] has captured the interest of practitioners because it so effectively describes a deep intuitive understanding of the dynamics of software maintenance projects. Discussion and enhancement of the concept is transforming the way that long-term software maintenance is *viewed*. But its lack of a sound theoretical basis (or even any scholarly examination), empirically based models, and practical implementation hinder its ability to transform how maintenance is *done*.

2.   The Technical Debt Metaphor

Technical debt refers to the effect of any incomplete, immature, or inadequate artifact in the software development lifecycle, for example, immature design, incomplete documentation, and so on. These artifacts remaining in a system affect subsequent development and maintenance activities, and so can be seen as a type of debt that the system developers owe the system, whose repayment may be demanded sooner or later. It is common that a software project incurs some debt in the development process because small amounts of debt can increase productivity. However, technical debt brings risks to the project, for example, compromised system architecture or less maintainable code. In addition, the existence of technical debt complicates software management as managers have to decide whether and how much debt should be paid and when. In order to make informed decisions, it is necessary to have thorough knowledge of the present and future value of the technical debt currently held by the project. Therefore, identifying, measuring, and monitoring technical debt would help managers make informed decisions, resulting in higher quality of maintained software and greater maintenance productivity.

Although the term may be fairly recent, the concept behind technical debt is not new. It is related to Lehman and Belady's [5] notion of *software decay* (increasing complexity due to change) and Parnas' [6] *software aging* phenomenon (the failure of a product to continue to meet changing needs). These issues have been studied for decades by software maintenance and quality researchers. The introduction of the technical debt metaphor provides a new way to talk about, manage, and measure these related concepts.

The term "technical debt" was first coined by Cunningham [7], in which he presented the metaphor of "going into debt" every time a new release of a system is shipped. The point was that a little debt can speed up software development in the short run, but every extra minute spent on not-quite-right code counts as interest on that debt [7]. This metaphor has been extended to refer to any imperfect artifact in the software lifecycle. Although technical debt has not been formally investigated, discussions about this topic are pervasive on the Web in such forms as personal blogs and online forums. The foci of the discussions vary from identification of technical debt to solutions for controlling it.

Technical debt can be described as either unintentional or intentional [8]. Unintentional debt occurs due to a lack of attention, for example, lack of adherence to development standards or missed test cases. Intentional debt is incurred proactively for tactical or strategic reasons such as to meet a delivery deadline. Technical debt can also be classified in terms of the phase in which it occurs in the software lifecycle, for example, design debt or testing debt [9]. Design debt refers to the integrity of the design as reflected in the source code itself. Testing debt refers to tests that were not developed or run against the code. From this perspective, a whole range of phenomena is related to technical debt. Some of these phenomena manifest themselves in obvious ways. For example,

- Documentation is partially missing;
- The project to-do list keeps growing;
- Minor changes require disproportionately large effort;
- Code cannot be updated because no one understands it anymore;
- It is too difficult to keep different portions of the system architecturally consistent.

These phenomena can be seen as symptoms of technical debt.

In order to manage technical debt, a way to quantify the concept is needed. One approach is to monitor the changes in software productivity during the software development process. In many cases, development organizations let their debt get out of control and spend most of their future development effort paying crippling "interest payments" in the form of harder-to-maintain and lower quality software. Since the interest payments hurt a team's productivity, the decrease in productivity can reflect how much debt an organization has.

Since technical debt is closely tied to software quality, metrics for software quality can also be used to measure technical debt. For example, if the software has defects or does not satisfy all the system requirements, then the defects will eventually have to be fixed and the requirements eventually implemented. Therefore, the number of defects currently in the system, or the number of pending requirements, is an indicator of technical debt. If the software is inflexible or overly complex, then future changes will be more expensive. From this point of view, coupling, cohesion, complexity, and depth of decomposition are metrics that can be applied to the problem of characterizing technical debt [10]. Ultimately, a good design is judged by how well it deals with changes [10], so time and effort required for changes (in particular the trend over time) is also an indicator of technical debt.

Technical debt can also be measured by characterizing the cost of paying the debt. For example, after determining what types of work are owed the system (e.g., architecture redesign, code refactoring, and documentation), the labor, time, and opportunity cost can be estimated for fixing the problems identified. This cost reflects the amount of technical debt currently in the system.

Strategies for paying off technical debt have also been discussed. One strategy is to pay the highest interest debt items first. In other words, this strategy focuses on the debt items that have severe potential future impact on the project. If the debt items with high interest are paid as soon as they are identified, the project avoids that high interest, which in some cases can lead to project failure or "bankruptcy." In terms of the overall cost—the total amount of interest that the project needs to pay—this strategy is not necessarily the optimal one, but it could lower the risk level of the project and keep technical debt under control. Another solution is to determine a breakeven point [4] along the timeline of the project at which technical debt should be paid. This strategy is based on the rationale that technical debt remaining in the system hurts the productivity of the project, which can be measured by the amount of functionality that the development team can implement per time unit. For example, suppose a software project manager, in planning the implementation of an enhancement, allocated relatively little time to analyzing and documenting the design upfront. As a result, the project delivered more functionality to market in the release in which the enhancement was implemented. However, the consequence is that the modules added and changed to implement that enhancement are more difficult to work with in the long run. This, then, is accumulated technical debt, which may slow down productivity later. A good design does require upfront time and effort, but it makes software flexible and easier to maintain for longer periods of time.

To extend this example, suppose we could estimate that the productivity (P) for a project in which enhancements are all designed and documented carefully is 10 requirements per day (assuming, in this context, that requirements per day is a reasonable measure of productivity) and it remains steady in the first 3 months. Thus the cumulative number of requirements that P can implement is 300 in the first month, 600 in the first 2 months, and 900 in the first 3 months. By contrast, the same project using a quick and dirty approach to designing enhancements (P') has higher productivity in the first month, but it decreases as the development proceeds. P' delivered 500 requirements in the first month, 700 in the first 2 months, and 900 in the first 3 months. With this trend, P' can no longer prevail in terms of the cumulative functionality after the third month. Therefore, in this example, the end of the third month is the breakeven point. Prior to this point, incurring technical debt yields benefit (early time to market) for P', while beyond this point the negative effect of technical debt invalidates such benefit and hence the debt should be paid (which, in this case, would involve reengineering and/or redocumenting the design, and possibly refactoring the code). This strategy stresses the need to determine whether it is cost-effective to incur debt, when it should be paid, and how much will be paid each time in order to minimize cost or maximize profit.

3. Related Work

The characteristics of technical debt warrant a strong relationship to several existing areas of active research, including software quality assessment, software effort estimation, and software risk management. A number of metrics and program analysis approaches have been proposed to assess, monitor, and predict software quality. Research results in effort estimation facilitate software project planning, investment analyses, and product pricing. Software risk management has been integrated into software development processes to improve software quality and productivity. Although research achievements are fruitful in each area, there is no work that has leveraged the capability of these three areas to address the technical debt management problem. However, any new work in the technical debt area must be informed by existing approaches to assessing software quality, estimating effort, and managing risk.

3.1   Software Project Risk Management

For financial debt, it is known whether a debtor needs to pay the interest and if so, the total amount of the interest can also be determined before he goes into debt. But this is usually not the case for technical debt. For example, the debt incurred by not completely testing a certain portion of the system never has to be paid back if that portion in fact has no defects. Similarly, if a particular module is never going to be modified in the future, then the debt incurred by failing to update its related documentation will save some time during modification of the module, but will not cause any problems if it is never repaid. Therefore, technical debt involves uncertainty that is not normally present with the analogous notion of financial debt.

Ideally, software managers can choose to incur technical debt only on those artifacts without interest, or delay payment on these artifacts while focusing on those that are subject to penalty. Nonetheless, the difficulty is, using the above examples, that it is rarely known beforehand if a particular portion of the system has defects or not, or if a particular module is ever going to need modification. In this sense, technical debt can be considered as a particular type of risk in software maintenance as it has the basic elements of a risk—the potential loss/penalty and the associated uncertainty. Therefore, the problem of measuring and managing technical debt is closely related to managing risk and making informed decisions about which delayed tasks need to be accomplished, and when.

Our approach to managing technical debt draws inspiration from approaches to software risk management proposed in the literature. Risk management approaches can generally be classified into methods for identifying risks, analyzing risks, or managing risks over time.

Risk identification approaches aim to identify potential problems related to the software project, product, or business. These approaches include intuitive methods such as brainstorming and history-based methods such as leveraging a risk taxonomy or list for risk identification. For example, Carr et al. proposed a risk identification approach based on the SEI taxonomy of software development risks [11]. The types of risks implied by technical debt fall into the product engineering category in the SEI taxonomy. Table I lists the major classes in this taxonomy and the elements in each class.

Risk analysis, or assessment, attempts to describe the identified risks in a way that will help stakeholders decide what actions to take. A common set of attributes to describe risks, as listed in Table II, is also proposed in the literature [12,13]. Our approach to technical debt management makes use of these attributes, with special emphasis on the attributes impact and probability. Other attributes of risks such as scope, class, and causes are included as well. The simplest metric scale for both probability and impact is an ordinal rating scale consisting of low, medium, and high [14]. Since the

TABLE I
SEI TAXONOMY OF SOFTWARE DEVELOPMENT RISKS [11]

Risk class	Product engineering	Development environment	Program constraints
Risk element	Requirements Design Code and unit test Integration and test Engineering specialties	Development process Development system Management process Management methods Work environment	Resources Contract Programming interfaces

TABLE II
RISK ATTRIBUTES [12,13]

Risk attribute	Description
Class	The type of the risk
Cause	The events that lead to the risk
Scope	The range in which the risk is considered
Impact	The severity of potential loss of the risk
Probability	The likelihood that the risk gets instantiated
Valid time period	The time frame in which the risk is valid

assignment of such values is highly subjective, some methods have been proposed to reduce the potential bias [15]. Better estimation of the impact and probability can be achieved using historical data that match current project characteristics. Based on the estimation of their impact and probability of occurrence, the risks can then be prioritized using a risk analysis matrix [16], tree-based techniques [17], or other risk models. We adopt a similar approach to quantifying technical debt, starting from rough estimation, refining the estimation using historical data, and finally prioritizing the technical debt items based on a combination of impact and probability.

Managing risks over time follows an iterative process that continues throughout the project [18]. This includes updating information about risks as they are handled and reevaluating risks as more information becomes available or context factors change. There are various strategies for risk management, generally classified into strategies for avoiding a risk, mitigating a risk, or transferring a risk to others. The decision is based on the results of risk assessment. It is to be noted that assessing risks for a project is not a one-time task because risks will change as a result of environmental change and actions taken to manage them. Therefore, risks should be continuously monitored to decide whether the risk is becoming more or less probable and whether the effects of the risk have changed [19]. The same is true for technical debt items, which can change with the context of the project.

3.2 Software Quality Assessment and Program Analysis

As mentioned in the introduction, technical debt refers to immature artifacts that fail to meet certain software quality criteria. Therefore, technical debt can in some cases be identified by comparing the quality of software artifacts with quality standards. However, software quality is a complex concept. On one hand, software quality has many attributes and different groups of people may have different views of software quality [20]. On the other hand, some attributes of quality, for example, maintainability and usability, are hard to assess directly. Therefore, software quality standards usually take the form of guidelines or heuristics. Thus, using such guidelines or heuristics to detect technical debt has to rely on human judgment and is inevitably subjective and difficult to quantify. Another approach to software quality assessment is to use software quality metrics. For example, lines of code can be used to measure the size of software, while cyclomatic complexity and fan-in/fan-out are used to measure software complexity. No matter what metrics are used, the relationship between the metrics and software quality attribute must be determined so that it is clear that software quality can be properly assessed using these metrics. Research regarding software quality metric evaluation [21–23] can be used to help select the appropriate metrics for a particular quality measurement goal.

Program analysis refers, in general, to any examination of source code that attempts to find patterns or anomalies thought to reveal specific behaviors of the software. Some types of program analysis focus on patterns that indicate poor programming practices and bad design choices. Such patterns, termed "bad code smells" [24], are shown to cause maintainability problems over time because they make the software less understandable, more complex, and harder to modify. Thus, code smells can be considered as a type of technical debt. Code smells can be categorized depending on their detection methods.

- *Primitive smells* are violations of predefined rules and development practices and can be directly detected based on the source code. An example of primitive smells are violations of coding rules that define how source code should be structured on different levels or which control structures should be used. A rule such as "one Java source file should not contain more than one Java class" can be translated into a code smell by constructing a rule statement out of its negative. Program analysis is able to detect these violations effectively.

- *Derived smells* are higher level design violations and require more complex computations and extractions of software quality metrics values from source code. They are computed based on Boolean expressions that include code metrics and thresholds. Based on established quality metrics, Marinescu and

Lanza [25] studied the disharmonies in software source code and proposed a set of criteria including metrics and threshold values to detect code smells. An example of a derived smell is a class that implements too much responsibility (known as a "God class"). The following expression evaluates if the "God class" smell is present:

$$WMC > 47, \quad ATFD > 5, \quad \text{and} \quad TCC < 0.33,$$

where WMC is the weighted methods per class, ATFD is the number of accesses to foreign class data, and TCC is tight class cohesion. These kinds of code smells require, on one hand, a rigorous definition of the metrics used (e.g., how are methods weighted when computing WMC?) and a set of baselines to define the included thresholds. Although this approach facilitates automated code smell detection, the metrics and thresholds should be tailored to improve accuracy in a particular domain [26].
- The last category of smells includes those that are not automatically detectable. These smells can only be discovered by a human inspector. A typical example is the quality (not the amount) of documentation present; a computer can neither judge if the documentation is easy to understand nor if it fits the actual implemented code statements.

Many bad smells, and the rules for automatically detecting them, are defined in the literature [24]. Examples of well-known bad smells include duplicated code, long methods, and inappropriate intimacy between classes. For many of these rules, thresholds are required to distinguish a bad smell from normal source code (e.g., how long does a method have to be before it smells bad?). With the rules and corresponding thresholds, many code smells can be detected by automatic means, and several smell detection tools exist [27].

3.3   Software Development Effort Estimation

The currency of choice in software project management is often effort, rather than dollars or euros or pounds or any other national currency. Effort is typically the largest component of cost in a software project, and is the resource that requires the most management. Thus, our approach to management of technical debt focuses on representing such concepts as principal and interest in terms of effort. This implies that methods for estimating the effort required for accomplishing various tasks are central to managing technical debt. Since the 1960s, various estimation techniques based on either formal estimation or expert estimation have been proposed, such as COCOMO [28], function point analysis [29], and Wideband Delphi [30].

The goal of effort estimation research is primarily to improve estimation accuracy. However, the accuracy of the existing approaches heavily depends on the context where the approaches are applied [31]. In addition, some approaches are too complicated to be applied though promising in their estimation accuracy. Hence, the dominant estimation approach in practice is still expert estimation [32]. Managing technical debt does not require more accurate or applicable effort estimation techniques than other areas of software project management, but the factors that go into choosing an estimation technique are similar. That is, estimation techniques that are appropriate for the domain, and that can be applied usefully in the context, are the most effective in any particular case.

4. Managing Technical Debt

In this section, we propose an initial technical debt management mechanism as a framework within which to develop theory and validate the approach. This mechanism is described below, and is designed to be flexible and to incorporate human judgment at all stages. In this way, it can easily be modified to incorporate results, understanding, new models, and theories emerging from future work in this area.

4.1 Identifying Technical Debt

The proposed approach to technical debt management centers around a "technical debt list." The list contains technical debt "items," each of which represents a task that was left undone, but that runs a risk of causing future problems if not completed. Examples of technical debt items include modules that need refactoring, testing that needs to be done, inspections/reviews that need to be done, documentation (including comments) that needs to be written or updated, architectural compliance issues, known latent defects that need to be removed, and so on. Each item includes a description of where (in the system) the debt item is and why that task needs to be done, and estimates of the principal and the interest. As with financial debt, the principal refers to the effort required to complete the task. The interest is composed of two parts. The "interest probability" is the probability that the debt, if not repaid, will make other work more expensive over a given period of time or a release. The "interest amount" is an estimate of the amount of extra work that will be needed if this debt item is not repaid. For example, the interest probability for a testing debt item is the probability that latent defects exist in the system that would have been detected if the testing activity had been completed. The interest amount would be the extra work required to deal with those defects later in the system's lifetime, over and above what it would have cost if they had been found during testing. The technical debt list must be reviewed and updated after each release, when items should be added as well as removed. Table III shows an example of a technical debt item.

Maintainers and managers can add items to the technical debt list at different points in the release process, depending on the type of debt (adapted from Ref. [9]):

- *Testing debt* items are added each time a decision is made to skip some set of tests (or reviews) for a particular release or module.
- *Defect debt* items are added each time a defect is found but not fixed in the current release.
- *Documentation debt* items are added each time a piece of software is modified but there is no corresponding modification to the associated documentation.
- *Design debt* items are generated when deficiencies in the code are identified, such as poor programming practices or violations of the system architecture.

4.2   Measuring Technical Debt

Initially, when a technical debt item is created, all three metrics (principal, interest probability, and interest amount) are assigned values of high, medium, or low. These coarse-grained estimates are sufficient for tracking the technical debt items and making preliminary decisions. More detailed estimates are not made until later, when they are required to do fine-grained planning and when more information is available upon which to base the estimates.

When more precise estimates are needed, estimation procedures are followed for each metric, based on the type of technical debt item. The details of these estimation procedures depend in part on the form and granularity of the historical data

TABLE III
TECHNICAL DEBT ITEM

ID	37
Date	3/31/2007
Responsible	Joe Blow
Type	Design
Location	Component X, especially function Y
Description	In the last release, function Y was added quickly and the implementation violates some elements of the architectural design
Estimated principal	Medium (medium level of effort to modify)
Estimated interest amount	High (if X has to be modified, this could cause lots of problems)
Estimated interest probability	Low (X not likely to be modified any time soon)

available, but general procedures have been defined for each type of technical debt item and each technical debt metric.

To estimate principal (i.e., the amount of effort required to complete a technical debt item task), historical effort data are used to achieve a more accurate estimation beyond the initial high/medium/low assessment. If an organization has very accurate, rich, detailed data on many projects, the estimation is very reliable. But even if the historical data are limited, an estimate can still be derived that is helpful in the technical debt decision-making process. Even an expert opinion-based estimate is useful in this context.

Interest probability addresses questions such as how likely it is that a defect will occur in the untested part, or that code containing a known error will be exercised, or that poorly documented code will have to be modified, and so on. Interest probability is also estimated using historical usage, change, and defect data. For example, the probability that a particular module, which has not been tested sufficiently, contains latent defects can be estimated based on the past defect profile of that module. Since the probability varies with different time frames, a time element must be attached to the probability. For example, a module may have a 60% probability of being changed over the next year, but a much lower probability of being changed in the next month.

Thus, estimation of principal and interest probability is fairly straightforward. The specific procedures for doing these estimations will vary depending on the form and nature of the historical data available, but such procedures can be established for any given maintenance environment. However, estimation of interest amount is more complicated. Interest amount refers to the amount of extra work that will be incurred as a result of not completing a technical debt item task, assuming that the item has an effect on future work. This quantity may be very hard to estimate with any certainty but, again, historical data can give sufficient insight for planning purposes. An example will help to illustrate the approach to estimating interest amount.

Suppose there is a technical debt item on the list that refers to a module, X, that needs refactoring. The interest amount in this case would quantify how much extra the next modification to X will cost if it is not refactored first. Suppose also that analysis of historical data shows that the average cost of the last N modifications to X is the quantity C. We can assume that the extra effort to modify X (i.e., the interest amount) is proportional to C. The coefficient of C will be a weighting factor, W, based on the initial rough estimate (in terms of high, medium, or low) of the interest amount. For example, suppose a value of 0.1 is assigned to W if the initial interest amount estimate is "low." This would imply that the "penalty" for not refactoring X before modifying it is about 10%. If the initial estimate is "medium," 0.5 could be the weighting factor, which would imply a 50% penalty. The more refined estimate for interest amount, then, would be

$$\text{Interest amount} = W \times C$$

This formula implies that, if the unrefactored module X does in fact have an effect on future work, the magnitude of that effect will be a percentage of the average cost of modifying X, where the percentage depends on how severe the penalty is thought to be. The severity of the penalty is captured by **W**, based on the initial coarse-grained estimate.

4.3 Monitoring Technical Debt

The goal of identifying and measuring technical debt is to facilitate decision making. There are two scenarios in which a technical debt list can be used to help management decide on various courses of action. The first is part of release planning, where a decision must be made as to whether, how much, and which technical debt items should be paid during the upcoming release. The second is ongoing monitoring of technical debt over time, independent of the release cycle. These two scenarios are described below.

Scenario 1: Significant work is planned for component X in the next release. Should some debt be paid down on component X at the same time? If so, how much and which items should be paid?

Assumptions: There is an up-to-date technical debt list that is sortable by component and has high, medium, and low values for principal and interest estimates for each item.

Step 1. Extract all technical debt items associated with component X.

Step 2. Reevaluate high/medium/low estimates for these items based on current plans for the upcoming release (e.g., some items may have a greatly reduced principal if they overlap with the planned work in the release).

Step 3. Do numeric estimates for all items with high interest probability and high interest amount.

Step 4. For each item considered in Step 3, compare cost (principal) with benefit (interest probability × interest amount) and eliminate any item for which the benefit does not outweigh the cost.

Step 5. Add up the estimated principal for all items left after Step 4. Decide if this cost can be reasonably absorbed into the next release. If not, use this analysis to justify the cost to management. If so, can more debt repayment be put into this release? If so, repeat Steps 3–5 with items with high interest probability and medium interest amount, and vice versa, then with medium for both probability and interest, and so on, until no more debt repayment can be absorbed by the release.

Example

System S has had two major releases: R1 and R2. The next major release, R3, is currently being planned. Since the first version, all technical debt items in S have been tracked and recorded in the technical debt list L, which is updated whenever S is modified. In the plan for R3, Module M will have significant changes. The budget for this release is 600 person-days, 2% of which can be used for paying off technical debt associated with M. According to L, there are five technical debt items in M. Table IV shows these items and their initial estimates of principal, interest probability, and interest amount.

Since most functions related with A are already planned for refactoring in release R3, we first update the estimated principle of A to low (signifying that paying off technical debt item A will impose very little effort beyond what is already planned for the release). After examining the release plan for R3, we decide that no other technical debt items are affected, and the coarse-grained estimates in Table IV do not need to be adjusted, with the exception of the principal for item A, as mentioned previously. However, in order to use this information for decision making, we need to be more precise and quantitative at this point. So, first, we assign 0.2, 0.5, and 0.8 to the interest probability levels—low, medium, and high—respectively. We also derive estimates for principal and interest amounts based on historical effort data. For example, we use data on past refactoring effort to estimate the effort to refactor the methods included in technical debt item A that are not already included in the release plan for R3. Note that these estimates are neither easy to create nor highly accurate. However, they are not created until needed in the analysis, and they provide as much information as is possible given the historical data available, which in any case will provide more insight than not tracking the debt at all. Table V shows the adjusted technical debt items and their numeric estimates.

We first examine item A because A has both high interest amount (6) and high interest probability (0.8). The benefit of paying off A is 4.8 (6×0.8), while the cost, that is, the principal, of paying off A is 4. Since the benefit of paying off A outweighs

TABLE IV
TECHNICAL DEBT ITEMS OF MODULE M IN SYSTEM R

Name	Type	Principal	Interest probability	Interest amount
A	Design debt	Medium	High	High
B	Design debt	High	Medium	High
C	Defect debt	Medium	Medium	Medium
D	Testing debt	Low	Low	Medium
E	Documentation debt	Low	Low	Low

TABLE V
RELEASE PLANNING PROCESS FOR TECHNICAL DEBT

Technical debt item	Principal/ cost	Interest probability	Interest amount	Benefit	Decision	Total cost	Step order
A	4 (low)	0.8	6	4.8	Pay off	4	①
~~B~~	~~10~~	~~0.5~~	~~4~~	~~2~~	Delay	4	②
C	6	0.5	13	6.5	Pay off	10	③
D	2	0.2	11	2.2	Pay off	12	④
E	Low	Low	Low	Low	Delay	Low	

the cost, we keep it on the list. The next item we consider is B, which has medium interest probability and high interest amount. Since the benefit of paying off B is less than the cost, we remove it from the list. Following the same procedure, we calculate the cost and benefit of C and D. According to the decisions we have made so far, A, C, and D will be paid off and the total cost is 12 person-days, which has reached the budget limit. Therefore, this process terminates. Although E is not considered because of the budget limit, we are confident on this decision because E is a debt item with low interest probability and low interest amount and hence will not cause big problems to the next release. Table V illustrated the decision-making process.

Scenario 2: Is technical debt increasing or decreasing for a system or for a component? Is there enough debt to justify devoting resources (perhaps an entire release cycle) to paying it down?

Approach: Plot various aggregated measures over time and look at the shape of curve to observe the trends. The aggregated measures include:
(1) total number of technical debt items,
(2) total number of high-principal items,
(3) total number of high interest (probability and amount) items,
(4) weighted total principal (TP), which is calculated by summing up over entire list (set three points for high, two for medium, one for low), and
(5) weighted total interest (TI) (add points for probability and amount).

Example

System X was first released 2 years ago. Since then, numerous modifications have been made. X currently has three minor releases, v1, v2, and v3. Since the first version, all technical debt items in S have been tracked and recorded in a technical debt list, which is updated whenever X is modified. The weighted TP and the weighted TI are calculated monthly, as shown in Table VI.

TABLE VI
TECHNICAL DEBT HISTORY IN SYSTEM X

	October 2009	November 2009	December 2009	January 2010	February 2010	March 2010	April 2010	May 2010	June 2010	July 2010	August 2010	September 2010
TP	5	8	13	18	30	34	7	8	12	15	20	22
TI	3	6	9	15	25	39	1	3	4	6	10	18

	October 2010	November 2010	December 2010	January 2011	February 2011	March 2011	April 2011	May 2011	June 2011	July 2011	August 2011	September 2011
TP	3	6	8	10	11	16	10	15	22	30	35	37
TI	1	4	9	14	17	19	4	6	15	26	40	50

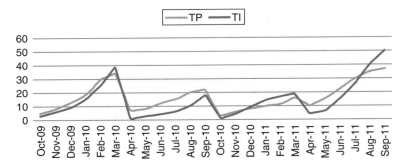

FIG. 1. Trends of technical debt in system X.

Based on the data in Table VI, we can plot charts to monitor the trends of technical debt remaining in X. Figure 1 is an example of the charts. From this chart, we can see that the amount of technical debt in X has an increasing tendency along the timeline, but it dropped to a lower level after each minor release, indicating that effort was devoted to paying down the debt in each release plan. Currently, technical debt has increased to a very high level. In addition, the amount of interest is higher than the amount of principle, which means maintenance of X is currently crippled by a high amount of technical debt. Therefore, it is time to pay down the debt.

This initial proposed approach to technical debt management (both identification and monitoring) relies heavily on the analysis and visualization of existing data from prior software development and maintenance efforts. The reliability and usefulness of the decision-making support that this approach provides increases with the quantity and quality of the data available. However, any amount of data will provide more support than is currently available. Thus, the approach is useful even with limited amounts of data, or even no data. Expert opinion, or a combination of opinion and limited data, can be substituted for any of the inputs to the approach that call for historical data. A benefit of the approach is that it utilizes software metrics data, to the extent that it is available, in new ways, further motivating the collection of this data.

5.   Open Research Issues

The technical debt concept, while intuitively appealing and helpful in facilitating discourse, currently lacks an underlying theory, models to aid its analysis, and mechanisms to facilitate its management. Thus, future work in this area needs to progress toward two related aims:

- A comprehensive technical debt theory must be developed that formalizes the relationship between the cost and benefit sides of the concept.
- Practical mechanisms must be developed and validated for exploiting the theory in management decision making.

The authors of this chapter are involved in a research agenda designed to address the above two aims. Specifically, two studies are currently underway, a retrospective study and a case study of a pilot of the technical debt management approach. The retrospective study will determine what types of benefits might have been incurred by a project had they tracked technical debt. The study is based on in-depth analysis of historical effort, defect, testing, and change data over several recent releases of an ongoing development project at one of our industrial partners. With help from project personnel in interpreting the data and adding historical context, we are analyzing all data available to reconstruct a technical debt list as it would have been built during a selected release if the project team had used the proposed technical debt management mechanism. Based on the reconstructed list, decisions will be simulated about the content of the subsequent release. Where the simulated decisions differ from the decisions actually made, the estimates for the affected technical debt items are used to determine the principal that would have been paid back and the interest that would have been avoided if the decisions had been made based on a technical debt list. This analysis will show whether a benefit would have been gained by using a technical debt list, and what factors contributed to that benefit. This analysis will be repeated with data from multiple releases.

While the retrospective study will provide evidence of a benefit from applying the technical debt management approach, it will not shed any light on the costs of the approach. This insight will come from a pilot of the approach on the same project, going forward. Before implementation of the technical debt mechanism in the chosen projects, baseline data will be collected in order to provide a basis for comparison. Such data will include basic effort, cost, and productivity data as well as qualitative data about the project's history of technical debt. The latter data will include the gathering of "stories" [33] about unexpected debt repayment, crises caused by unpaid debt (or at least recognized as such *post hoc*), and decisions that had been made based upon an implicit understanding of technical debt.

Once the baseline data are collected, the technical debt mechanism will be tailored to the specific work practices in the projects. Details of the procedures for using and maintaining the technical debt list will depend on the types and formats of the software process data available, and the tools used to manage that data. A simple tool will be implemented to aid in managing the list and to collect data on its use. The list will be kept under version control, along with other project documents. Project personnel will be trained on using the technical debt list. The process of implementation will be closely monitored, including all issues raised and their resolutions.

In the first release cycle, during which the projects will be tracking technical debt for the first time, detailed qualitative and quantitative data will be collected concerning the amount of time project personnel spend using the technical debt list, the kinds of problems and questions that come up, and the usefulness of the approach from the point of view of the project personnel. After the first release, detailed focus groups will be conducted with each project, aimed at characterizing in more detail the amount of work required to carry out the approach, the confidence that personnel have in the eventual benefits, and any benefits already observed. This will also provide an opportunity to modify the approach based on feedback. Data will then be collected over successive releases to determine the benefits of the approach over time. These data will include documentation of decisions made concerning technical debt, the principal and interest paid and/or avoided, the costs of using the technical debt list, its contribution to decision making, and the rate at which technical debt items are added and removed from the list. Much of this data will be qualitative in nature, and will contribute to an open, mixed-methods case study design. All data, both qualitative and quantitative, will be analyzed using an iterative approach involving coding and comparing pieces of evidence in order to build well-grounded propositions. This approach is similar to grounded theory; however, the process will start with well-defined research questions and will not be completely open. The questions guiding the data analysis are:

- What factors contributed to the costs of measuring and monitoring technical debt?
- In what ways did technical debt information contribute to decision making?

A natural outcome of the retrospective and pilot studies will be a set of suggestions for improvement to the management mechanism. However, the challenge here will be to evolve the management mechanism in a way that is general and flexible enough to be valuable in any environment (with proper tailoring, of course). The key to meeting this challenge is to triangulate findings between multiple study settings; that is beyond the single case study that is currently underway. Comparing the evolution of the mechanism in the two settings will allow identification of modifications that are essential to support the core concepts of technical debt, and of those that are needed to support technical debt management in a particular setting. Both types of modifications are necessary, but it is essential to be able to differentiate between the two.

The findings from the retrospective and case studies will be the primary input to the evolution of the management mechanism. As new factors and relationships are identified in the cost–benefit models, these factors and relationships must be incorporated into the management mechanism. Incorporating new concepts could take the form of additions to the technical debt item template, modifications to the decision procedures, new types of technical debt, modified estimation procedures, or changes to any other part of the management mechanism.

6. Conclusion

The problem of managing the aging of software systems during maintenance is not new. Typically, tight maintenance budgets and schedules inevitably result in modifications that do not fully take quality requirements into account. Using the technical debt metaphor to reason about this phenomenon allows practitioners and managers to fully account for it in planning and decision making. However, there are many obstacles to doing this easily. We have attempted in this chapter to propose a way forward toward using a technical debt lens to facilitate maintenance management. More work lies ahead in validating and refining this approach in practice, as well as broadening the metaphor to include all sources of technical debt.

REFERENCES

[1] S.M. Dekleva, Software maintenance: 1990 status, Software Maintenance Res. Pract. 4 (1992) 15.
[2] M.J.C. Sousa, H.M. Moreira, A survey on the software maintenance process, in: International Conference on Software Maintenance, Bethesda, MD, USA, 1998, pp. 265–274.
[3] B.P. Lientz, E.B. Swanson, G.E. Tompkins, Characteristics of application software maintenance, Commun. ACM 21 (1978) 6.
[4] M. Fowler, Technical Debt. Available: http://www.martinfowler.com/bliki/TechnicalDebt.html, 2003.
[5] M.M. Lehman, L.A. Belady (Eds.), Program Evolution: Processes of Software Change, Academic Press Professional, Inc, San Diego, CA, USA, 1985.
[6] D.L. Parnas, Software aging, in: 16th International Conference on Software Engineering, Sorrento, Italy, 1994.
[7] W. Cunningham, The WyCash Portfolio management system, in: Addendum to the Proceedings on Object-Oriented Programming Systems, Languages, and Applications, 1992, pp. 29–30.
[8] S. McConnell, 10x Software Development. Available: http://forums.construx.com/blogs/stevemcc/archive/2007/11/01/technical-debt-2.aspx, 2007.
[9] J. Rothman, An Incremental Technique to Pay off Testing Technical Debt. Available: http://www.stickyminds.com/sitewide.asp?Function=edetail&ObjectType=COL&ObjectId=11011&tth=DYN&tt=siteemail&iDyn=2, 2006.
[10] J. Shore, Quality with a Name. Available: http://jamesshore.com/Articles/Quality-With-a-Name.html, 2006.
[11] M.J. Carr, S. Konda, I. Monarch, C.F. Walker, F.C. Ulrich, Taxonomy-Based Risk Identification, Software Engineering Institute, Pittsburgh, 1993, CMU/SEI-93-TR-6.
[12] R. Fairley, Risk management for software projects, IEEE Software 11 (1994) 57–67.
[13] C. Chapman, S. Ward, Project Risk Management: Processes, Techniques and Insights, first ed., John Wiley & Sons, West Sussex, UK, 1996.

[14] Airmic, A risk management standard, available at http://www.theirm.org/publications/documents/Risk_Management_Standard_030820.pdf, 2002.

[15] D. Hillson, D. Hulett, Assessing risk probability: alternative approaches, in: Proceedings of PMI Global Congress, Prague, Czech Republic, 2004.

[16] P.E. Engert, Z.F. Lansdowne, Risk Matrix User's Guide, The Mitre Corporation, Bedford, MA, USA, 1999. Available at http://www.mitre.org/work/sepo/toolkits/risk/ToolsTechniques/files/UserGuide220.pdf.

[17] J. Ansell, F. Wharton, Risk: Analysis, Assessment and Management, John Wiley & Sons, Chichester, 1992.

[18] I. Sommerville, Software Engineering, eighth ed., Addison-Wesley, Harlow, UK, 2007.

[19] S. McConnell, Software Project Survival Guide, Microsoft Press, Redmond, WA, USA, 1998.

[20] B. Kitchenham, L. Pfleeger, Software quality: the elusive target, IEEE Software 13 (1996) 12–21.

[21] J. Tian, M. Zelkowitz, Complexity measure evaluation and selection, IEEE Trans. Software Eng. 21 (1995) 641–650.

[22] K. El Emam, et al., The confounding effect of class size on the validity of object-oriented metrics, IEEE Trans. Software Eng. 27 (2001) 630–650.

[23] G. Koru, T. Jeff, Comparing high-change modules and modules with the highest measurement values in two large-scale open-source products, IEEE Trans. Software Eng. 31 (2005) 625–642.

[24] M. Fowler, et al., Refactoring. Improving the Design of Existing Code, Addison Wesley, Boston, MA, USA, 1999.

[25] M. Lanza, et al., Object-Oriented Metrics in Practice, Springer, Berlin, 2006.

[26] Y. Guo, et al., Domain-specific tailoring of code smells: an empirical study, in: Proceedings of the 32nd ACM/IEEE International Conference on Software Engineering, 2010, Vancouver, Canada, pp. 167–170.

[27] E. van Emden, L. Moonen, Java quality assurance by detecting code smells, in: 9th Working Conference on Reverse Engineering, Richmond, VA, USA, 2002.

[28] B.W. Boehm, Software Engineering Economics, Prentice-Hall, Englewood Cliffs, NJ, 1981.

[29] I.I. Standard, ISO-20926 Software Engineering—Unadjusted Functional Size Measurement Method—Counting Practices Manual, 2003.

[30] A. Stellman, J. Greene, Applied software project management, 2005.

[31] M. Jørgensen, Estimation of software development work effort: evidence on expert judgment and formal models, Int. J. Forecasting 23 (2007) 449–462.

[32] M. Jørgensen, A review of studies on expert estimation of software development effort, J. Systems and Software, 70 (2004) 37–60.

[33] W.G. Lutters, C.B. Seaman, The value of war stories in debunking the myths of documentation in software maintenance, Inform. Software Technol. 49 (2007) 12.

A Taxonomy and Survey of Energy-Efficient Data Centers and Cloud Computing Systems

ANTON BELOGLAZOV

Cloud Computing and Distributed Systems (CLOUDS) Laboratory, Department of Computer Science and Software Engineering, The University of Melbourne, Melbourne, VIC 3010, Australia

RAJKUMAR BUYYA

Cloud Computing and Distributed Systems (CLOUDS) Laboratory, Department of Computer Science and Software Engineering, The University of Melbourne, Melbourne, VIC 3010, Australia

YOUNG CHOON LEE

Centre for Distributed and High Performance Computing, School of Information Technologies, The University of Sydney, Sydney, NSW 2600, Australia

ALBERT ZOMAYA

Centre for Distributed and High Performance Computing, School of Information Technologies, The University of Sydney, Sydney, NSW 2600, Australia

Abstract

Traditionally, the development of computing systems has been focused on performance improvements driven by the demand of applications from consumer, scientific, and business domains. However, the ever-increasing energy

ADVANCES IN COMPUTERS, VOL. 82
ISSN: 0065-2458/DOI: 10.1016/B978-0-12-385512-1.00003-7

consumption of computing systems has started to limit further performance growth due to overwhelming electricity bills and carbon dioxide footprints. Therefore, the goal of the computer system design has been shifted to power and energy efficiency. To identify open challenges in the area and facilitate future advancements, it is essential to synthesize and classify the research on power- and energy-efficient design conducted to date. In this study, we discuss causes and problems of high power/energy consumption, and present a taxonomy of energy-efficient design of computing systems covering the hardware, operating system, virtualization, and data center levels. We survey various key works in the area and map them onto our taxonomy to guide future design and development efforts. This chapter concludes with a discussion on advancements identified in energy-efficient computing and our vision for future research directions.

1. Introduction

The primary focus of designers of computing systems and the industry has been on the improvement of the system performance. According to this objective, the performance has been steadily growing driven by more efficient system design and increasing density of the components described by Moore's law [1]. Although the performance per watt ratio has been constantly rising, the total power drawn by computing systems is hardly decreasing. Oppositely, it has been increasing every year that can be illustrated by the estimated average power use across three classes of servers presented in Table I [2]. If this trend continues, the cost of the energy consumed by a server during its lifetime will exceed the hardware cost [3]. The problem is even worse for large-scale compute infrastructures, such as clusters and data centers. It was estimated that in 2006 IT infrastructures in the United States consumed about 61 billion kWh for the total electricity cost about 4.5 billion dollars [4]. The estimated energy consumption is more than double from what was consumed by IT in 2000. Moreover, under current efficiency trends, the energy consumption tends to double again by 2011, resulting in 7.4 billion dollars annually.

Energy consumption is not only determined by hardware efficiency, but it is also dependent on the resource management system deployed on the infrastructure and the efficiency of applications running in the system. This interconnection of the energy consumption and different levels of computing systems can be seen in Fig. 1. Energy efficiency impacts end-users in terms of resource usage costs, which are typically determined by the total cost of ownership (TCO) incurred by a resource provider. Higher power consumption results not only in boosted electricity bills but also in additional requirements to a cooling system and power delivery infrastructure, that is, uninterruptible power supplies (UPS), power distribution units (PDU), and so on. With the growth of computer components density, the cooling problem becomes crucial, as more heat has to be dissipated for a square meter. The problem is

TABLE I
ESTIMATED AVERAGE POWER CONSUMPTION PER SERVER CLASS (W/U) FROM 2000 TO 2006 [2]

Server class	2000	2001	2002	2003	2004	2005	2006
Volume	186	193	200	207	213	219	225
Mid-range	424	457	491	524	574	625	675
High-end	5534	5832	6130	6428	6973	7651	8163

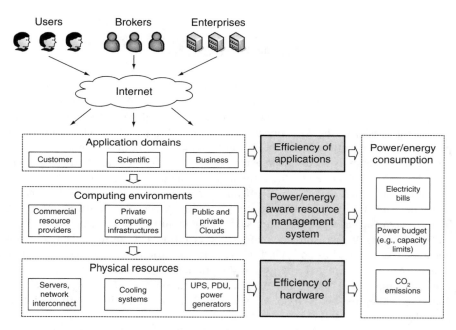

FIG. 1. Energy consumption at different levels in computing systems.

especially important for 1U and blade servers. These types of servers are the most difficult to cool because of high density of the components, and thus lack of space for the air flow. Blade servers bring the advantage of more computational power in less rack space. For example, 60 blade servers can be installed into a standard 42U rack [5]. However, such system requires more than 4000 W to supply the resources and cooling system compared to the same rack filled by 1U servers consuming 2500 W. Moreover, the peak power consumption tends to limit further performance improvements due to constraints of power distribution facilities. For example, to power a server rack in a typical data center, it is necessary to provide about 60 A [6]. Even if the cooling problem can be addressed for future systems, it is likely that delivering current in such data centers will reach the power delivery limits.

Apart from the overwhelming operating costs and the total cost of acquisition (TCA), another rising concern is the environmental impact in terms of carbon dioxide (CO_2) emissions caused by high energy consumption. Therefore, the reduction of power and energy consumption has become a first-order objective in the design of modern computing systems. The roots of energy-efficient computing, or Green IT, practices can be traced back to 1992, when the U.S. Environmental Protection Agency launched Energy Star, a voluntary labeling program which is designed to identify and promote energy-efficient products in order to reduce the greenhouse gas emissions. Computers and monitors were the first labeled products. This has led to the widespread adoption of the sleep mode in electronic devices. At that time, the term "green computing" was introduced to refer to energy-efficient personal computers [7]. At the same time, the Swedish confederation of professional employees has developed the TCO certification program—a series of end-user and environmental requirements for IT equipment including video adapters, monitors, keyboards, computers, peripherals, IT systems, and even mobile phones. Later, this program has been extended to include requirements on ergonomics, magnetic and electrical field emission levels, energy consumption, noise level, and use of hazardous compounds in hardware. The Energy Star program was revised in October 2006 to include stricter efficiency requirements for computer equipment, along with a tiered ranking system for approved products.

There are a number of industry initiatives aiming at the development of standardized methods and techniques for the reduction of the energy consumption in computer environments. They include Climate Savers Computing Initiative (CSCI), Green Computing Impact Organization, Inc. (GCIO), Green Electronics Council, The Green Grid, International Professional Practice Partnership (IP3), with membership of companies such as AMD, Dell, HP, IBM, Intel, Microsoft, Sun Microsystems, and VMware.

Energy-efficient resource management has been first introduced in the context of battery-powered mobile devices, where energy consumption has to be reduced in order to improve the battery lifetime. Although techniques developed for mobile devices can be applied or adapted for servers and data centers, this kind of systems requires specific methods. In this chapter, we discuss ways to reduce power and energy consumption in computing systems, as well as recent research works that deal with power and energy efficiency at the hardware and firmware, operating system (OS), virtualization, and data center levels. The main objective of this work is to give an overview of the recent research advancements in energy-efficient computing, identify common characteristics, and classify the approaches. On the other hand, the aim is to show the level of development in the area and discuss open research challenges and direction for future work. The reminder of this chapter is organized as follows: in the next section, power and energy models are introduced; in Section 3, we discuss problems caused by high power and energy consumption; in Sections 4–8, we present the taxonomy and survey of the research in energy-efficient design of computing systems, followed by a conclusion and directions for future work in Section 9.

2. Power and Energy Models

To understand power and energy management mechanisms, it is essential to clarify the terminology. Electric current is the flow of electric charge measured in amperes. Amperes define the amount of electric charge transferred by a circuit per second. Power and energy can be defined in terms of work that a system performs. Power is the rate at which the system performs the work, while energy is the total amount of work performed over a period of time. Power and energy are measured in watts (W) and watt-hour (Wh), respectively. Work is done at the rate of 1 W when 1 A is transferred through a potential difference of 1 V. A kilowatt-hour (kWh) is the amount of energy equivalent to a power of 1 kW (1000 W) being applied for one hour. Formally, power and energy can be defined as in (1) and (2):

$$P = \frac{W}{T},\tag{1}$$

$$E = PT,\tag{2}$$

where P is power, T is a period of time, W is the total work performed during that period of time, and E is energy. The difference between power and energy is very important because a reduction of the power consumption does not always reduce the consumed energy. For example, the power consumption can be decreased by lowering the CPU performance. However, in this case, a program may require longer time to complete its execution consuming the same amount of energy. On one hand, a reduction of the peak power consumption results in decreased costs of the infrastructure provisioning, such as costs associated with capacities of UPS, PDU, power generators, cooling system, and power distribution equipment. On the other hand, decreased energy consumption leads to a reduction of the electricity bills. The energy consumption can be reduced temporarily using dynamic power management (DPM) techniques or permanently applying static power management (SPM). DPM utilizes the knowledge of the real-time resource usage and application workloads to optimize the energy consumption. However, it does not necessarily decrease the peak power consumption. In contrast, SPM includes the usage of highly efficient hardware equipment, such as CPUs, disk storage, network devices, UPS, and power supplies. These structural changes usually reduce both the energy and peak power consumption.

2.1 Static and Dynamic Power Consumption

The main power consumption in complementary metal-oxide-semiconductor (CMOS) circuits comprises static and dynamic power. The static power consumption, or leakage power, is caused by leakage currents that are present in any active circuit, independently of clock rates and usage scenarios. This static power is mainly determined by the type of transistors and process technology. The reduction of the static power requires improvements of the low-level system design; therefore, it is not in the focus of this chapter. More details regarding possible ways to improve the energy efficiency at this level can be found in the survey by Venkatachalam and Franz [8].

Dynamic power consumption is created by circuit activity (i.e., transistor switches, changes of values in registers, etc.) and depends mainly on a specific usage scenario, clock rates, and I/O activity. The sources of the dynamic power consumption are short-circuit current and switched capacitance. Short-circuit current causes only 10–15% of the total power consumption and so far no way has been found to reduce this value without compromising the performance. Switched capacitance is the primary source of the dynamic power consumption; therefore, the dynamic power consumption can be defined as in (3):

$$P_{\text{dynamic}} = aCV^2f, \tag{3}$$

where a is the switching activity, C is the physical capacitance, V is the supply voltage, and f is the clock frequency. The values of switching activity and capacitance are determined by the low-level system design. Whereas the combined reduction of the supply voltage and clock frequency lies in the roots of the widely adopted DPM technique called dynamic voltage and frequency scaling (DVFS). The main idea of this technique is to intentionally downscale the CPU performance, when it is not fully utilized, by decreasing the voltage and frequency of the CPU that in the ideal case should result in a cubic reduction of the dynamic power consumption. DVFS is supported by most modern CPUs including mobile, desktop, and server systems. We will discuss this technique in detail in Section 5.2.1.

2.2 Sources of Power Consumption

According to data provided by Intel Labs [5], the main part of power consumed by a server is accounted for the CPU, followed by the memory and losses due to the power supply inefficiency (Fig. 2). The data show that the CPU no longer dominates power consumption by a server. This resulted from the continuous improvement of the CPU power efficiency and application of power-saving techniques (e.g., DVFS) that enable active low-power modes. In these modes, a CPU consumes a fraction of the total power, while preserving the ability to execute programs. As a result, current

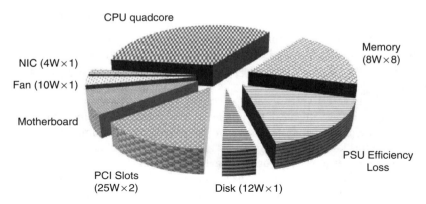

FIG. 2. Power consumption by server's components [5].

desktop and server CPUs can consume less than 30% of their peak power in low-activity modes, leading to dynamic power range of more than 70% of the peak power [9]. In contrast, dynamic power ranges of all other server's components are much narrower: less than 50% for dynamic random access memory (DRAM), 25% for disk drives, 15% for network switches, and negligible for other components [10]. The reason is that only the CPU supports active low-power modes, whereas other components can only be completely or partially switched off. However, the performance overhead of a transition between active and inactive modes is substantial. For example, a disk drive in a spun-down, deep-sleep mode consumes almost no power, but a transition to active mode incurs a latency that is 1000 times higher than the regular access latency. Power inefficiency of the server's components in the idle state leads to a narrow overall dynamic power range of 30%. This means that even if a server is completely idle, it will still consume more than 70% of its peak power.

Another reason for the reduction of the fraction of power consumed by the CPU relatively to the whole system is the adoption of multi-core architectures. Multi-core processors are much more efficient than conventional single-core processors. For example, servers built with recent Quad-core Intel Xeon processor can deliver 1.8 teraflops at the peak performance, using less than 10 kW of power. To compare with, Pentium processors in 1998 would consume about 800 kW to achieve the same performance [5].

The adoption of multi-core CPUs along with the increasing use of virtualization technologies and data-intensive applications resulted in the growing amount of memory in servers. In contrast to the CPU, DRAM has a narrower dynamic power range and power consumption by memory chips is increasing. Memory is packaged in dual in-line memory modules (DIMMs), and power consumption by these modules varies from 5 to 21 W per DIMM, for DDR3 and fully buffered DIMM (FB-DIMM) memory technologies [5]. Power consumption by a server with eight 1 GB DIMMs is about 80 W. Modern large servers currently use 32 or 64 DIMMs that leads to power consumption by memory higher than by CPUs. Most of the power management techniques are focused on the CPU; however, the constantly increasing frequency and capacity of memory chips raise the cooling requirements apart from the problem of high energy consumption. These facts make memory one of the most important server components that have to be efficiently managed. New techniques and approaches to the reduction of the memory power consumption have to be developed in order to address this problem.

Power supplies transform alternating current (AC) into direct current (DC) to feed server's components. This transformation leads to significant power losses due to the inefficiency of the current technology. The efficiency of power supplies depends on their load. They achieve the highest efficiency at loads within the range of 50–75%. However, most data centers normally create a load of 10–15% wasting the majority of the consumed electricity and leading to the average power losses of 60–80% [5]. As a result, power supplies consume at least 2% of the US electricity production. More efficient power supply design can save more than a half of the energy consumption.

The problem of the low average utilization also applies to disk storages, especially when disks are attached to servers in a data center. However, this can be addressed by moving the disks to an external centralized storage array. Nevertheless, intelligent policies have to be used to efficiently manage a storage system containing thousands of disks. This creates another direction for the research work aimed at the optimization of the resource, power, and energy usage in server farms and data centers.

2.3   Modeling Power Consumption

To develop new policies for DPM and understand their impact, it is necessary to create a model of dynamic power consumption. Such a model has to be able to predict the actual value of the power consumption by a system based on some run-time system characteristics. One of the ways to accomplish this is to utilize power monitoring capabilities that are built-in modern computer servers. This instrument provides the ability to monitor power usage of a server in real time and collect accurate statistics of the power usage. Based on this data, it is possible to derive a power consumption model for a particular system. However, this approach is complex and requires the collection of statistical data for each target system.

Fan et al. [10] have found a strong relationship between the CPU utilization and total power consumption by a server. The idea behind the proposed model is that the power consumption by a server grows linearly with the growth of the CPU utilization from the value of the power consumption in the idle state up to the power consumed when the server is fully utilized. This relationship can be expressed as in (4):

$$P(u) = P_{\text{idle}} + (P_{\text{busy}} - P_{\text{idle}}) \times u, \tag{4}$$

where P is the estimated power consumption, P_{idle} is the power consumption by an idle server, P_{busy} is the power consumed by the server when it is fully utilized, and u is the current CPU utilization. The authors have also proposed an empirical non-linear model given in (5):

$$P(u) = P_{\text{idle}} + (P_{\text{busy}} - P_{\text{idle}})(2u - u^r), \tag{5}$$

where r is a calibration parameter that minimizes the square error and has to be obtained experimentally. For each class of machines of interest, a set of calibration experiments must be performed to fine tune the model.

Extensive experiments on several thousands of nodes under different types of workloads (Fig. 3) have shown that the derived models accurately predict the power consumption by server systems with the error below 5% for the linear model and 1% for the empirical model. The calibration parameter r has been set to 1.4 for the presented results. These precise results can be explained by the fact that the CPU is the main power consumer in servers and, in contrast to the CPU, other system components (e.g., I/O, memory) have narrow dynamic power ranges or their activities correlate with the CPU activity . For example, current server processors can reduce power consumption up to 70% by switching to low-power-performance modes [9].

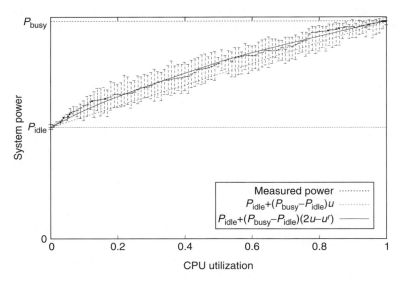

FIG. 3. Power consumption to CPU utilization relationship [10].

However, dynamic power ranges of other components are much narrower: $< 50\%$ for DRAM, 25% for disk drives, and 15% for network switches.

This accurate and simple power model enables easy prediction of the power consumption by a server supplied with CPU utilization data and power consumption values at the idle and maximum CPU utilization states. Therefore, it is especially important that the increasing number of server manufactures publish actual power consumption figures for their systems at different utilization levels [11]. This is driven by the adoption of the ASHRAE Thermal Guideline [12] that recommends providing power ratings for the minimum, typical and full CPU utilization.

Dhiman et al. [13] have found that although regression models based on just CPU utilization are able to provide reasonable prediction accuracy for CPU-intensive workloads, they tend to be considerably inaccurate for prediction of power consumption caused by I/O- and memory-intensive applications. The authors have proposed a power modeling methodology based on Gaussian mixture models that predicts power consumption by a physical machine running multiple virtual machine (VM) instances. To perform predictions, in addition to the CPU utilization, the model relies on run-time workload characteristics such as the number of instructions per cycle (IPC) and the number of memory accesses per cycle (MPC). The proposed approach requires a training phase to perceive the relationship between the workload metrics and the power consumption. The authors have evaluated the proposed model via experimental studies involving different workload types. The obtained experimental results have shown that the model predicts the power consumption with high accuracy ($<10\%$ prediction error), which is consistent over all the tested workloads. The proposed model outperforms regression models by a factor of 5 for specific workload types. This proves the importance of architectural metrics like IPC and MPC as compliments to the CPU utilization for the power consumption prediction.

3. Problems of High Power and Energy Consumption

The energy consumption by computing facilities raises various monetary, environmental, and system performance concerns. A recent study on the power consumption of server farms [2] has shown that in 2005 the electricity use by servers worldwide—including their associated cooling and auxiliary equipment—costed 7.2 billion dollars. The study also indicates that the electricity consumption in that year had doubled compared to the consumption in 2000. Clearly, there are environmental issues with the generation of electricity. The number of transistors integrated into today's Intel Itanium 2 processor reaches nearly 1 billion. If this rate continues, the heat (per cm^2) produced by future processors would exceed that of the surface of the Sun [14], resulting in poor system performance. The scope of energy-efficient design is not limited to main computing components (e.g., processors, storage devices, and visualization facilities), but it can expand into a much larger range of resources associated with computing facilities including auxiliary equipments, water used for cooling, and even physical/floor space occupied by these resources.

While recent advances in hardware technologies including low-power processors, solid state drives, and energy-efficient monitors have alleviated the energy consumption issue to a certain degree, a series of software approaches have significantly contributed to the improvement of energy efficiency. These two approaches (hardware and software) should be seen as complementary rather than competitive. User awareness is another non-negligible factor that should be taken into account when discussing Green IT. User awareness and behavior in general considerably affect computing workload and resource usage patterns; this in turn has a direct relationship with the energy consumption of not only core computing resources but also auxiliary equipment such as cooling/air conditioning systems. For example, a computer program developed without paying much attention to its energy efficiency may lead to excessive energy consumption and may contribute to higher heat emission resulting in increases in the energy consumption for cooling.

Traditionally, power- and energy-efficient resource management techniques have been applied to mobile devices. It was dictated by the fact that such devices are usually battery-powered, and it is essential to apply power and energy management to improve their lifetime. However, due to the continuous growth of the power and energy consumption by servers and data centers, the focus of power and energy management techniques has been switched to these systems. Even though the problems caused by high power and energy consumption are interconnected, they have their specifics and have to be considered separately. The difference is that the peak power consumption determines the cost of the infrastructure required to maintain the system's operation, whereas the energy consumption accounts for electricity bills. Let us discuss each of these problems in detail.

3.1   High Power Consumption

The main reason of the power inefficiency in data centers is low average utilization of the resources. To show this, we have analyzed the data provided as a part of the CoMon project,[1] a monitoring infrastructure for PlanetLab.[2] We have used the data of

---

[1] http://comon.cs.princeton.edu/
[2] http://www.planet-lab.org/

the CPU utilization by more than a thousand servers located at more than 500 places around the world. The data have been collected in 5 minute intervals during the period from 10 to 19 May 2010. The distribution of the data over the mentioned 10 days along with the characteristics of the distribution are presented in Fig. 4. The data confirm the observation made by Barroso and Holzle [9]: the average CPU utilization is below 50%. The mean value of the CPU utilization is 36.44% with 95% confidence interval from 36.40% to 36.47%. The main run-time reasons of underutilization in data centers are variability of the workload and statistical effects. Modern service applications cannot be kept on fully utilized servers, as even non-significant workload fluctuation will lead to performance degradation and failing to provide the expected quality of service (QoS). However, servers in a non-virtualized data center are unlikely to be completely idle because of background tasks (e.g., incremental backups), or distributed data bases or file systems. Data distribution helps to tackle load-balancing problem and improves fault tolerance. Furthermore, despite the fact that the resources have to be provisioned to handle theoretical peak loads, it is very unlikely that all the servers of a large-scale data centers will be fully utilized simultaneously.

Systems where average utilization of resources less than 50% represent huge inefficiency, as most of the time only a half of the resources are actually in use. Although the resources on average are utilized by less than 50%, the infrastructure

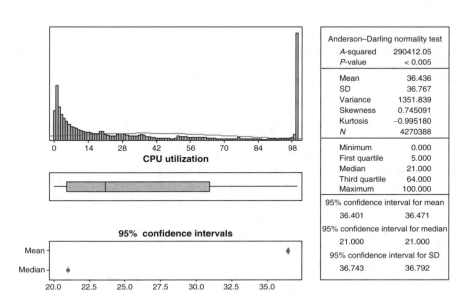

FIG. 4. The CPU utilization of more than 1000 PlanetLab nodes over a period of 10 days.

has to be built to handle the peak load, which rarely occurs in practice. In such systems, the cost of over-provisioned capacity is very significant and includes expenses on extra capacity of cooling systems, PDU, generators, power delivery facilities, UPS, and so on. The less the average resource utilization in a data center, the more expensive the data center becomes as a part of the TCO, as it has to support peak loads and meet the requirements to the peak power consumption [10]. Moreover, the peak power consumption can constrain further growth of power density, as power requirements already reach 60 A for a server rack [6]. If this tendency continues, further performance improvements can be bounded by the power delivery capabilities.

Another problem of high power consumption and increasing density of server's components (i.e., 1U, blade servers) is the heat dissipation. Much of the electrical power consumed by computing resources gets turned into heat. The amount of heat produced by an integrated circuit depends on how efficient the component's design is, and the voltage and frequency at which the component operates. The heat generated by the resources has to be dissipated to keep them within their safe thermal state. Overheating of the components can lead to a decrease of their lifetime and high error-proneness. Moreover, power is required to feed the cooling system operation. For each watt of power consumed by computing resources, an additional 0.5–1 W is required for the cooling system [6]. For example, to dissipate 1 W consumed by a high-performance computing (HPC) system at the Lawrence Livermore National Laboratory (LLNL), 0.7 W of additional power is needed for the cooling system [15]. Moreover, modern high-density servers, such as 1U and blade servers, further complicate cooling because of the lack of space for airflow within the packages. These facts justify the significant concern about the efficiency and real-time adaptation of the cooling system operation.

3.2   High Energy Consumption

The way to address high power consumption is the minimization of the peak power required to feed a completely utilized system. In contrast, the energy consumption is defined by the average power consumption over a period of time. Therefore, the actual energy consumption by a data center does not affect the cost of the infrastructure. However, it is reflected in the cost of electricity consumed by the system, which is the main component of data center operating costs. Furthermore, in most data centers, 50% of consumed energy never reaches the computing resources: it is consumed by the cooling facilities or dissipated in conversions within the UPS and PDU systems. With the current tendency of continuously growing energy consumption and costs associated with it, the point when operating costs exceed the cost of computing resources themselves in few years can be reached soon. Therefore, it is crucial to develop and apply energy-efficient resource management strategies in data centers.

Except for high operating costs, another problem caused by the growing energy consumption is high CO_2 emissions, which contribute to the global warming. According to Gartner [16] in 2007, the Information and Communications Technology (ICT) industry was responsible for about 2% of global CO_2 emissions, which is equivalent to the aviation. According to the estimation by the U.S. Environmental Protection Agency (EPA), current efficiency trends lead to the increase of annual CO_2 emissions from 42.8 million metric tons ($MMTCO_2$) in 2007 to 67.9 $MMTCO_2$ in 2011. Intense media coverage has raised the awareness of people around the climate change and greenhouse effect. More and more customers start to consider the "green" aspect in selecting products and services. Besides the environmental concern, businesses have begun to face risks caused by being non-environment friendly. The reduction of CO_2 footprints is an important problem that has to be addressed in order to facilitate further advancements in computing systems.

4. Taxonomy of Power/Energy Management in Computing Systems

A large volume of research has been done in the area of power and energy-efficient resource management in computing systems. As power and energy management techniques are closely connected, from this point we will refer to them as power management. As shown in Fig. 5, the high-level power management techniques can be divided into static and dynamic. From the hardware point of view,

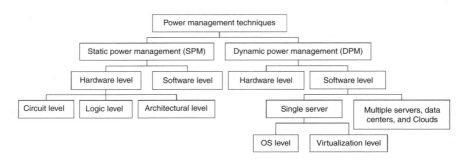

FIG. 5. High-level taxonomy of power and energy management.

SPM contains all the optimization methods that are applied at the design time at the circuit, logic, architectural, and system levels [17]. Circuit level optimizations are focused on the reduction of the switching activity power of individual logic gates and transistor level combinational circuits by the application of a complex gate design and transistor sizing. Optimizations at the logic level are aimed at the switching activity power of logic-level combinational and sequential circuits. Architecture level methods include the analysis of the system design and subsequent incorporation of power optimization techniques in it. In other words, this kind of optimization refers to the process of efficient mapping of a high-level problem specification onto a register-transfer level design. Apart from the optimization of the hardware-level system design, it is extremely important to carefully consider the implementation of programs that are supposed to run in the system. Even with perfectly designed hardware, poor software design can lead to dramatic performance and power losses. However, it is impractical or impossible to analyze power consumption caused by large programs at the operator level, as not only the process of compilation or code generation but also the order of instructions can have an impact on power consumption. Therefore, indirect estimation methods can be applied. For example, it has been shown that faster code almost always implies lower energy consumption [18]. Nevertheless, methods for guaranteed synthesizing of optimal algorithms are not available, and this is a very difficult research problem.

This chapter focuses on DPM techniques that include methods and strategies for run-time adaptation of a system's behavior according to current resource requirements or any other dynamic characteristic of the system's state. The major assumption enabling DPM is that systems experience variable workloads during their operation allowing the dynamic adjustment of power states according to current performance requirements. The second assumption is that the workload can be predicted to a certain degree. As shown in Fig. 6, DPM techniques can be distinguished by the level at which they are applied: hardware or software. Hardware DPM varies for different hardware components, but usually can be classified as dynamic performance scaling (DPS), such as DVFS, and partial or complete dynamic component deactivation (DCD) during periods of inactivity. In contrast, software DPM techniques utilize interface to the system's power management and according to their policies apply hardware DPM. The introduction of the Advanced Power Management (APM)[3] and its successor, the Advanced Configuration and Power Interface (ACPI),[4] has drastically simplified the software power management and resulted in broad research studies in this area. The problem of power-efficient

---

[3] http://en.wikipedia.org/wiki/Advanced_power_management
[4] http://www.acpi.info/

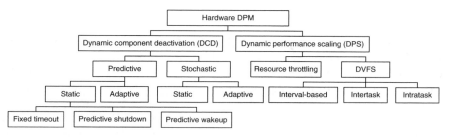

Fig. 6. DPM techniques applied at the hardware and firmware levels.

resource management has been investigated in different contexts of device-specific management, OS-level management of virtualized and non-virtualized servers, followed by multiple-node system such as homogeneous and heterogeneous clusters, data centers, and Clouds.

DVFS creates a broad dynamic power range for the CPU enabling extremely low-power active modes. This flexibility has led to the wide adoption of this technique and appearance of many policies that scale CPU performance according to current requirements, while trying to minimize performance degradation [19]. Subsequently, these techniques have been extrapolated on multiple-server systems providing coordinated performance scaling across them [20]. However, due to narrow overall dynamic power range of servers in a data center, it has been found beneficial to consolidate workload to a limited number of servers and switch off or put to sleep/hibernate state idle nodes [21].

Another technology that can improve the utilization of resources, and thus reduce the power consumption, is virtualization of computer resources. The virtualization technology allows one to create several VMs on a physical server and, therefore, reduce the amount of hardware in use and improve the utilization of resources. The concept originated with the IBM mainframe OSs of the 1960s, but was commercialized for x86-compatible computers only in the 1990s. Several commercial companies and open-source projects now offer software packages to enable a transition to virtual computing. Intel Corporation and AMD have also built proprietary virtualization enhancements to the x86 instruction set into each of their CPU product lines to facilitate virtualized computing. Among the benefits of virtualization are improved fault and performance isolation between applications sharing the same computer node (a VM is viewed as a dedicated resource to the customer); the ability to relatively easily move VMs from one physical host to another using live or off-line migration; and support for hardware and software heterogeneity. The ability to reallocate VMs at run-time enables dynamic consolidation of the workload, as VMs can be moved to a minimal number of physical nodes, while idle nodes can be switched to power-saving modes.

Terminal servers have also been used in Green IT practices. When using terminal servers, users connect to a central server; all of the computing is done at the server level but the end-user experiences a dedicated computing resource. It is usually combined with thin clients, which use up to one-eighth the amount of energy of a normal workstation, resulting in a decrease of the energy consumption and costs. There has been an increase in the usage of terminal services with thin clients to create virtual laboratories. Examples of terminal server software include Terminal Services for Windows, the Aqua Connect Terminal Server for Mac, and the Linux Terminal Server Project (LTSP) for the Linux operating system. Thin clients possibly are going to gain a new wave of popularity with the adoption of the Software as a Service (SaaS) model, which is one of the kinds of Cloud computing [22], or Virtual Desktop Infrastructures (VDI) heavily promoted by virtualization software vendors.[5]

Traditionally, an organization purchases its own computing resources and deals with the maintenance and upgrades of the outdated hardware and software, resulting in additional expenses. The recently emerged Cloud computing paradigm [22] leverages virtualization technology and provides the ability to provision resources on-demand on a pay-as-you-go basis. Organizations can outsource their computation needs to the Cloud, thereby eliminating the necessity to maintain own computing infrastructure. Cloud computing naturally leads to power efficiency by providing the following characteristics:

- Economy of scale due to elimination of redundancies.
- Improved utilization of the resources.
- Location independence—VMs can be moved to a place where energy is cheaper.
- Scaling up/down and in/out—the resource usage can be adjusted to current requirements.
- Efficient resource management by the Cloud provider.

One of the important requirements for a Cloud computing environment is providing reliable QoS. It can be defined in terms of service level agreements (SLA) that describe such characteristics as minimal throughput, maximal response time, or latency delivered by the deployed system. Although modern virtualization

---

[5] VMware View (VMware VDI) Enterprise Virtual Desktop Management, http://www.vmware.com/ products/view/; Citrix XenDesktop Desktop Virtualization, http://www.citrix.com/virtualization/desktop/ xendesktop.html; Sun Virtual Desktop Infrastructure Software, http://www.sun.com/software/vdi/

technologies can ensure performance isolation between VMs sharing the same physical computing node, due to aggressive consolidation and variability of the workload, some VMs may not get the required amount of resource when requested. This leads to performance losses in terms of increased response times, timeouts, or failures in the worst case. Therefore, Cloud providers have to deal with the power-performance trade-off—minimization of the power consumption while meeting the QoS requirements.

The following sections detail different levels of the presented taxonomy: in Section 5, we discuss power optimization techniques that can be applied at the hardware level. We survey the approaches proposed for power management at the OS level in Section 6, followed by the discussion of modern virtualization technologies and their impact on power-aware resource management in Section 7, and the recent approaches applied at the data center level in Section 8.

5. Hardware and Firmware Level

As shown in Fig. 6, DPM techniques applied at the hardware and firmware level can be broadly divided into two categories: dynamic component deactivation (DCD) and dynamic performance scaling (DPS). DCD techniques are built upon the idea of the clock gating of parts of an electronic component or complete disabling during periods of inactivity.

The problem could be easily solved if transitions between power states would cause negligible power and performance overhead. However, transitions to low-power states usually lead to additional power consumption and delays caused by the reinitialization of the components. For example, if entering a low-power state requires shutdown of the power supply, returning to the active state will cause a delay consisting of turning on and stabilization of the power supply and clock, reinitialization of the system, and restoring the context [23]. In the case of non-negligible transitions, efficient power management turns into a difficult online optimization problem. A transition to low-power state is worthwhile only if the period of inactivity is longer than the aggregated delay of transitions from and into the active state, and the saved power is higher than the required to reinitialize the component.

5.1 Dynamic Component Deactivation

Computer components that do not support performance scaling and can only be deactivated require techniques that will leverage the workload variability and disable the component when it is idle. The problem is trivial in the case of a negligible transition overhead. However, in reality such transitions lead not only to delays, which can degrade performance of the system, but also to additional power draw. Therefore, to be effective, a transition has to be done only if the idle period is long enough to compensate the transition overhead. In most real-world systems, there is a limited or no knowledge of the future workload. Therefore, a prediction of an effective transition has to be done according to historical data or some system model. A large volume of research has been done to develop efficient methods to solve this problem [23,24]. As shown in Fig. 6, the proposed DCD techniques can be divided into predictive and stochastic.

Predictive techniques are based on the correlation between the past history of the system behavior and its near future. The efficiency of such techniques is highly dependent on the actual correlation between past and future events and the quality of tuning for a particular workload type. A non-ideal prediction can result in an over- or underprediction. An overprediction means that the actual idle period is shorter than the predicted, leading to a performance penalty. However, an underprediction means that the actual idle period is longer than the predicted. This case does not have any influence on the performance; however, it results in reduced energy savings.

Predictive techniques can be further split into static and adaptive. Static techniques utilize some threshold of a real-time execution parameter to make predictions of idle periods. The simplest policy is called fixed timeout. The idea is to define the length of time, after which a period of inactivity can be treated as long enough to do a transition to a low-power state. Activation of the component is initiated once the first request to a component is received. The policy has two advantages: it can be applied to any workload type, and over- and under-predictions can be controlled by adjusting the value of the timeout threshold. However, disadvantages are obvious: the policy requires adjustment of the threshold value for each workload, it always leads to a performance loss on the activation, and the energy consumed from the beginning of an idle period to the timeout is wasted. Two ways to overcome the drawbacks of the fixed timeout policy have been proposed: predictive shutdown and predictive wakeup.

Predictive shutdown policies address the problem of the missed opportunity to save energy within the timeout. These policies utilize the assumption that previous periods of inactivity are highly correlated with the nearest future. According to the analysis of the historical information, they predict the length of the next idle period before it actually begins. These policies are highly dependent on the actual workload and the strength of the correlation between past and future events. History-based predictors have been shown to be more efficient and less safe than timeouts [25]. Predictive wakeup techniques aim to eliminate the performance penalty on the activation. The transition to the active state is predicted based on the past history and performed before an actual user request [26]. This technique increases the energy consumption but reduces performance losses on wakeups.

All the static techniques are inefficient in cases when the system workload is unknown or can vary over time. To address this problem, adaptive predictive techniques have been introduced. The basic idea is to dynamically adjust the parameters, which are fixed for the static techniques, according to the prediction quality that they have provided in the past. For example, the timeout value can be increased if for the last several intervals the value has led to overpredictions. Another way to provide the adaptation is to maintain a list of possible values of the parameter of interest and assign weights to the values according to their efficiency at previous intervals. The actual value is obtained as a weighted average over all the values in the list. In general, adaptive techniques are more efficient than static when the type of the workload is unknown *a priori*. Several adaptive techniques are discussed in the paper by Douglis et al. [27].

Another way to deal with non-deterministic system behavior is to formulate the problem as a stochastic optimization, which requires building an appropriate probabilistic model of the system. For instance, in such a model, system requests and power state transitions are represented as stochastic processes and can be modeled as Markov processes. At any moment, a request arrives with some probability and a device power state transition occurs with another probability obtained by solving the stochastic optimization problem. It is important to note that the results, obtained using the stochastic approach, are expected values, and there is no guarantee that the solution will be optimal for a particular case. Moreover, constructing a stochastic model of the system in practice may not be straightforward. If the model is not accurate, the policies using this model may not provide the efficient system control.

5.2   Dynamic Performance Scaling

DPS includes different techniques that can be applied to computer components supporting dynamic adjustment of their performance proportionally to the power consumption. Instead of complete deactivations, some components, such as the CPU, allow gradual reductions or increases of the clock frequency along with adjustments of the supply voltage in cases when the resource is not fully utilized. This idea lies in the roots of the widely adopted DVFS technique.

5.2.1   Dynamic Voltage and Frequency Scaling

Although the CPU frequency can be adjusted separately, frequency scaling by itself is rarely worthwhile as a way to conserve switching power. Saving the most power requires dynamic voltage scaling too, because of the V^2 component and the fact that modern CPUs are strongly optimized for low voltage states. Dynamic voltage scaling is usually used in conjunction with frequency scaling, as the frequency that a chip may run at is related to the operating voltage. The efficiency of some electrical components, such as voltage regulators, decreases with a temperature increase, so the power used may increase with temperature. Since increasing power use may raise the temperature, increases in voltage or frequency may raise the system power demand even faster than the CMOS formula indicates, and vice versa. DVFS reduces the number of instructions a processor can issue in a given amount of time, thus reducing the performance. This, in turn, increases the run-time of program segments which are significantly CPU bound. Hence, it creates a challenge of providing the optimal energy/performance control, which has been extensively investigated by scientists in recent years. Some of the research works will be reviewed in the following sections.

Although the application of DVFS may seem to be straightforward, real-world systems raise many complexities that have to be considered. First of all, due to complex architectures of modern CPUs (i.e., pipelining, multilevel cache, etc.), the prediction of the required CPU clock frequency that will meet application's performance requirements is not trivial. Another problem is that in contrast to the theory, power consumption by a CPU may not be quadratic to its supply voltage. For example, it is shown that some architectures may include several supply voltages that power different parts of the chip, and even if one of them can be reduced, overall power consumption will be dominated by the larger supply voltage [8]. Moreover, the execution time of a program running on the CPU may not be inversely proportional to the clock frequency, and DVFS may result in non-linearities in the execution time [28]. For example, if a program is memory or I/O bounded, the CPU speed will not have a dramatic effect on the execution time. Furthermore, slowing down the CPU may lead to changes in the order, in which the tasks are scheduled [8]. In summary, DVFS can provide substantial energy savings; however, it has to be applied carefully, as the result may significantly vary for different hardware and software system architectures.

Approaches that apply DVFS to reduce energy consumption by a system can be divided into interval-based, inter- and intratask [28]. Interval-based algorithms are similar to adaptive predictive DCD approaches in that they also utilize the knowledge of the past periods of the CPU activity [29,30]. Depending on the utilization of the CPU during previous intervals, they predict the utilization in the near future and appropriately adjust the voltage and clock frequency. Wierman et al. [31] and Andrew et al. [32] have conducted analytical studies of speed scaling algorithms in processor sharing systems. They have proved that no online energy-proportional speed scaling algorithm can be better than two-competitive comparing to the offline optimal algorithm. Moreover, they have found that sophistication in the design of speed scaling algorithms does not provide significant performance improvements; however, it dramatically improves robustness to errors in estimation of workload parameters. Intertask approaches instead of relying on coarse-grained data on the CPU utilization distinguish different tasks running in the system and assign them different speeds [33,34]. The problem is easy to solve if the workload is known *a priori* or constant over the whole period of a task execution. However, the problem becomes non-trivial when the workload is irregular. In contrast to intertask, intratask approaches leverage fine-grained information about the structure of programs and adjust the processor frequency and voltage within the tasks [35,36]. Such policies can be implemented by splitting a program execution into timeslots and assigning different CPU speeds to each of them. Another way to apply such policies is to implement them at the compiler level. This kind of approaches utilizes the compiler's knowledge of a program's structure to make inferences about possible periods for the clock frequency reduction.

5.3   Advanced Configuration and Power Interface

Many DPM algorithms, such as timeout-based as well as other predictive and stochastic policies, can be implemented in hardware as a part of an electronic circuit. However, a hardware implementation highly complicates the modification and reconfiguration of the policies. Therefore, there are strong reasons to shift the implementation to the software level. In 1996 to address this problem, Intel, Microsoft, and Toshiba have published the first version of the Advanced Configuration and Power Interface (ACPI) specification—an open standard defining a unified OS-centric device configuration and power management interface. In contrast to previous basic input/output system (BIOS) central, firmware-based, and platform-specific power management systems, ACPI describes platform-independent interfaces for hardware discovery, configuration, power management, and monitoring.

ACPI is an attempt to unify and improve the existing power and configuration standards for hardware devices. The standard brings DPM into the OS control and requires an ACPI-compatible OS to take over the system and have the exclusive control of all aspects of the power management and device configuration responsibilities. The main goals of ACPI are to enable all computing systems to implement DPM capabilities, and simplify and accelerate the development of power-managed systems. It is important to note that ACPI does not put any constraints on particular power management policies, but provides an interface that can be used by software developers to leverage flexibility in adjustment of the system's power states.

ACPI defines a number of power states that can be applied in the system at run-time. The most important states in the context of DPM are C-states and P-states. C-states are the CPU power states C0–C3 that denote the operating state, halt, stop-clock, and sleep mode accordingly. While a processor operates, it can be in one of several power-performance states (P-state). Each of these states designates a particular combination of DVFS settings. P-states are implementation-dependent, but P0 is always the highest performance state, with P_1 to P_n being successively lower performance states, up to an implementation-specific limit of n no greater than 16. P-states have become known as SpeedStep in Intel processors, PowerNow!, or Cool'n'Quiet in AMD processors, and PowerSaver in VIA processors. ACPI is widely used by OSs, middleware, and software on top of them to manage power consumption according to their specific policies.

6. Operating System Level

In this section, we discuss research works that deal with power-efficient resource management at the OS level. The taxonomy of the characteristics used to classify the works is presented in Fig. 7. To highlight the most important characteristics of the works, they are summarized in Table II (the full table is given in Appendix A).

6.1   The On-Demand Governor (Linux Kernel)

Pallipadi and Starikovskiy [19] have developed an in-kernel real-time power manager for the Linux OS called the on-demand governor. The manager continuously monitors the CPU utilization multiple times per second and sets a clock frequency and supply voltage pair that corresponds to current performance requirements keeping the CPU approximately 80% busy to handle fast changes in the workload. The goal of the on-demand governor is to keep the performance loss due to reduced frequency to the minimum. Modern CPU frequency scaling technologies provide extremely low latency allowing dynamic adjustment of the power consumption matching the variable workload with almost negligible performance overhead. For example, Enhanced Intel Speedstep Technology enables frequency switching with the latency as low as 10 ms. To accommodate different requirements of diverse systems, the on-demand governor can be tuned via the specification of the rate at which the CPU utilization is checked and the value of the upper utilization threshold, which is set to 80% by default.

The on-demand governor effectively handles multiprocessor SMP systems as well as multi-core and multithreading CPU architectures. The governor manages each CPU individually and can manage different cores in the CPU separately if this is supported by the hardware. In cases when different processor cores in a CPU are dependent on each other in terms of frequency, they are managed together as a single entity. In order to support this design, the on-demand governor sets the frequency of all the cores based on the highest utilization among the cores in the group.

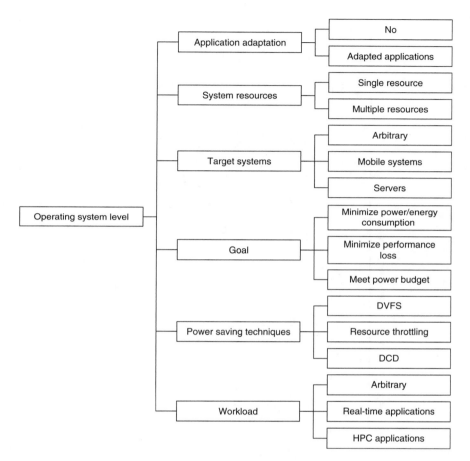

FIG. 7. Operating system level taxonomy.

There are a number of improvements that are currently under investigation, including parallel calculation of the utilization and a dedicated work queue. The original governor samples the utilization of all of the processors in the system in a centralized way that can become a significant overhead with increase in the number of CPUs. To overcome this problem, the authors in [19] have proposed a parallel sampling independently for each CPU. Another improvement that can increase the performance for multiprocessor systems is to have dedicated kernel threads for the governor and do sampling and changing of frequencies in the context of a particular kernel thread.

TABLE II

OPERATING SYSTEM LEVEL RESEARCH WORKS

Project name	System resources	Target systems	Goal	Power-saving techniques
The on-demand governor [19]	CPU	Arbitrary	Minimize power consumption, minimize performance loss	DVFS
ECOsystem [37,38]	CPU, memory, disk storage, network interface	Mobile systems	Achieve target battery lifetime	Resource throttling
Nemesis OS [39]	CPU, memory, disk storage, network interface	Mobile systems	Achieve target battery lifetime	Resource throttling
GRACE [40,41]	CPU, network interface	Mobile systems	Minimize energy consumption, satisfy performance requirements	DVFS, resource throttling
Linux/RK [42]	CPU	Real-time systems	Minimize energy consumption, satisfy performance requirements	DVFS
Coda and Odyssey [43]	CPU, network interface	Mobile systems	Minimize energy consumption through application degradation	Resource throttling
PowerNap [44]	System wide	Server systems	Minimize power consumption, minimize performance loss	DCD

6.2   ECOsystem

Zeng et al. [37,38] have proposed and developed ECOsystem—a framework for managing energy as a first-class OS resource aimed at battery-powered devices. The authors' fundamental assumption is that applications play an important role in energy distribution opportunities that can be leveraged only at the application level. ECOsystem provides an interface to define a target battery lifetime and applications' priorities used to determine the amount of energy that will be allocated to applications at each time frame.

The authors split OS-level energy management into two dimensions. Along the first dimension, there is a variety of system devices (e.g., CPU, memory, disk storage, network interface) that can consume energy concurrently. The other dimension spans applications that share the system devices and cause the energy consumption. To address the problem of accounting the energy usage by both devices and applications, the authors have introduced a new measurement unit called currentcy. One unit of currentcy represents the right to consume a certain amount of energy during a fixed period of time. When the user sets the target battery lifetime and prioritizes the applications, ECOsystem transforms these data into an appropriate amount of currentcy and determines how much currentcy should be allocated to each application at each time frame. The length of the timeframe has been empirically determined as 1 s that is sufficient to achieve smooth energy allocation. An application expends the allocated amount of currentcy by utilizing the CPU, performing disk and memory accesses and consuming other system resources. An application can accumulate currentcy up to a specified limit. When an expenditure of an application exceeds the allocated amount of currentcy, none of the associated processes are scheduled or otherwise serviced.

The system has been implemented as a modified Linux kernel and has been experimentally evaluated. The obtained results show that the proposed model can be effectively used to meet different energy goals, such as achieving a target battery lifetime and proportional energy distribution among competing applications.

6.3   Nemesis OS

Neugebauer and McAuley [39] have developed the resource-centric Nemesis OS—an OS for battery-powered devices that strives to provide a consistent QoS for time-sensitive application, such as multimedia applications. Nemesis provides fine-grained control and accounting for energy usage over all the system resources: the CPU, memory, disk, and network bandwidth.

To implement per-process resource usage accounting, the OS has been vertically structured: most of the system's functions, protocol stacks, and device drivers are implemented in user-level shared libraries that execute in the applications' processes. This design allows accurate and easy accounting for the energy consumption caused by individual applications.

The goal of Nemesis is to address the problem of battery lifetime management. To achieve the target battery lifetime specified by the user, the system relies on the cooperation with applications. If the current energy consumption rate exceeds the threshold that can lead to failing to meet the user's expectations, the system charges the applications according to their current energy usage. The applications should interpret the charges as feedback signals and adapt their behavior. The applications are supposed to limit their resource usage according to the data provided by the OS. However, not all application may support the adaptation. In this case, the user can prioritize the applications leading to shutdowns of the low-priority tasks. Currently, Nemesis supports a number of platforms including Intel 486, Pentium, Pentium Pro and Pentium II-based PCs, DEC Alpha workstations and evaluation boards, and StrongARM SA-110-based network computers.

6.4   The Illinois GRACE Project

Sachs et al. [40,41] have created the Illinois GRACE project (Global Resource Adaptation through CoopEration). They have proposed saving energy through coordinated adaptation at multiple system layers according to changes in the applications' demand for system resources. The authors have proposed three levels of adaptation: global, per-application, and internal adaptation. The global adaptation takes into account all the applications running in the system and all the system layers. This level of adaptation responses to significant changes in the system, such as an application entry or exit. The per-application adaptation considers each application in isolation and is invoked every time frame adapting all the system resources to the application's demands. The internal adaptation focuses on different system resources separately that are possibly shared by multiple applications and adapts the states of the resources. All the adaptation levels are coordinated in order to ensure adaptation decisions that are effective across all levels.

The framework supports adaptations of the CPU performance (DVSF), applications (frame rate and dithering), and soft CPU scaling (CPU time allocation). The second generation of the framework (GRACE-2) focuses on a hierarchical adaptation for mobile multimedia systems. Moreover, it leverages the adaptation of the application behavior depending on the resource constraints. GRACE-2 apart from the CPU adaptation enforces network bandwidth constraints and minimizes the network transmission energy. The approach has been implemented as a part of the Linux kernel and requires applications to be able to limit their resource usage at run-time in order to leverage the per-application adaptation technique. There is only a limited support for legacy applications.

The experimental results show that the application adaptation provides significant benefits over the global adaptation when the network bandwidth is constrained. Energy savings in a system with the CPU and network adaptations when adding the application adaptation reach 32% (22% on average). When both the CPU and application adaptations are added to a system with the global adaptation, the energy savings have been found to be more than additive.

6.5   Linux/RK

Rajkumar et al. [42] have proposed several algorithms for application of DVFS in real-time systems and have implemented a prototype as a modified Linux kernel— Linux/Resource Kernel (Linux/RK). The objective is to minimize the energy consumption, while maintaining the performance isolation between applications. The authors have proposed four alternative DVFS algorithms that are automatically selected by the system when appropriate.

SystemClock Frequency Assignment (Sys-Clock) is suitable for systems where the overhead of voltage and frequency scaling is too high to be performed at every context switch. A single clock frequency is selected at the admission of an application and kept constant until the set of applications running in the system changes. Priority-Monotonic Clock Frequency Assignment (PM-Clock) is suitable for systems with a low voltage and frequency scaling overhead allowing the adjustment of the voltage and frequency settings at each context switch. Each application is assigned its own constant clock frequency, which is enabled when the application is allocated a CPU time frame. Optimal Clock Frequency Assignment (Opt-Clock) uses a non-linear optimization model to determine the optimal frequency for each application that minimizes the energy consumption. Due to high computational complexity, this technique is suitable only for the offline usage. Dynamic PM-Clock (DPM-Clock) suits systems where the average execution time of an application is significantly less than the worst case. The authors have conducted experimental studies to evaluate the proposed algorithms. The results show that Sys-Clock, PM-Clock, and DPM-Clock provide up to 50% energy savings.

6.6   Coda and Odyssey

Flinn and Satyanarayanan [43] have explored the problem of managing limited computing resources and battery lifetime in mobile systems, as well as addressing the variability of the network connectivity. They have developed two systems: Coda and Odyssey that implement adaptation across multiple system levels. Coda implements application-transparent adaptation in the context of a distributed file system, which does not require any modification of legacy applications to run in the system.

Odyssey is responsible for initiation and managing application adaptations. This kind of adaptation allows adjustment of the resource consumption by the cost of the output data quality, which is mostly suitable for multimedia applications. For example, in cases of constrained resources video data can be processed or transferred over network in a lower resolution or sound quality can be reduced.

Odyssey introduces a term fidelity that defines the degree to which the output data corresponds to the original quality. Each application can specify acceptable levels of fidelity that can be requested by Odyssey when the resource usage has to be limited. When Odyssey notifies an application about a change of the resource availability, the application has to adjust its fidelity to match the requested level. For energy-aware adaptation, it is essential that reductions in fidelity lead to energy savings that are both significant and predictable. The evaluation results show that this approach allows the extension of the battery lifetime up to 30%. A limitation of such a system is that all the necessary applications have to be modified in order to support the proposed approach.

6.7   PowerNap

Meisner et al. [44] have proposed an approach for power conservation in server systems based on fast transitions between active and low-power states. The goal is to minimize power consumption by a server while it is in an idle state. Instead of addressing the problem of achieving energy-proportional computing as proposed by Barroso and Holzle [9], the authors require only two power states (sleep and fully active) for each system component. The other requirements are fast transitions between the power states and very low-power consumption in the sleep mode.

To investigate the problem, the authors have collected fine-grained utilization traces of several servers serving different workloads. According to the data, the majority of idle periods are shorter than 1 s with the mean length in the order of hundreds of milliseconds, whereas busy periods are even shorter falling below 100 ms for some workloads. The main idea of the proposed approach is to leverage short idle periods that occur due to the workload variability. To estimate the characteristics of the hardware suitable for the proposed technique, the authors have constructed a queueing model based on characteristics of the collected utilization traces. They have found that if the transition time is less than 1 ms, it becomes negligible and power savings vary linearly with the utilization for all workloads. However, with the growth of the transition time, power savings decrease and the performance penalty becomes higher. When the transition time reaches 100 ms, the relative response time for low utilization can grow up to 3.5 times in comparison to a system without power management, which is clearly unacceptable for real-world systems.

The authors have concluded that if the transition time is less than 10 ms, power savings are approximately linear to the utilization and significantly outperform the effect from DVFS for low utilization (<40%). However, the problem is that the requirement for the transition time being less than 10 ms cannot be satisfied with the current technological level. According to the data provided by the authors, modern servers can ensure the transition time of 300 ms, which is far from the required 10 ms. The proposed approach is similar to the fixed timeout DCD technique, but adapted to fine-grained management. Therefore, all the disadvantages of the fixed timeout technique are inherited by the proposed approach, that is, a constant performance penalty on wakeups and an overhead in cases when an idle period is shorter than the transition time to and from a low-power state. The authors have reported that if the stated requirements are satisfied, the average server power consumption can be reduced by 74%.

7. Virtualization Level

The virtualization level enables the abstraction of an OS and applications running on it from the hardware. Physical resources can be split into a number of logical slices called VMs. Each VM can accommodate an individual OS creating for the user a view of a dedicated physical resource and ensuring the performance and failure isolation between VMs sharing a single physical machine. The virtualization layer lies between the hardware and OS and, therefore, a virtual machine monitor (VMM) takes the control over resource multiplexing and has to be involved in the system's power management. There are two ways of how a VMM can participate in the power management:

1. A VMM can act as a power-aware OS without distinction between VMs: monitor the overall system's performance and appropriately apply DVFS or any DCD techniques to the system components.
2. Another way is to leverage OS's specific power management policies and application-level knowledge, and map power management calls from different VMs on actual changes in the hardware's power state or enforce system-wide power limits in a coordinated manner.

We will discuss these techniques in detail in the following sections.

7.1 Virtualization Technology Vendors

In this section, we discuss three of the most popular virtualization technology solutions: the Xen hypervisor,[6] VMware solutions,[7] and Kernel-based virtual machine (KVM).[8] All of these systems support the first described way to perform power management; however, none allows the coordination of VMs' specific calls for power state changes. Section 7.2 discusses an approach proposed by Stoess et al. [45] that utilizes both system-wide power control and fine-grained application-specific power management performed by guest OSs.

Other important capabilities supported by the mentioned virtualization solutions are offline and live migrations of VMs. They enable transferring VMs from one physical host to another, and thus have facilitated the development of different techniques for VM consolidation and load balancing that will be discussed in Section 8.

7.1.1 Xen

The Xen hypervisor is an open-source virtualization technology developed collaboratively by the Xen community and engineers from over 20 innovative data center solution vendors [46]. Xen is licensed under the GNU General Public License (GPL2) and available at no charge in both source and object formats. Xen's support for power management is similar to what is provided by the Linux's on-demand governor described in Section 6.1. Xen supports ACPI's P-states implemented in the cpufreq driver [47]. The system periodically measures the CPU utilization, determines an appropriate P-state, and issues a platform-dependent command to make a change in the hardware's power state. Similarly to the Linux's power management subsystem, Xen contains four governors:

- Ondemand—chooses the best P-state according to current resource requirements.
- Userspace—sets the CPU frequency specified by the user.
- Performance—sets the highest available clock frequency.
- Powersave—sets the lowest clock frequency.

Apart from P-states, Xen also incorporates the support for C-states (CPU sleeping states) [47]. When a physical CPU does not have any task assigned, it is switched to

---

[6] http://www.xen.org/
[7] http://www.vmware.com/
[8] http://www.linux-kvm.org/

a C-state. When a new request comes, the CPU is switched back to the active state. An issue is to determine which C-state to enter: deeper C-states provide higher energy saving by the cost of higher transition latencies. At this moment, by default Xen puts the CPU into the first C-state, which provides the least transition delay. However, the user can specify a C-state to enter. As the CPU wakes up upon receiving a load, it always gets an inevitable performance penalty. The policy is a fixed timeout DCD implying all its disadvantages described in Section 5.1.

Besides P- and C-states, Xen also supports offline and live migration of VMs, which can be leveraged by power-aware dynamic VM consolidation algorithms. Migration is used to transfer a VM between physical hosts. Offline migration moves a VM from one host to another by suspending, copying the VM's memory contents, and then resuming the VM on the destination host. Live migration allows transferring a VM without a suspension. From the user side such migration should be inconspicuous. To perform a live migration, both hosts must be running Xen and the destination host must have sufficient resources (e.g., memory capacity) to accommodate the VM after the transmission. At the destination host Xen starts a new VM instance that forms a container for the VM to be migrated. Xen cyclically copies memory pages to the destination host, continuously refreshing the pages that have been updated on the source. When it notices that the number of modified pages is not shrinking anymore, it stops the source instance and copies the remaining memory pages. Once it is completed, the new VM instance is started. To minimize the migration overhead, the hosts are usually connected to a network attached storage (NAS) or similar storage solution, which eliminates the necessity to copy disk contents. The developers argue that the final phase of a live migration, when both instances are suspended, typically takes approximately 50 ms. Given such a low overhead, the live migration technology has facilitated the development of various energy conservation dynamic VM consolidation approaches proposed by researchers around the world.

7.1.2 VMware

VMware ESX Server and VMware ESXi are enterprise-level virtualization solutions offered by VMware, Inc. Similar to Xen, VMware supports host-level power management via DVFS. The system monitors the CPU utilization and continuously applies appropriate ACPI's P-states [48]. VMware VMotion and VMware Distributed Resource Scheduler (DRS) are two other services that operate in conjunction with ESX Server and ESXi [49]. VMware VMotion enables live migration of VMs between physical nodes, which can be initiated programmatically or manually by system administrators. VMware DRS monitors the resource usage in a pool of servers and uses VMotion to continuously rebalance VMs according to the current workload and load-balancing policy.

VMware DRS contains a subsystem called VMware Distributed Power Management (DPM) to reduce power consumption by a pool of servers by dynamically switching off spare servers [49,50]. Servers are powered back when there is a rising demand for resources. VMware DPM utilizes live migration to reallocate VMs keeping the minimal number of servers powered on. VMware ESX Server and VMware ESXi are free for use, whereas other components of VMware Infrastructure have a commercial license.

7.1.3   Kernel-based Virtual Machine (KVM)

KVM is a virtualization platform, which is implemented as a module of the Linux kernel [51]. Under this model, Linux works as a hypervisor and all the VMs are regular processes scheduled by the Linux scheduler. This approach reduces the complexity of the hypervisor implementation, as scheduling and memory management are handled by the Linux kernel.

KVM supports the S4 (hibernate) and S3 (sleep/stand by) power states.[9] S4 does not require any specific support from KVM: on hibernation, the guest OS dumps the memory state to a hard disk and initiates powering off the computer. The hypervisor translates this signal into termination of the appropriate process. On the next boot, the OS reads the saved memory state from the disk, resumes from the hibernation, and reinitializes all the devices. During the S3 state, memory is kept powered, and thus the content does not need to be saved to a disk. However, the guest OS must save the states of the devices, as they should be restored on a resume. During the next boot, the BIOS should recognize the S3 state and instead of initializing the devices, but jump directly to the restoration of the saved device states. Therefore, the BIOS has to be modified in order to support such behavior.

7.2   Energy Management for Hypervisor-based VMs

Stoess et al. [45] have proposed a framework for energy management in virtualized servers. Typically, energy-aware OSs assume the full knowledge and full control over an underlying hardware, implying device- or application-level accounting for the energy usage. However, in virtualized systems, a hardware resource is shared among multiple VMs. In such an environment, device control and accounting information are distributed across the system, making it infeasible for an OS to take the full control over the hardware. This results in the inability of energy-aware

---

[9] http://www.linux-kvm.org/page/PowerManagement

OSs to invoke their policies in the system. The authors have proposed mechanisms for fine-grained guest OS-level energy accounting and allocation. To encompass the diverse demands on energy management, the authors have proposes to use the notion of energy as the base abstraction in the system, an approach similar to the currentcy model in ECOsystem described in Section 6.2.

The prototypical implementation comprises two subsystems: a host-level resource manager and an energy-aware OS. The host-level manager enforces system-wide power limits across VM instances. The power limits can be dictated by a battery or a power generator, or by thermal constraints imposed by reliability requirements and the cooling system capacity. The manager determines power limits for each VM and device type, which cannot be exceeded to meet the defined power constraints. The complementary energy-aware OS is capable of fine-grained application-specific energy management. To enable application-specific energy management, the framework supports accounting and control not only for physical but also for virtual devices. This enables guest resource management subsystems to leverage their application-specific knowledge.

Experimental results presented by the authors show that the prototype is capable of enforcing power limits for energy-aware and energy-unaware guest OSs. Three areas are considered to be prevalent for future work: devices with multiple power states, processors with support for hardware-assisted virtualization, and multi-core architectures.

8. Data Center Level

In this section we discuss recent research efforts in the area of power management at the data center level. Most of the approaches to dealing with the energy-efficient resource management at the data center level are based on the idea of consolidating the workload into the minimum of physical resources. Switching off idle resources leads to the reduced energy consumption, as well as the increased utilization of resources; therefore, lowering the TCO and speeding up Returns On Investments (ROI).

However, to meet the SLA requirements, the consolidation has to be done intelligently in order to minimize both the energy consumption and performance degradation. In the following sections we survey different approaches to addressing the problem of effectively managing the energy-performance trade-off in virtualized and non-virtualized data centers. The characteristics used to classify the approaches are presented in Fig. 8 Table III illustrates the most significant characteristics of the reviewed research works (the full table is given in Appendix B).

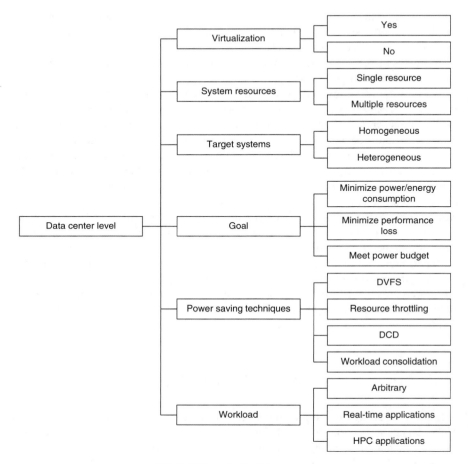

Fɪɢ. 8. Data center level taxonomy.

8.1   Implications of Cloud Computing

Cloud computing has become a very promising paradigm for both consumers and providers in various areas including science, engineering, and not to mention business. A Cloud typically consists of multiple resources possibly distributed and heterogeneous. Although the notion of a Cloud has existed in one form or another for some time now (its roots can be traced back to the mainframe era [66]), recent advances in virtualization technologies and the business trend of reducing the TCO in particular have made it much more appealing compared to when it was first introduced. There are

TABLE III
DATA CENTER LEVEL RESEARCH WORKS

Project name	Virtualization	System resources	Goal	Power-saving techniques
Load balancing and unbalancing for power and performance in cluster-based system [21]	No	CPU, disk storage, and network interface	Minimize power consumption, minimize performance loss	Server power switching
Managing energy and server resources in hosting centers [52]	No	CPU	Minimize power consumption, minimize performance loss	Workload consolidation, server power switching
Energy-efficient server clusters [20]	No	CPU	Minimize energy consumption, satisfy performance requirements	DVFS, server power switching
Energy-aware consolidation for Cloud computing [53]	No	CPU, disk storage	Minimize energy consumption, satisfy performance requirements	Workload consolidation, server power switching
Optimal power allocation in server farms [54]	No	CPU	Allocate the available power budget to minimize mean response time	DVFS
Environment-conscious scheduling of HPC applications [55]	No	CPU	Minimize energy consumption and CO_2 emissions, maximize profit	DVFS, leveraging geographical distribution of data centers
VirtualPower: coordinated power management in virtualized enterprise systems [56]	Yes	CPU	Minimize energy consumption, satisfy performance requirements	DFVS, soft scaling, VM consolidation, and server power switching
Coordinated multilevel power management for the data center [57]	Yes	CPU	Minimize power consumption, minimize performance loss while meeting power budget	DVFS, VM consolidation, and server power switching
Power and performance management of virtualized computing environments via lookahead control [58]	Yes	CPU	Minimize power consumption, minimize performance loss	DVFS, VM consolidation, and server power switching
Resource allocation using virtual clusters [59]	Yes	CPU	Maximize resource utilization, satisfy performance requirements	Resource throttling

(continued)

TABLE III (*Continued*)

Project name	Virtualization	System resources	Goal	Power-saving techniques
Multitiered on-demand resource scheduling for VM-based data center [60]	Yes	CPU, memory	Maximize resource utilization, satisfy performance requirements	Resource throttling
Shares- and utilities-based power consolidation in virtualized server environments [61]	Yes	CPU	Minimize power consumption, minimize performance loss	DFVS, soft scaling
pMapper: power and migration cost aware application placement in virtualized systems [62]	Yes	CPU	Minimize power consumption, minimize performance loss	DVFS, VM consolidation, and server power switching
Resource pool management: reactive versus proactive [63]	Yes	CPU, memory	Maximize resource utilization, satisfy performance requirements	VM consolidation, server power switching
GreenCloud: energy-efficient and SLA-based management of Cloud resources [64,65]	Yes	CPU	Minimize energy consumption, satisfy performance requirements	Leveraging heterogeneity of Cloud data centers, DVFS

many benefits from the adoption and deployment of Clouds, such as scalability and reliability; however, Clouds in essence aim to deliver more economical solutions to both parties (consumers and providers). By economical, we mean that consumers only need to pay per their use and providers can capitalize poorly utilized resources.

From the provider's perspective, the maximization of their profit is a high priority. In this regard, the minimization of energy consumption plays a crucial role. Recursively, energy consumption can be much reduced by increasing the resource utilization. Large profit-driven Cloud service providers typically develop and implement better power management, since they are interested in taking all necessary means to reduce energy costs to maximize their profit. It has been shown that a reduction in the energy consumption by more effectively dealing with resource provisioning (avoidance of resource under/over provisioning) can be obtained [68]. Another problem is that Cloud applications require movements of large data sets between the infrastructure and consumers; thus it is essential to consider both compute and network aspects of the energy efficiency [67]. Energy usage in large-scale computing systems like Clouds yields many other concerns, such as carbon emissions and system reliability. In the following sections we show how recent research addresses the mentioned problems.

8.2   Non-virtualized Systems

8.2.1   Load Management for Power and Performance in Clusters

Pinheiro et al. [21] have proposed a technique for managing a cluster of physical machines with the objective of minimizing the power consumption while providing the required QoS. The authors have presented a new direction of research as all previous works deal with power efficiency in mobile systems or load balancing in clusters. The main technique to minimize power consumption is the load concentration, or unbalancing, while switching idle computing nodes off. The approach requires dealing with the power-performance trade-off, as performance of applications can be degraded due to the workload consolidation. The authors use the throughput and execution time of applications as constraints for ensuring the QoS. The nodes are assumed to be homogeneous. The algorithm periodically monitors the load and decides which nodes should be turned on or off to minimize the power consumption by the system while providing expected performance. To estimate the performance, the authors apply a notion of demand for resources, where resources include CPU, disk, and network interface. This notion is used to predict performance degradation and throughput due to workload migration based on historical data. However, the demand estimation is static—the prediction does not consider possible demand changes over time. Moreover, due to sharing of the resource by several applications, the estimation of the resource demand for each application can be complex when the total demand exceeds 100% of the available resource capacity. For this reason, throughput degradation is not estimated in the experimental study. To determine the time to add or remove a node, the authors introduce a total demand threshold that is set statically for each resource. Additionally, this threshold is supposed to solve the problem of the latency caused by a node addition, but may lead to performance degradation in the case of fast demand growth.

The actual load balancing is not handled by the system and has to be managed by the applications. The resource management algorithm is executed on a master node that creates a single point of failure and might become a performance bottleneck in a large system. In addition, it is claimed that reconfiguration operations are time-consuming and the implementation of the algorithm adds or removes only one node at a time that may also be a reason for slow reaction in large-scale environments.

The authors have also investigated the cooperation between applications and OS in terms of power management decisions. They found that it can help achieve more efficient control. However, the requirement for such cooperation leads to loss of the approach generality. Generality is also reduced as the system has to be configured for each application. However, this problem can be eliminated by the application of the virtualization technology. To evaluate the approach, the authors have conducted several experimental studies with two workload types: web applications and compute-intensive applications. The approach can be applied to multi-service mixed-workload environments with fixed SLA.

8.2.2   Managing Energy and Server Resources in Hosting Centers

Chase et al. [52] have studied the problem of managing resources in Internet hosting centers. Resources are shared among multiple service applications with specified SLA—the throughput and latency. The authors have developed an OS for an Internet hosting center (Muse) that is a supplement for the OSs of the individual servers and supposed to manage and coordinate interactions between the data center's components. The main distinction from previous research on resource management in hosting centers is that the objective is not just to schedule resources efficiently but also to minimize the consumption of electrical power by the system components. In this study, this approach is applied to data centers in order to reduce: operating costs (power consumption by computing resources and cooling system); CO_2 emissions, and thus the impact on the environment; thermal vulnerability of the system due to cooling failures or high service load; and over-provisioning in capacity planning. Muse addresses these problems by automatically scaling back the power demand (and therefore waste heat) when appropriate. Such a control over the resource usage optimizes the trade-off between the service quality and price, allowing the support of flexible SLA negotiated between consumers and the resource provider.

The main challenge is to determine resource demand of each application at its current request load level, and to allocate resources in the most efficient way. To deal with this problem, the authors apply an economic framework: the system allocates resources in a way that maximizes the "profit" by balancing the cost of each resource unit against the estimated utility, or the "revenue" that is gained from allocating that resource unit to a service. Services "bid" for the resources in terms of the volume and quality. This enables negotiation of the SLA according to the available budget and current QoS requirements, that is, balancing cost of resource usage (energy cost) and benefit gained due to the usage of this resource. This enables a data center to improve the energy efficiency under a fluctuating workload, dynamically match the load and power consumption, and respond gracefully to resource shortages.

The system maintains an active set of servers selected to serve requests for each service. Network switches are dynamically reconfigured to change the active set when necessary. Energy consumption is reduced by switching idle servers to power-saving states (e.g., sleep, hibernation). The system is targeted at the web workload, which leads to a "noise" in the load data. The authors address this problem by applying the statistical "flip-flop" filter, which reduces the number of unproductive realloca-tions and leads to a more stable and efficient control.

This work has created a foundation for numerous studies in the area of power-efficient resource allocation at the data center level; however, the proposed approach has several weaknesses. The system deals only with the CPU management, but does not take into account other system resources such as memory, disk storage, and network interface. It utilizes APM, which is an outdated standard for Intel-based systems, while currently adopted by industry standard is ACPI. The thermal factor is not considered as well as the latency due to switching physical nodes on/off. The authors have pointed out that the management algorithm is stable, but it turns out to be relatively expensive during significant changes in the workload. Moreover, heterogeneity of the software configuration requirements is not handled, which can be addressed by applying the virtualization technology.

8.2.3   Energy-Efficient Server Clusters

Elnozahy et al. [20] have explored the problem of power-efficient resource management in a single-service environment for web applications with fixed SLA (response time) and automatic load-balancing running in a homogeneous cluster. The motivation for the work is the reduction of operating costs and improvement of the error-proneness due to overheating. Two power management mechanisms that are applied switching physical nodes on and off (vary-on vary-off, VOVO) and DVFS of the CPU.

The authors have proposed five policies for the resource management: independent voltage scaling (IVS), coordinated voltage scaling (CVS), VOVO, combined policy (VOVO-IVS), and coordinated combined policy (VOVO-CVS). The last mentioned policy is stated to be the most advanced and is provided with a detailed description and mathematical model for determining CPU frequency thresholds. The thresholds define when it is appropriate to turn on an additional physical node or turn off an idle node. The main idea of the policy is to estimate total CPU frequency required to provide the expected response time, determine the optimal number of physical nodes, and proportionally set the frequency for all the nodes.

The experimental results show that the proposed IVS policy can provide up to 29% energy savings and is competitive with more complex schemes for some workloads. VOVO policy can produce saving up to 42%, whereas CVS policy in conjunction with VOVO (VOVO-CVS) results in 18% higher savings that are obtained using VOVO separately. However, the proposed approach is limited in the following factors. The transition time for starting up an additional node is not considered. Only a single application is assumed to be run in the cluster and the load-balancing is supposed to be done by an external system. Moreover, the algorithm is centralized that creates a single point of failure and reduces the system scalability. The workload data are not approximated, which can lead to inefficient decisions due to fluctuations in the demand. No other system resources except for CPU are considered in resource management decisions.

8.2.4   Energy-Aware Consolidation for Cloud Computing

Srikantaiah et al. [53] have investigated the problem of dynamic consolidation of applications serving small stateless requests in data centers to minimize the energy consumption. First of all, the authors have explored the impact of the workload consolidation on the energy-per-transaction metric depending on both CPU and disk utilizations. The obtained experimental results show that the consolidation influences the relationship between energy consumption and utilization of resources in a non-trivial manner. The authors have found that the energy consumption per transaction results in "U"-shaped curve. When the utilization is low, due to high fraction of the idle state, the resource is not efficiently used leading to a more expensive in terms of the energy-performance metric. However, high resource utilization results in an increased cache miss rate, context switches, and scheduling conflicts. Therefore, the energy consumption becomes high due to the performance degradation and consequently longer execution time. For the described experimental setup, the optimal points of utilization are at 70% and 50% for CPU and disk utilizations, respectively.

According to the obtained results, the authors stated that the goal of the energy-aware consolidation is to keep servers well utilized, while avoiding the performance degradation due to high utilization. They modeled the problem as a multidimensional bin packing problem, in which servers are represented by bins, where each resource (CPU, disk, memory, and network) considered as a dimension of the bin. The bin size along each dimension is defined by the determined optimal utilization level. The applications with known resource utilizations are represented by objects with an appropriate size in each dimension. The minimization of the number of bins leads to the minimization of the energy consumption due to switching off idle nodes. However, the model does not capture a possible application performance degradation due to the consolidation. Moreover, the energy consumption may depend on a particular set of application combined on a computer node.

The authors have proposed a heuristic for the defined bin packing problem. The heuristic is based on the minimization of the sum of the Euclidean distances of the current allocations to the optimal point at each server. As a request for an execution of a new application is received, the application is allocated to a server using the proposed heuristic. If the capacity of the active servers is fulfilled, a new server is switched on, and all the applications are reallocated using the same heuristic in an arbitrary order. According to the experimental results, the energy used by the proposed heuristic is about 5.4% higher than optimal. The proposed approach is suitable for heterogeneous environments; however, it has several shortcomings. First of all, resource requirements of applications are assumed to be known *a priori* and constant. Moreover, migration of state-full applications between nodes incurs performance and energy overheads, which are not considered by the authors. Switching servers on/off also leads to significant costs that must be considered for a real-world system. Another problem with the approach is the necessity in an experimental study to obtain the optimal points of the resource utilizations for each server. Furthermore, the decision about keeping the upper threshold of the resource utilization at the optimal point is not justified as the utilization above the threshold can symmetrically provide the same energy-per-transaction level.

8.2.5   Optimal Power Allocation in Server Farms

Gandhi et al. [54] have studied the problem of allocating an available power budget to servers in a virtualized heterogeneous server farm to minimize the mean response time for HPC applications. The authors have investigated how server's CPU frequency scaling techniques affect the server's power consumption. They have conducted experiments applying DFS (T-states), DVFS (P-states), and DVFS + DFS (coarse-grained P-states combined with fine-grained T-states) for CPU-intensive workloads. The results show a linear power-to-frequency relationship for the DFS and DVFS techniques and cubic square relationship for DVFS + DFS.

Given the power-to-frequency relationship, the authors have investigated the problem of finding the optimal power allocation as a problem of determining the optimal frequencies of the servers' CPUs, while ensuring the minimization of the mean response time. To investigate the effect of different factors on the mean response time, the authors have introduced a queuing model that allows prediction of the mean response time as a function of the power-to-frequency relationship, arrival rate, peak power budget, and so on. The model allows determining the optimal power allocation for every possible configuration of the above factors.

The approach has been experimentally evaluated against different types of workloads. The results show that an efficient power allocation can significantly vary for different workloads. To gain the best performance constrained by a power budget, it is not always optimal to run a small number of servers at their maximum speed. Oppositely, depending on the workload it can be more efficient to run more servers but at lower performance levels. The experimental results show that efficient power allocation can substantially improve server farm performance—up to a factor of 5 and by a factor of 1.4 on average.

8.2.6   Environment-Conscious Scheduling of HPC Applications

Garg et al. [55] have investigated the problem of energy and CO_2 efficient scheduling of HPC applications in geographically distributed Cloud data centers. The aim is to provide HPC users with the ability to leverage high-end computing resources supplied by Cloud computing environments on demand and on a pay-as-you-go basis. The authors have addressed the problem in the context of a Cloud resource provider and presented heuristics for energy-efficient meta-scheduling of applications across heterogeneous resource sites. Apart from reducing the maintenance costs, which results in a higher profit for a resource provider, the proposed approach decreases CO_2 footprints. The proposed scheduling algorithms take into account energy cost, carbon emission rate, workload, and CPU power efficiency, which change across different data centers depending on their location, design, and resource management system.

The authors have proposed five scheduling policies: two of which minimize CO_2 emissions, two maximize the profit of resource providers, and the last one is a multiobjective policy that minimizes CO_2 emissions and maximizes the profit.

The multiobjective policy finds for each application a data center that provides the least CO_2 emissions across data centers able to complete an application by the deadline. Then from all the application-data center pairs, the policy chooses one, which results in the maximal profit. These steps are repeated until all the applications are scheduled. The energy consumption is also reduced by applying DVFS for all the CPUs in data centers.

The proposed heuristics have been evaluated using simulations of different scenarios. The experimental results have shown that the energy-centric policies allow the reduction of energy costs by 33% on average. The proposed multiobjective algorithm can be effectively applied when limitations of CO_2 emissions are desired by resource providers or forced by governments. This algorithm leads to a reduction of the carbon emission rate, while maintaining a high level of the profit.

8.3   Virtualized Systems

8.3.1   VirtualPower: Coordinated Power Management

Nathuji and Schwan [56] have investigated the problem of power-efficient resource management in large-scale virtualized data centers. This is the first time when power management techniques have been explored in the context of virtualized systems. The authors have pointed out the following benefits of virtualization: improved fault and performance isolation between applications sharing the same resource; ability to relatively easy move VMs between physical hosts applying live or offline migration; and support for hardware and software heterogeneity, which they investigated in their previous work [69]. Besides the hardware scaling and VMs consolidation, the authors apply a new power management technique in the context of virtualized systems called "soft resource scaling." The idea is to emulate hardware scaling by providing a VM less time for utilizing the resource using the VMM's scheduling capability. "Soft" scaling is useful when hardware scaling is not supported or provides a very small power benefit. The authors have found that combination of "hard" and "soft" scaling may provide higher power savings due to usually limited number of hardware scaling states.

The goals of the proposed approach are support for the isolated and independent operation of guest VMs, and control and coordination of diverse power management policies applied by the VMs to resources. The system intercepts guest VMs' ACPI calls to perform changes in power states, map them on "soft" states and uses as hints for actual changes in the hardware's power state. In this way, the system supports guest VM's system level or application level specific power management policies, while maintaining the isolation between multiple VMs sharing the same physical node.

The authors have proposed splitting the resource management into local and global policies. At the local level, the system coordinates and leverages power management policies of guest VMs at each physical machine. An example of such a policy is the on-demand governor integrated into the Linux kernel. At this level, the QoS is maintained as decisions about changes in power states are issued externally, by guest OS-specific policies. However, the drawback of such a solution is that the power management may be inefficient due to a legacy or non-power-aware guest OS. Moreover, power management decisions are usually done with some slack and the aggregated slack will grow with the number of VMs leading to under-optimal management. The authors have described several local policies aimed at the minimization of power consumption under QoS constraints, and at power capping. The global policies are responsible for managing multiple physical machines and use the knowledge of rack- or blade-level characteristics and requirements. These policies consolidate VMs using migration in order to offload resources and place them into power saving states. The experiments conducted by the authors show that the usage of the proposed system leads to efficient coordination of VM- and application-specific power management policies, and reduces the power consumption up to 34% with little or no performance penalties.

8.3.2 *Coordinated Multilevel Power Management*

Raghavendra et al. [57] have investigated the problem of power management for a data center environment by combining and coordinating five diverse power management policies. The authors argue that although a centralized solution can be implemented to handle all aspects of power management, it is more likely for a business environment that different solutions from multiple vendors are applied. In this case, it is necessary to solve the problem of the coordination between individual controllers to provide correct, stable, and efficient control. The authors classify existing solutions by a number of characteristics including the objective function, performance constraints, hardware/software, and local/global types of policies. The range of solutions that fall into this taxonomy can be very wide. Therefore, instead of trying to address the whole space, the authors focus on five individual solutions and propose five appropriate power management controllers. They have explored the problem in terms of control theory and applied a feedback control loop to coordinate the controllers' actions.

The efficiency controller optimizes the average power consumption by individual servers. The controller monitors the utilization of resources and based on these data predicts future demand and appropriately adjusts the P-state of the CPU. The server manager implements power capping at the server level. It monitors power consumption by a server and reduces the P-state if the power budget is violated. The enclosure manager and the group manager implement power capping at the enclosure and data center level, respectively. They monitor individual power consumptions across a collection of machines and dynamically reprovision power across them to maintain the group power budget. The power budgets can be provided by system designers based on thermal or power delivery constraints, or by high-level power managers. The VM controller reduces power consumption across multiple physical nodes by dynamically consolidating VMs and switching idle servers off. The authors provide integer programming model for the problem of the VM allocation optimization. However, the proposed model does not provide a protection from unproductive migrations due to workload fluctuations and does not show how SLA can be guaranteed in cases of fast changes in the workload. Furthermore, the transition time for reactivating servers and the ability to handle multiple system resources apart from the CPU are not considered.

The authors have provided experimental results, which show the ability of the system to reduce the power consumption under different workloads. The authors have pointed out an interesting outcome of the experiment: the actual power savings can vary depending on the workload, but "the benefits from coordination are qualitatively similar for all classes of workloads." In summary, the authors have presented a system coordinating different power management policies. However, the proposed system is not able to ensure meeting QoS requirements as well as variable SLA from different applications. Therefore, the solution is suitable for enterprise environments, but not for Cloud computing providers, where more reliable QoS and a comprehensive support for SLA are essential.

8.3.3 Power and Performance Management via Lookahead Control

Kusic et al. [58] have explored the problem of power- and performance-efficient resource management in virtualized computing systems. The problem is narrowed to the dynamic provisioning of VMs for multitiered web applications according to the current workload (number of incoming requests). The SLA for each application are defined as the request processing rate. The clients pay for the provided service and receive a refund in a case of violated SLA as a penalty to the resource provider. The objective is to maximize the resource provider's profit by minimizing both power consumption and SLA violation. The problem is stated as a sequential optimization and addressed using the limited lookahead control (LLC). Decision variables to be optimized are the following: the number of VMs to be provisioned for each service;

the CPU share allocated to each VM; the number of servers to switch on or off; and a fraction of the incoming workload to distribute across the servers hosting each service.

The workload is assumed to be quickly changing, which means that resource allocations must be adapted over short time periods—"in order of 10 seconds to a few minutes." Such requirement makes essential the high performance of the optimization controller. The authors have also incorporated in the model time delays and incurred costs for switching hosts and VMs on/off. Switching hosts on/off as well as resizing and dynamic consolidation of VMs via offline migration are applied as power-saving mechanisms. However, DVFS is not performed due to low-power reduction effect as argued by the authors.

The authors have applied Kalman filter to estimate the number of future requests, which is used to predict the future system state and perform necessary reallocations. The authors have provided a mathematical model for the optimization problem. The utility function is risk-aware and includes risks of "excessive switching caused by workload variability" as well as transient power consumption and opportunity costs. However, the proposed model requires simulation-based learning for the application-specific adjustments: processing rate of VMs with different CPU shares must be known *a priori* for each application. This fact limits the generality of the approach. Moreover, due to the complexity of the model, the optimization controller execution time reaches 30 min even for a small experimental setup (15 hosts), which is not suitable for large-scale real-world systems. The authors have applied neural networks to improve the performance; however, the provided experimental results are only for 10 hosts, and thus are not enough to prove the applicability of such a technique. The experimental results show that a server cluster managed using LLC saves 26% in the power consumption costs over a 24-h period when compared to an uncontrolled system. Power savings are achieved with SLA violations of 1.6% of requests.

8.3.4   *Resource Allocation Using Virtual Clusters*

Stillwell et al. [59] have studied the problem of the resource allocation for HPC applications in virtualized homogeneous clusters. The objective is to maximize the resource utilization, while optimizing user-centric metric that encompasses both performance and fairness, which is referred to as the yield. The idea is to design a scheduler focusing on a user-centric metric. The yield of a job is "a fraction of its maximum achievable compute rate that is achieved." A yield of 1 means that the job consumes computational resources at its peak rate.

To formally define the basic resource allocation problem, the authors have assumed that an application requires only one VM instance; the application's computational power and memory requirements are static and known *a priori*. The authors have defined a Mixed Integer Programming Model that describes the problem. However, the solution of the model requires an exponential time, and thus can be obtained only for small instances of the problem. The authors have proposed several heuristics to solve the problem and evaluated them experimentally across different workloads. The results show that the multi-capacity bin packing algorithm that sorts tasks in descending order by their largest resource requirement outperforms or equals to all the other evaluated algorithms in terms of minimum and average yield as well as failure rate.

Subsequently, the authors have relaxed the stated assumptions and considered the cases of parallel applications and dynamic workloads. The researchers have defined a Mixed Integer Programming Model for the first case and adapted the previously designed heuristics to fit into the model. The second case allows migration of applications to address the variability of the workload, but the cost of migration is simplified and considered as a number of bytes required to transfer over network. To limit the overhead due to VM migration, the authors fix the amount of bytes that can be reallocated at one time. The authors have provided a Mixed Integer Programming Model for the defined problem; however, no heuristic has been proposed to solve large-scale problem instances. Limitations of the proposed approach are that no other system resources except for the CPU are considered in the optimization and that the applications' resource needs are assumed to be known *a priori*, which is not typical in practice.

8.3.5   Multitiered On-Demand Resource Scheduling

Song et al. [60] have studied the problem of the efficient resource allocation in multiapplication virtualized data centers. The objective is to improve the utilization of resources leading to the reduced energy consumption. To ensure the QoS, the resources are allocated to applications proportionally according to the application priorities. Each application can be deployed using several VMs instantiated on different physical nodes. In resource management decisions, only the CPU and RAM utilizations are taken into account. In cases of limited resources, the performance of a low-priority application is intentionally degraded and the resources are allocated to critical applications. The authors have proposed scheduling at three levels: the application-level scheduler dispatches requests among application's VMs; the local level scheduler allocates resources to VMs running on a physical node according to their priorities; and the global-level scheduler controls the resource "flow" among the applications. Rather than apply VM migration to implement the global resource "flow," the authors preinstantiate VMs on a group of physical nodes and allocate fractions of the total amount of resources assigned to an application to different VMs.

The authors have presented a linear programming model for the resource allocation problem and a heuristic for this model. They have provided experimental results
for three different applications running on a cluster: a web application, a database,
and a virtualized office application showing that the approach allows the satisfaction
of the defined SLA. One of the limitations of the proposed approach is that it
requires machine learning to obtain the utility functions for applications. Moreover,
it does not utilize VM migration to adapt the allocation at run-time. The approach is
suitable for enterprise environments, where application can have explicitly defined
priorities.

8.3.6 Shares- and Utilities-based Power Consolidation

Cardosa et al. [61] have investigated the problem of the power-efficient VM
allocation in virtualized enterprise computing environments. They leverage min,
max, and shares parameters, which are supported by the most modern VM managers. Min and max allow the user to specify minimum and maximum of CPU time
that can be allocated to a VM. Shares parameter determines proportions, in which
CPU time will be allocated to VMs sharing the same resource. Such approach suits
only enterprise environments, as it does not support strict SLA and requires the
knowledge of the application priorities.

The authors have provided a mathematical formulation of the optimization
problem. The objective function to be optimized includes the power consumption
and utility gained from the execution of a VM, which is assumed to be known
a priori. The authors provide several heuristics for the defined model and experimental results. A basic strategy is to place all the VMs at their maximum resource
requirements in a first-fit manner and leave 10% of the spare capacity to handle the
future growth of the resource usage. The algorithm leverages the heterogeneity of
the infrastructure by sorting physical machines in the increasing order of the power
cost per unit of capacity. The limitations of the basic strategy are that it does not
leverage relative priorities of different VMs, it always allocates a VM at its maximum resource requirements, and uses only 90% of a server's capacity. This algorithm has been used as the benchmark policy and improved throughout the paper
eventually culminating in the recommended PowerExpandMinMax algorithm.
In comparison to the basic policy, this algorithm uses the value of profit that can
be gained by allocating an amount of resource to a particular VM. It leverages the
ability to shrink a VM to minimum resource requirements when necessary and
expand it when it is allowed by the spare capacity and can bring additional profit.
The power consumption cost incurred by each physical server is deducted from the
profit to limit the number of servers in use.

The authors have evaluated the proposed algorithms on a range of large-scale simulations and a small real data center testbed. The experimental results show that the PowerExpandMinMax algorithm consistently outperforms the other policies across a broad spectrum of inputs—varying VM sizes and utilities, varying server capacities, and varying power costs. One of the experiments on a real testbed showed that the overall utility of the data center can be improved by 47%. A limitation of this work is that migration of VMs is not applied in order to adapt the allocation of VMs at run-time—the allocation is static. Another problem is that no other system resources except for CPU are handled by the model. Moreover, the approach requires static definition of the application priorities that limits the applicability in real-world environments.

8.3.7   pMapper: Power and Migration Cost Aware Application Placement

Verma et al. [62] have investigated the problem of dynamic placement of applications in virtualized systems, while minimizing the power consumption and maintaining the SLA. To address the problem, the authors have proposed the pMapper application placement framework. It consists of three managers and an arbitrator, which coordinates their actions and makes allocation decisions. Performance Manager monitors the applications' behavior and resizes VMs according to current resource requirements and the SLA. Power Manager is in charge of adjusting hardware power states and applying DVFS. Migration Manager issues instructions for live migration of VMs in order to consolidate the workload. Arbitrator has a global view of the system and makes decisions about new placements of VMs and determines which VMs and which nodes should be migrated to achieve this placement. The authors claim that the proposed framework is general enough to be able to incorporate different power and performance management strategies under SLA constraints.

The authors have formulated the problem as a continuous optimization: at each time frame, the VM placement should be optimized to minimize the power consumption and maximize the performance. They make several assumptions to solve the problem, which are justified by experimental studies. The first of them is the performance isolation, which means that a VM can be seen by an application running on that VM as a dedicated physical server with the characteristics equal to the VM parameters. The second assumption is that the duration of a VM live migration does not depend on the background load, and the cost of migration can be estimated based on the VM size and profit decrease caused by an SLA violation. The moreover, the solution does not focus on specific applications and can be applied to any kind of the workload. Another assumption is that the power minimization algorithm can minimize the power consumption without knowing the actual amount of power consumed by the application.

The authors have presented several algorithms to solve the defined problem. They have defined it as a bin packing problem with variable bin sizes and costs. The bins, items to pack, and bin costs represent servers, VMs, and power consumption of servers, respectively. To solve the bin packing problem, first-fit decreasing algorithm (FFD) has been adapted to work for differently sized bins with item-dependent cost functions. The problem has been divided into two subproblems: in the first part, new utilization values are determined for each server based on the cost functions and required performance; in the second part, the applications are placed onto servers to fill the target utilization. This algorithm is called min Power Packing (mPP). The first phase of mPP solves the cost minimization problem, whereas the second phase solves the application placement problem. mPP has been adapted to reduce the migration cost by keeping track of the previous placement while solving the second phase. This variant is termed mPPH. Finally, the placement algorithm has been designed that optimizes the power and migration cost trade-off (pMaP). A VM is chosen to be migrated only if the revenue due to the new placement exceeds the migration cost. pMap searches the space between the old and new placements and finds a placement that minimizes the overall cost (sum of the power and migration costs). The authors have implemented the pMapper architecture with the proposed algorithms and performed extensive experiments to validate the efficiency of the approach. The experimental results show that the approach allows saving about 25% of power relatively to the Static and Load Balanced Placement algorithms. The researchers have suggested several directions for the future work such as the consideration of memory bandwidth, a more advanced application of idle states, and an extension of the theoretical formulation of the problem.

8.3.8   Resource Pool Management: Reactive Versus Proactive

Gmach et al. [63] have studied the problem of the energy-efficient dynamic consolidation of VMs in enterprise environments. The authors have proposed a combination of a trace-based workload placement controller and a reactive migration controller. The trace-based workload placement controller collects data on resource usage by VMs instantiated in the data center and uses this historical information to optimize the allocation, while meeting the specified QoS requirements. This controller performs multiobjective optimization by trying to find a new placement of VMs that will minimize the number of servers needed to serve the workload, while limiting the number of VM migrations required to achieve the new placement. The bound on the number of migrations is supposed to be set by the system administrator depending on the acceptable VM migration overhead. The controller places VMs according to their peak resource usage over the period since the previous reallocation, which is set to 4 hours in the experimental study.

The reactive migration controller continuously monitors the resource utilization of physical nodes and detects when the servers are overloaded or underloaded. In contrast to the trace-based workload placement controller, it acts based on the real-time data on the resource usage and adapts the allocation in a small scale (every minute). The objective of this controller is to rapidly respond to fluctuations in the workload. The controller is parameterized by two utilization thresholds that determine overload and underload conditions. An overloading occurs when the utilization of CPU or memory of a server exceeds a given threshold. An underloading occurs when the CPU or memory usage averaged over all the physical nodes falls below a specified threshold. The threshold values are statically set according to the workload analysis and QoS requirements.

The authors have proposed several policies based on different combinations of the described optimization controllers with different utilization thresholds. The simulation-driven evaluation using 3 months of real-world workload traces for 138 SAP applications has shown that the best results can be achieved by applying both optimization controllers simultaneously. The best policy invokes the workload placement controller every 4 hours, and when the servers are detected to be lightly utilized. The migration controller is executed in parallel to tackle the overloading and underloading of servers when they occur. This policy provides minimal CPU violation penalties and requires 10–20% more CPU capacity than the ideal case.

8.3.9 GreenCloud: Energy-Efficient and SLA-based Management Cloud Resources

Buyya et al. [64] have proposed the GreenCloud project aimed at the development of energy-efficient provisioning of Cloud resources, while meeting QoS requirements defined by the SLA established through a negotiation between providers and consumers. The project has explored the problem of power-aware allocation of VMs in Cloud data centers for application services based on user QoS requirements such as deadline and budget constraints [65]. The authors have introduced a real-time virtual machine model. Under this model, a Cloud provider provisions VMs for requested real-time applications and ensures meeting the specified deadline constraints.

The problem is addressed at several levels. At the first level, a user submits a request to a resource broker for provisioning resources for an application consisting

of a set of subtasks with specified CPU and deadline requirements. The broker
translates the specified resource requirements into a request for provisioning VMs
and submits the request to a number of Cloud data centers. The data centers return
the price of provisioning VMs for the broker's request if the deadline requirement
can be fulfilled. The broker chooses the data center that provides the lowest price of
resource provisioning. The selected data center's VM provisioner allocates the
requested VMs to the physical resources, followed by launching the user's applications. The authors have proposed three policies for scheduling real-time VMs in a
data center using DVFS to reduce the energy consumption, while meeting the
deadline constraints and maximizing the request acceptance rate. The Lowest-
DVS policy adjusts the CPU's P-state to the lowest level, ensuring that all the
real-time VMs meet their deadlines. The δ-Advanced-DVS policy over-scales the
CPU speed up to δ% to increase the acceptance rate. The Adaptive-DVS policy uses
an M/M/1 queueing model to calculate the optimal CPU speed if the arrival rate and
service time of real-time VMs can be estimated in advance.

The proposed approach has been evaluated via simulations using the CloudSim
toolkit [70]. The simulations results have shown that the δ-Advanced-DVS shows
the best performance in terms of profit per unit of the consumed power, as the CPU
performance is automatically adjusted according to the system load. The performance of the Adaptive-DVS is limited by the simplified queueing model.

9. Conclusions and Future Directions

In recent years, energy efficiency has emerged as one of the most important design
requirements for modern computing systems, ranging from single servers to data
centers and Clouds, as they continue to consume enormous amounts of electrical
power. Apart from high operating costs incurred by computing resources, this leads to
significant emissions of CO_2 into the environment. For example, currently, IT infrastructures contribute about 2% of the total CO_2 footprints. Unless energy-efficient
techniques and algorithms to manage computing resources are developed, IT's contribution in the world's energy consumption and CO_2 emissions is expected to rapidly
grow. This is obviously unacceptable in the age of climate change and global warming.
To facilitate further developments in the area, it is essential to survey and review the
existing body of knowledge. Therefore, in this chapter, we have studied and classified
various ways to achieve the power and energy efficiency in computing systems.
Recent research advancements have been discussed and categorized across the hardware, OS, virtualization, and data center levels.

It has been shown that intelligent management of computing resources can lead to
a significant reduction of the energy consumption by a system, while still meeting

the performance requirements. A relaxation of the performance constraints usually results in a further decrease of the energy consumption. One of the significant advancements that have facilitated the progress in managing single computing servers is the implementation of the ability to dynamically adjust the voltage and frequency of the CPU (DVFS), followed by the subsequent introduction and implementation of ACPI. These technologies have enabled the run-time software control over the power consumption by the CPU traded for the performance. In this work, we have surveyed and classified various approaches to control the power consumption by a system from the OS level applying DVFS and other power saving techniques and algorithms. A number of research efforts aimed at the development of efficient algorithms for managing the CPU power consumption have resulted in the mainstream adoption of DVFS in a form of the implementation in a kernel module of the Linux OS. The main idea of the technique is to monitor the CPU utilization, and continuously adjust its clock frequency and supply voltage to match the current performance requirements.

The virtualization technology has further advanced the area by introducing the ability to encapsulate the workload in VMs and consolidate them to a single physical server, while providing fault and performance isolation between individual VMs. The consolidation has become especially effective after the adoption of multi-core CPUs in computing environments, as numerous VMs can be allocated to a single physical node leading to the improved utilization of resources and reduced energy consumption compared to a multi-node setup. Besides the consolidation, leading virtualization vendors (i.e., Xen, VMware) similarly to the Linux OS implement continuous DVFS.

The power management problem becomes more complicated when considered from the data center level. In this case the system is represented by a set of interconnected computing nodes that need to be managed as a single resource in order to optimize the energy consumption. The efficient resource management is extremely important for data centers and Cloud computing systems comprising multiple computing nodes, as due to a low average utilization of resources, the cost of energy consumed by computing nodes and a supporting infrastructure (e.g., cooling systems, power supplies, PDU) leads to an inappropriately high TCO. We have classified and discussed a number of recent research works that deal with the problem of the energy-efficient resource management in non-virtualized and virtualized data centers. Due to a narrow dynamic power range of servers, the most effective power saving technique is to allocate the workload to the minimum number of physical servers and switch idle servers off. This technique improves the utilization of resources and eliminates the power consumed by idle servers, which accounts for up to 70% of the power consumption by fully utilized servers. In virtualized environments and Clouds, live and offline VM migration offered by the virtualization technology have enabled the technique of dynamic consolidation of VMs according to their current performance requirements. However, applying VM migration leads to energy and performance overheads, requiring a careful analysis and intelligent techniques to eliminate non-productive migrations that can occur due to workload variation and violations of the SLA negotiated between Cloud providers and their customers. Common limitations of most of the surveyed research works are that no other system resource except for the CPU are considered in the optimization; the transition overhead caused by switching power states of resources and the VM migration overhead are not handled leading to performance degradation; VM migration is not applied to optimize the allocation in run-time. In summary, a more generic solution suitable for modern Cloud computing environments should comply with the following requirements:

- Virtualization of the infrastructure to support hardware and software heterogeneity and simplify the resource provisioning.
- The application of VM migration to continuously adapt the allocation and quickly respond to changes in the workload.
- The ability to handle multiple applications with different SLA owned by multiple users.
- Guaranteed meeting of the QoS requirements for each application.
- The support for different kinds of applications creating, mixed workloads.
- The decentralization and high performance of the optimization algorithm to ensure scalability and fault tolerance.
- The optimization of resource provisioning considering multiple system resources, such as the CPU, memory, disk storage, and network interface.

Apart from satisfying the listed requirements, for future research in the area, we propose the investigation of the following directions. First of all, due to the wide adoption of multi-core CPUs, it is important to develop energy-efficient resource management approaches that will leverage such architectures. Apart from the CPU and memory, another significant energy consumer in data centers is the network interconnect infrastructure. Therefore, it is crucial to develop intelligent techniques to manage network resources efficiently. One of the ways to achieve this for virtualized data centers is to continuously optimize network topologies established between VMs, and thus reduce the network communication overhead and the load of network devices. Regarding the low-level system design, it is important to improve the efficiency of power supplies and develop hardware components supporting the performance scaling proportionally to the power consumption. A reduction of the transition overhead caused by switching between different power states and the VM migration overhead can also greatly advance the energy-efficient resource management and should be addressed by future research.

Another future research direction is the investigation of Cloud federations comprising geographically distributed data centers. For example, efficient distribution of the workload across geographically distributed data centers can reduce the costs by dynamically reallocating the workload to a place where the computing resources, energy and/or cooling are cheaper (e.g., solar energy during daytime across different time zones, efficient cooling due to climate conditions). Other important directions for future research are the investigation of a fine-grained user's control over the power consumption/CO_2 emissions in Cloud environments, and support for flexible SLA negotiated between resource providers and users. Building on the strong foundation of prior works, new research projects are starting to investigate advanced resource management and power-saving techniques. Nevertheless, there are still many open research challenges that are becoming even more prominent in the age of Cloud computing.

ACKNOWLEDGMENTS

We would like to thank Adam Wierman (California Institute of Technology), Kresimir Mihic (Stanford University), and Saurabh Kumar Garg (University of Melbourne) for their constructive comments and suggestions on improving the Chapter.

OPERATING SYSTEM LEVEL RESEARCH WORKS

Project name	Approach/algorithm	Application adaptation	System resources	Target systems	Goal	Power saving techniques	Workload	Implementation
The on-demand governor [19]	The OS continuously monitors the CPU utilization and sets the frequency and voltage according to performance requirements	No	CPU	Arbitrary	Minimize power consumption, minimize performance loss	DVFS	Arbitrary	Part of Linux kernel
ECOsystem [37,38]	The system determines overall amount of currency and distributes it between applications according to their priorities. Applications expend currency by utilizing the resources	Applications cooperate with the OS using power-based API	CPU, memory, disk storage, network interface	Mobile systems	Achieve target battery lifetime	Resource throtting	Arbitrary	Modified Linux kernel (introduced a new kernel thread kenrgd)
Nemesis OS [39]	Nemesis notifies applications if their energy consumption exceeds the threshold, the applications must adapt their behavior	Applications adapt their behavior according to signals from the OS	CPU, memory, disk storage, network interface	Mobile systems	Achieve target battery lifetime	Resource throtting	Real-time applications	New operating system, source codes are available for downloading
GRACE [40,41]	Three levels of application adaptation: global, per-application, and internal. All the adaptation levels are coordinated to ensure effective adaptation	Applications adapt their behavior according to signals from the OS	CPU, network interface	Mobile systems	Minimize energy consumption, satisfy performance requirements	DVFS, resource throtting	Real-time multimedia applications	Extension of Linux OS
Linux/RK [42]	Four proposed four alternative DVFS algorithms, each is suitable for different system characteristics and is selected automatically	No	CPU	Real-time systems	Minimize energy consumption, satisfy performance requirements	DVFS	Arbitrary	Real-time extensions to the Linux kernel
Coda and Odyssey [43]	Coda implements application-transparent adaptation in the context of a distributed file system. Odyssey implements application adaptation allowing adjustment of the resource consumption by the cost of output data quality	Applications adapt their behavior according to signals from the OS	CPU, network interface	Mobile systems	Minimize energy consumption allowing application data degradation	Resource throtting	Multimedia applications	Coda is implemented as a package for Linux, Odyssey is integrated into Linux
PowerNap [44]	Leveraging short idle periods in the resource utilization using fast transitions to system-wide low-power states	No	System-wide	Server systems	Minimize power consumption, minimize performance loss	DCD	Arbitrary	Extension to Linux OS

APPENDIX B

Data Center Level Research Works

Project name	Virtualization	Approach/algorithm	System resources	Target systems	Goal	XPower saving techniques	Workload	Implementation
Load balancing and unbalancing for power and performance in cluster-based system [21]	No	The system periodically monitors the load and decides which nodes should be turned on or off to minimize power consumption by the system, while providing expected performance	CPU, disk storage, network interface	Homogeneous	Minimize power consumption, minimize performance loss	Server power switching	Arbitrary	Extension of Linux
Managing energy and server resources in hosting centers [52]	No	Economical framework: the system allocates resources in a way to maximize "profit" by balancing the cost of each resource unit against the estimated utility or "revenue" that is gained from allocating that resource unit to a service. Energy consumption is reduced by switching idle servers to power-saving states	CPU	Homogeneous	Minimize power consumption, minimize performance loss	Workload consolidation, server power switching	Web applications	Extension of FreeBSD OS
Energy-efficient server clusters [20]	No	The system estimates total CPU frequency required to provide expected response time, determine the optimal number of physical nodes and set the proportional frequency on all the nodes. The thresholds define when it is appropriate to turn on an additional physical node or turn off an idle node	CPU	Homogeneous	Minimize energy consumption, satisfy performance requirements	DVFS, server power switching	Web applications	Simulation
Energy-aware consolidation for Cloud computing [53]	No	Applications are allocated to servers using a heuristic for multidimensional bin packing, resulting in the desired workload distribution across servers. If a request cannot be allocated, a new server is turned on and all requests are reallocated using the same heuristic	CPU, disk storage	Heterogeneous	Minimize energy consumption, satisfy performance requirements	Workload consolidation, server power switching	Online services	Simulation
Optimal power allocation in server farms [54]	No	A queueing model is used to predict the mean response time as a function of the power-to-frequency relationship, arrival rate, peak power budget, and so on. The model determines the optimal power allocation for every possible configuration of the above factors	CPU	Heterogeneous	Allocate the available power budget to minimize mean response time	DVFS	Web applications	Simulation
Environment-conscious scheduling of HPC applications [55]	No	Five heuristics for scheduling HPC applications across geographically distributed Cloud data centers to minimize the energy consumption and carbon emissions, and maximize the resource provider's profit	CPU	Heterogeneous	Minimize energy consumption and CO_2 emissions, maximize profit	DVFS, leveraging geographical distribution of data centers	HPC applications	Simulation

(continued)

APPENDIX B (*Continued*)

Project name	Virtualization	Approach/algorithm	System resources	Target systems	Goal	XPower saving techniques	Workload	Implementation
VirtualPower: coordinated power management in virtualized enterprise systems [56]	Yes	Hierarchical power management: at the local level, the system coordinates and leverages power management policies of guest VMs; global policies are responsible for managing multiple physical machines and have knowledge of rack- or blade-level characteristics and requirements	CPU	Heterogeneous	Minimize energy consumption, satisfy performance requirements	DFVS, soft scaling, VM consolidation, server power switching	Arbitrary	Extension of Xen
Coordinated multilevel power management for the data center [57]	Yes	A combination of five individual power management solutions that are coordinatively act across a collection of machines and dynamically reprovision power to meet the power budget	CPU	Heterogeneous	Minimize power consumption, minimize performance loss, and meet power budget	DVFS, VM consolidation, and server power switching	Arbitrary	Combining and cooperation of five independent commercial solutions
Power and performance management of virtualized computing environments via lookahead control [58]	Yes	The behavior of each application is captured using simulation-based learning. A limited lookahead control (LLC) is applied to estimate future system states over a prediction horizon using Kalman filter	CPU	Heterogeneous	Minimize power consumption, minimize loss	DVFS, VM consolidation, and server power switching	Online services	VMware API, Linux shell commands, and IPMI
Resource allocation using virtual clusters [59]	Yes	Several heuristics to solve the resource allocation problem. The multi-capacity bin packing algorithm that sorts tasks in descending order by their largest resource requirement outperforms or equals to all the other evaluated algorithms in terms of minimum and average yield, as well as failure rate	CPU	Homogeneous	Maximize resource utilization, satisfy performance requirements	Resource throttling	HPC applications	Extension of Xen
Multitiered on-demand resource scheduling for VM-based data center [60]	Yes	Three scheduling levels: the application-level scheduler dispatches requests among application's VMs; the local level scheduler allocates resources to VMs running on a physical node according to their priorities; the global-level scheduler controls the resource "flow" among applications	CPU, memory	Heterogeneous	Maximize resource utilization, satisfy performance requirements	Resource throttling	Arbitrary	Extension of Xen
Shares and utilities-based power consolidation in virtualized server environments [61]	Yes	The hypervisor distributes resources among VMs according to a sharing-based mechanism, assuming that the minimum and maximum amounts of resources that can be allocated to a VM are specified	CPU	Heterogeneous	Minimize power consumption, minimize performance loss	DFVS, soft scaling	Arbitrary	Extension of VMware ESX

Name		Description	Resources	Architecture	Objective	Technique	Workload	Testbed
pMapper: power and migration cost aware application placement in virtualized systems [62]	Yes	Heuristics for continuous optimization of VM placement. Performance Manager monitors applications behavior and resize VMs according to current resource requirements and the SLA. Power Manager adjusts hardware power states and applies DVFS. Migration Manager issues instructions for live migration of VMs. Arbitrator makes decisions about new placements of VMs and determines VMs to migrate	CPU	Heterogeneous	Minimize power consumption, minimize performance loss	DVFS, VM consolidation, and server power switching	Arbitrary	Extension of VMware ESX
Resource pool management: reactive versus proactive [63]	Yes	A combination of two optimization controllers: proactive global optimization using the workload placement controller and reactive adaptation using the migration controller	CPU, memory	Heterogeneous	Maximize resource utilization, satisfy performance requirements	VM consolidation, server power switching	Arbitrary	Simulation
GreenCloud: energy-efficient and SLA-based management of Cloud resources [64,65]	Yes	Heuristics for scheduling real-time VMs in Cloud data centers applying DVFS in order to minimize the energy consumption, while meeting the deadline constraints of applications	CPU	Heterogeneous	Minimize energy consumption, satisfy performance requirements	Leveraging heterogeneity of Cloud data centers, DVFS	HPC applications	Simulation

REFERENCES

[1] G.E. Moore, Cramming more components onto integrated circuits, Proc. IEEE 86 (1) (1998) 82–85.
[2] J.G. Koomey, Estimating Total Power Consumption by Servers in the US and the World, Analytics Press, Oakland, CA, 2007.
[3] L. Barroso, The Price of Performance, ACM Press, Queue, 2005, vol. 3 (7), p. 53.
[4] R. Brown, E. Masanet, B. Nordman, B. Tschudi, A. Shehabi, J. Stanley, et al., Report to Congress on Server and Data Center Energy Efficiency: Public Law 109–431, Lawrence Berkeley National Laboratory, Berkeley, CA, USA, 2008.
[5] L. Minas, B. Ellison, Energy Efficiency for Information Technology: How to Reduce Power Consumption in Servers and Data Centers, Intel Press, USA, 2009.
[6] P. Ranganathan, P. Leech, D. Irwin, J. Chase, Ensemble-level power management for dense blade servers, in: Proceedings of the 33rd International Symposium on Computer Architecture (ISCA 2006), 2006, pp. 66–77.
[7] S. Rowe, Usenet archives. http://groups.google.com/group/comp.misc/browse_thread/thread/5c4db94663b5808a/f99158e3743127f9, 1992.
[8] V. Venkatachalam, M. Franz, Power reduction techniques for microprocessor systems, ACM Comput. Surv. CSUR 37 (3) (2005) 195–237.
[9] L.A. Barroso, U. Holzle, The case for energy-proportional computing, Computer 40 (12) (2007) 33–37.
[10] X. Fan, W.D. Weber, L.A. Barroso, Power provisioning for a warehouse-sized computer, in: Proceedings of the 34th Annual International Symposium on Computer Architecture (ISCA 2007), ACM New York, NY, USA, 2007, pp. 13–23.
[11] M. Blackburn, Five Ways to Reduce Data Center Server Power Consumption, The Green Grid, USA, 2008.
[12] American Society of Heating and Refrigerating and Air-Conditioning Engineers, Thermal Guidelines for Data Processing Environments, ASHRAE, Atlanta, GA, USA, 2004.
[13] G. Dhiman, K. Mihic, T. Rosing, A system for online power prediction in virtualized environments using gaussian mixture models, in: Proceedings of the 47th ACM/IEEE Design Automation Conference, Anaheim, CA, USA, 2010, pp. 807–812.
[14] G. Koch, Discovering multi-core: extending the benefits of Moore's law, Technology 1 (2005).
[15] F. Petrini, J. Moreira, J. Nieplocha, M. Seager, C. Stunkel, G. Thorson, et al., What are the future trends in high-performance interconnects for parallel computers? in: Proceedings of the 12th Annual IEEE Symposium on High Performance Interconnects, 2004, p. 3.
[16] C. Pettey, Gartner estimates ICT industry accounts for 2 percent of global CO_2 emissions, http://www.gartner.com/it/page.jsp?id=503867, 2007.
[17] S. Devadas, S. Malik, S. Devadas, S. Malik, A survey of optimization techniques targeting low power VLSI circuits, in: Proceedings of the 32nd ACM/IEEE Conference on Design Automation, 1995, pp. 242–247.
[18] V. Tiwari, P. Ashar, S. Malik, Technology mapping for low power, in: Proceedings of the 30th Conference on Design Automation, 1993, pp. 74–79.
[19] V. Pallipadi, A. Starikovskiy, The ondemand governor, in: Proceedings of the Linux Symposium, 2006, vol. 2.
[20] E. Elnozahy, M. Kistler, R. Rajamony, Energy-efficient server clusters, Power Aware Comput. Syst. 2325 (2003) 179–197.
[21] E. Pinheiro, R. Bianchini, E.V. Carrera, T. Heath, Load balancing and unbalancing for power and performance in cluster-based systems, in: Proceedings of the Workshop on Compilers and Operating Systems for Low Power, 2001, pp. 182–195.

[22] R. Buyya, C.S. Yeo, S. Venugopal, J. Broberg, I. Brandic, Cloud computing and emerging IT platforms: vision, hype, and reality for delivering computing as the 5th utility, Future Generation Comput. Syst. 25 (6) (2009) 599–616.

[23] L. Benini, A. Bogliolo, G.D. Micheli, A survey of design techniques for system-level dynamic power management, IEEE Trans. VLSI Syst. 8 (3) (2000) 299–316.

[24] S. Albers, Energy-efficient algorithms, Commun. ACM 53 (5) (2010) 86–96.

[25] M.B. Srivastava, A.P. Chandrakasan, R.W. Brodersen, Predictive system shutdown and other architectural techniques for energy efficient programmable computation, IEEE Trans. VLSI Syst. 4 (1) (1996) 42–55.

[26] C.H. Hwang, A.C. Wu, A predictive system shutdown method for energy saving of event-driven computation, ACM Trans. Des. Autom. Electron. Syst. 5 (2) (2000) 241.

[27] F. Douglis, P. Krishnan, B. Bershad, Adaptive disk spin-down policies for mobile computers, Comput. Syst. 8 (4) (1995) 381–413.

[28] G. Buttazzo, Scalable applications for energy-aware processors, in: Embedded Software, 2002, pp. 153–165.

[29] M. Weiser, B. Welch, A. Demers, S. Shenker, Scheduling for reduced CPU energy, Mobile Comput. (1996) 449–471.

[30] K. Govil, E. Chan, H. Wasserman, Comparing algorithm for dynamic speed-setting of a low-power CPU, in: Proceedings of the 1st Annual International Conference on Mobile Computing and Networking (MobiCom 2005), Berkeley, CA, USA, 1995, p. 25.

[31] A. Wierman, L.L. Andrew, A. Tang, Power-aware speed scaling in processor sharing systems, in: Proceedings of the 28th Conference on Computer Communications (INFOCOM 2009), Rio, Brazil, 2009.

[32] L.L. Andrew, M. Lin, A. Wierman, Optimality, fairness, and robustness in speed scaling designs, in: Proceedings of ACM International Conference on Measurement and Modeling of International Computer Systems (SIGMETRICS 2010), New York, USA, 2010.

[33] A. Weissel, F. Bellosa, Process cruise control: event-driven clock scaling for dynamic power management, in: Proceedings of the 2002 International Conference on Compilers, Architecture, and Synthesis for Embedded Systems, Grenoble, France, 2002, p. 246.

[34] K. Flautner, S. Reinhardt, T. Mudge, Automatic performance setting for dynamic voltage scaling, Wireless Netw. 8 (5) (2002) 507–520.

[35] S. Lee, T. Sakurai, Run-time voltage hopping for low-power real-time systems, in: Proceedings of the 37th Annual Design Automation Conference, Los Angeles, CA, USA, 2000, pp. 806–809.

[36] J.R. Lorch, A.J. Smith, Improving dynamic voltage scaling algorithms with PACE, ACM SIGMETRICS Perform. Eval. Rev. 29 (1) (2001) 61.

[37] H. Zeng, C.S. Ellis, A.R. Lebeck, A. Vahdat, ECOSystem: managing energy as a first class operating system resource, ACM SIGPLAN Notices 37 (10) (2002), 132.

[38] H. Zeng, C.S. Ellis, A.R. Lebeck, Experiences in managing energy with ecosystem, IEEE Pervasive Comput. 4 (1) (2005) 62–68.

[39] R. Neugebauer, D. McAuley, Energy is just another resource: energy accounting and energy pricing in the nemesis OS, in: Proceedings of the 8th IEEE Workshop on Hot Topics in Operating Systems, Elmau/Oberbayern, Germany, 2001, pp. 59–64.

[40] D.G. Sachs, W. Yuan, C.J. Hughes, A. Harris, S.V. Adve, D.L. Jones, et al., GRACE: a hierarchical adaptation framework for saving energy, University of Illinois at Urbana-Champaign, Technical Report, UIUCDCS, 2003, pp. 2004–2409.

[41] V. Vardhan, D.G. Sachs, W. Yuan, A.F. Harris, S.V. Adve, D.L. Jones, et al., Integrating fine-grained application adaptation with global adaptation for saving energy, in: International Workshop on Power-Aware Real-Time Computing, Jersey City, NJ, 2005.

[42] R. Rajkumar, K. Juvva, A. Molano, S. Oikawa, Resource kernels: a resource-centric approach to real-time and multimedia systems, in: Readings in Multimedia Computing and Networking, Morgan Kaufmann Publishers Inc., 2001, pp. 476–490.

[43] J. Flinn, M. Satyanarayanan, Managing battery lifetime with energy-aware adaptation, ACM Trans. Comput. Syst. 22 (2) (2004) 179.

[44] D. Meisner, B.T. Gold, T.F. Wenisch, PowerNap: eliminating server idle power, ACM SIGPLAN Notices 44 (3) (2009) 205–216.

[45] J. Stoess, C. Lang, F. Bellosa, Energy management for hypervisor-based virtual machines, in: Proceedings of the USENIX Annual Technical Conference, Santa Clara, CA, USA, USENIX Association, 2007, pp. 1–14.

[46] P. Barham, B. Dragovic, K. Fraser, S. Hand, T. Harris, A. Ho, et al., Xen and the art of virtualization, in: Proceedings of the 19th ACM Symposium on Operating Systems Principles (SOSP 2003), Bolton Landing, NY, USA, 2003, p. 177.

[47] G. Wei, J. Liu, J. Xu, G. Lu, K. Yu, K. Tian, The on-going evolutions of power management in Xen, Intel Corporation, 2009, Technical Report.

[48] VMware Inc., vSphere resource management guide, 2009.

[49] VMware Inc., How VMware virtualization right-sizes IT infrastructure to reduce power consumption, 2009.

[50] VMware Inc., VMware® distributed power management concepts and use, 2010.

[51] Qumranet Inc., KVM: kernel-based virtualization driver, White Paper, 2006.

[52] J.S. Chase, D.C. Anderson, P.N. Thakar, A.M. Vahdat, R.P. Doyle, Managing energy and server resources in hosting centers, in: Proceedings of the 18th ACM Symposium on Operating Systems Principles. ACM New York, NY, USA, 2001, pp. 103–116.

[53] S. Srikantaiah, A. Kansal, F. Zhao, Energy aware consolidation for cloud computing, in: Proceedings of the Workshop on Power Aware Computing Systems (HotPower 2008), San Diego, CA, USA, 2008.

[54] A. Gandhi, M. Harchol-Balter, R. Das, C. Lefurgy, Optimal power allocation in server farms, in: Proceedings of the 11th International Joint Conference on Measurement and Modeling of Computer Systems. ACM New York, NY, USA, 2009, pp. 157–168.

[55] S.K. Garg, C.S. Yeo, A. Anandasivam, R. Buyya, Environment-conscious scheduling of HPC applications on distributed cloud-oriented data centers, J. Parallel Distributed Comput, ISSN: 0743-7315, Elsevier Press, Amsterdam, The Netherlands, 2010.

[56] R. Nathuji, K. Schwan, Virtualpower: coordinated power management in virtualized enterprise systems, ACM SIGOPS Oper. Syst. Rev. 41 (6) (2007) 265–278.

[57] R. Raghavendra, P. Ranganathan, V. Talwar, Z. Wang, X. Zhu, No "power" struggles: coordinated multi-level power management for the data center, SIGARCH Comput. Archit. News 36 (1) (2008) 48–59.

[58] D. Kusic, J.O. Kephart, J.E. Hanson, N. Kandasamy, G. Jiang, Power and performance management of virtualized computing environments via lookahead control, Cluster Comput. 12 (1) (2009) 1–15.

[59] M. Stillwell, D. Schanzenbach, F. Vivien, H. Casanova, Resource allocation using virtual clusters, in: Proceedings of the 9th IEEE/ACM International Symposium on Cluster Computing and the Grid (CCGrid 2009), Shanghai, China, 2009, pp. 260–267.

[60] Y. Song, H. Wang, Y. Li, B. Feng, Y. Sun, Multi-Tiered On-Demand resource scheduling for VM-Based data center, in: Proceedings of the 9th IEEE/ACM International Symposium on Cluster Computing and the Grid (CCGrid 2009), Shanghai, China, 2009, pp. 148–155.

[61] M. Cardosa, M. Korupolu, A. Singh, Shares and utilities based power consolidation in virtualized server environments, in: Proceedings of the 11th IFIP/IEEE Integrated Network Management (IM 2009), Long Island, NY, USA, 2009.

[62] A. Verma, P. Ahuja, A. Neogi, pMapper: power and migration cost aware application placement in virtualized systems, in: Proceedings of the 9th ACM/IFIP/USENIX International Conference on Middleware, Springer-Verlag, New York, 2008, pp. 243–264.

[63] D. Gmach, J. Rolia, L. Cherkasova, A. Kemper, Resource pool management: reactive versus proactive or let's be friends, Comput. Netw. 53 (17) (2009), pp. 2905–2922.

[64] R. Buyya, A. Beloglazov, J. Abawajy, Energy-efficient management of data center resources for cloud computing: a vision, architectural elements, and open challenges, in: Proceedings of the 2010 International Conference on Parallel and Distributed Processing Techniques and Applications (PDPTA 2010), Las Vegas, USA, July 12–15, 2010.

[65] K.H. Kim, A. Beloglazov, R. Buyya, Power-aware provisioning of cloud resources for real-time services, in: Proceedings of the 7th International Workshop on Middleware for Grids, Clouds and e-Science (MGC 2009), Urbana Champaign, IL, USA, 2009, pp. 1–6.

[66] D.F. Parkhill, The Challenge of the Computer Utility, Addison-Wesley, Reading, MA, 1966.

[67] J. Baliga, R. Ayre, K. Hinton, R.S. Tucker, Green cloud computing: balancing energy in processing, storage and transport, in: Proceedings of the IEEE, 99(1), IEEE Press, USA, 2011, pp. 149-167.

[68] M. Armbrust, A. Fox, R. Griffith, A.D. Joseph, R. Katz, A. Konwinski, et al., A view of cloud computing, Commun. ACM 53 (4) (2009) 50–58.

[69] R. Nathuji, C. Isci, E. Gorbatov, Exploiting platform heterogeneity for power efficient data centers, in: Proceedings of the 4th International Conference on Autonomic Computing (ICAC 2007), Jacksonville, FL, USA, 2007, p. 5.

[70] R.N. Calheiros, R. Ranjan, A. Beloglazov, C.A.F.D. Rose, R. Buyya, CloudSim: a toolkit for modeling and simulation of cloud computing environments and evaluation of resource provisioning algorithms, in: Software: Practice and Experience, Wiley Press, New York, USA, 41 (1) (2011), pp. 23–50.

Applications of Mobile Agents in Wireless Networks and Mobile Computing

SERGIO GONZÁLEZ-VALENZUELA

Department of Electrical and Computer Engineering, The University of British Columbia, Vancouver, BC, Canada

MIN CHEN

School of Computer Science and Engineering, Seoul National University, Korea

VICTOR C.M. LEUNG

Department of Electrical and Computer Engineering, The University of British Columbia, Vancouver, BC, Canada

Abstract

We examine the applicability of mobile software codes to perform networking tasks in wireless and mobile computing environments. We contend that the advent of wireless technologies during the past decade has turned computer networks increasingly complex to manage. In particular, factors such as context awareness and user mobility are now crucial in the design of communications protocols used by portable devices with moderate to severe bandwidth and battery power limitations. Unlike hard-coded communication protocols that fulfill a specific need, mobile software agents can be deployed to deal with a range of tasks and can be designed to efficiently adapt to diverse circumstances. We present our latest advancements in the areas of mobile *ad hoc* networking and wireless sensor networks using mobile agents (MAs). We also elaborate on the importance of engineering an efficient migration strategy as the single most distinctive proceeding that an MA performs to operate efficiently. In addition, we describe the *Wiseman* system for scripting MAs that can perform networking tasks in both homogeneous and heterogeneous wireless network environments. Monitoring, tracking, and E-healthcare applications are discussed and evaluated at length.

1. Introduction

Many definitions have been offered throughout the literature to describe mobile agents (MAs). Essentially, a software agent differentiates itself from a regular computer program by having the ability to observe and estimate the current state of the environment where it executes, deciding how to act based on this information and then performing a corresponding action [1]. In addition to this, an MA has the distinctive feature of being able to arrange for its forwarding from one device to another. Conversely, regular programs do not incorporate any feedback mechanism when making a decision and do not possess the mobility feature. There are many types of MAs, but they are generally categorized as being at the opposite side of the communications mechanisms plane, in which shared memory is the simplest scheme, as illustrated in Fig. 1. Message passing is the oldest and most employed data communications mechanism, whereby a network device encapsulates information in a tight fashion before transmitting it. However, devices can also forward either interpretable programs or executable binary codes that encapsulate instructions for local or remote execution. We are particularly interested in the applicability of interpretable programs that are parsed and executed by virtual machines implemented by networked devices.

1.1 Foundations of Mobile Agent Systems

Early discussions in this area argued that there are no MA applications, but rather applications that benefit from the use of MAs [2], which has proven a sensible statement after more than a decade of research into the subject. Similarly, MAs can be regarded as the enabling technology for a networking application. In general, security issues have proven to be the most discouraging factor toward a wider

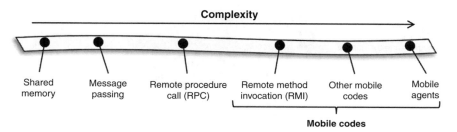

Fig. 1. Data communications mechanisms.

adoption of MA technology [3–5]. In other words, opening the doors to seemingly benign, interpretable programs make networked devices susceptible to a number of malicious attacks. As a result, we observe that certain types of networks have benefited more than others from implementing MA-based applications in real systems. In general, closed networks provide a secure environment to deploy MA technology and benefit from its unique features. Thus, not only the application type but also the network environment plays an important role for deciding how an MA-based solution should realize one or more tasks. Figure 2 illustrates the implementation types that software agents can take.

The most important characteristic of the MA approach and software agents in general is that it allows *programmability*, thus enabling an MA-based system to change its operation on demand to adapt the circumstances determined by the underlying environment. For example, a network with sufficient bandwidth can support the deployment of many MAs collaborating to achieve a number of tasks. Nevertheless, a sudden bandwidth shortage as sensed by these agents could activate a low-usage mode of operation, whereby only a few agents perform only the most crucial tasks. It follows that the MAs' policies can be either static or variable. By the same token, the most important benefit introduced by the mobility feature of a software agent is that it enables better bandwidth usage by moving the processing element to the location where the data to be analyzed resides. For example, moving a 500 KB program to process 100 MB of data at a remote location is more bandwidth

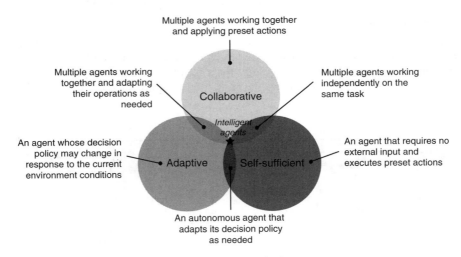

Fig. 2. Implementation types of software agents.

efficient than carrying out the reverse procedure. However, it is also clear that implementing an efficient migration policy is crucial in achieving this bandwidth-saving goal.

Thus far, we have pinpointed some key aspects that are relevant to deploying MAs: flexibility to implement diverse applications, adaptability to deal with unforeseen situations, efficient migration mechanisms to improve performance, an application-dependent strategy, and preference for closed-network deployment. It is straightforward to see that MAs are best suited for highly specialized applications in access-restricted networks that are subject to unexpected, variable conditions, and resource constraints. As a result, we turn our attention to exploring the applicability of MAs to support diverse tasks in wireless and mobile networks. These types of networks possess some or all the peculiarities just mentioned. In particular, we direct the focus of our investigations to wireless sensor networks (WSN) and *ad hoc* networks created by portable devices. However, to better understand the relevance of investigating MA applicability in these networks, we present a concise discussion on the advantages and disadvantages of MA technology, followed by a brief historical perspective with concerning previous research efforts involving MA technology, its shortcomings, the current state of affairs, and what we can expect to see in the near future.

1.2   Advantages and Disadvantages of Using MAs

The benefits and drawbacks of the MA approach were extensively discussed in the initial years of its research. In general, there are some advantages that are attributable to all agent types, whereas others are more specific. For instance, compactness is oftentimes referred to as an inherent MA characteristic, though this is not always the case. For instance, an MA coded to perform a complex brokering task requires that a significant amount of functionality be implemented into it to deal with a wide variety of possible situations for the transactions it supports. However, MAs used for active networking tasks (e.g., routing) can be significantly more compact because they are targeted at specific tasks with well-known outcomes. Another advantage regularly associated to using agents is bandwidth savings, which can be achieved if an efficient agent migration policy is employed. However, it is possible that the bandwidth overhead incurred by moving a relatively large agent could offset the one incurred by using a simple message-passing scheme, depending on the application. Still, the bandwidth-savings potential remains by far one of the most compelling reasons for using agents [6].

Figure 3 exemplifies the bandwidth savings-feature by showing both a traditional and an MA-based approach for collecting data in a WSN. In the first case, the occurrence of an event as sensed by individual WSN nodes initiates the

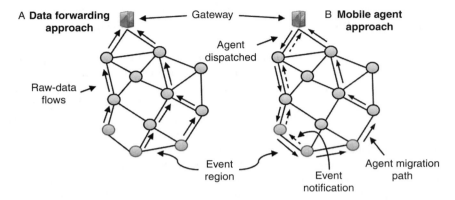

FIG. 3. Raw data forwarding versus mobile agent processing.

corresponding client–server interactions to send raw data to the WSN gateway or sink for subsequent analysis. In this approach, each client–server session incurs one data flow from source to destination, leading to higher bandwidth utilization. Moreover, this method places a higher burden in the nodes closer to the WSN gateway because their links observe heavy data traffic as compared to the wireless links located farther away from the gateway. Conversely, the mobile agent system (MAS) approach dispatches an agent to the WSN's region of interest (ROI) where the event was observed. Once there, the MA processes data and sends back to the WSN gateway either a concise assessment of the situation or a digest of the analyzed data. This has the benefit of incurring a single traffic flow, in contrast to the client–server approach that observes multiple flows.

In addition to enabling bandwidth savings, MAs can also help reduce processing delay. Revisiting the example shown in Fig. 3, the actual data pooling process triggered by an event in a WSN region might require multiple interactions between the WSN gateway and the nodes involved. This obeys to the possibility of having a relatively large amount of data that have to be progressively transferred if, say, the first data block yields no conclusive results and one block or more need to be pooled from the corresponding devices until a result is found. Conversely, in the MA approach, the codes that actually process data migrate to the devices that triggered the event, and the analysis is realized *in situ*, so that no messages or data need to be sent back and forth from the devices to the WSN gateway. In addition, if a result is not found, the MA can migrate to another node to immediately begin analyzing more data, whereas using the message-passing approach entails initiating a new session between the WSN gateway and another device, followed by the respective data transfer process. It is clear that the MA approach incurs less delay during its migration process than consecutively forwarding raw data segments. Resilience is yet another advantage that an MA-based solution can incorporate in environments whose behavior is unstable or highly uncertain. For instance, whereas a message-passing scheme incurs significant signaling to recover from failures during an ongoing data transfer session under adverse circumstances (e.g., in the presence of a noisy-channel, or frequent disconnections), an MA-based solution could have the agent monitor the channel conditions until the circumstances are favorable to migrate back to the WSN sink with the desired information.

The previous discussion provides some compelling reasons in favor of using MAs to solve distinct networking tasks. In fact, it is easy to see that these advantages are highly appealing for the case of wireless and mobile networks. However, there are important counterarguments against MA technology. For instance, bandwidth savings can only be achieved if the size of one or more MAs performing a task is sufficiently compact to offset the bandwidth otherwise incurred by employing the message-passing mechanism. This might be hard to achieve if the MA is coded to provide added resilience, thereby sacrificing compactness as per the extra codes that implement this added feature. Another aspect that adds complexity to an MA-based solution is the migration strategy employed to visit multiple nodes, either throughout the network or in a portion thereof. An inefficient migration strategy incurs added bandwidth because of the total number of times that one or more MAs hop to accomplish a certain task. However, a carefully engineered migration strategy would ostensibly be capable of achieving better results. It thus follows that large-sized MAs implementing an inefficient migration strategy would result detrimental to the overall system's performance. In addition, the effectiveness with which an MA solution provides resilience depends directly on the programmer's ability to anticipate and deal with situations that the MA could encounter. In the message-passing mechanism, the respective communications protocol daemon running into an unexpected situation could simply reschedule the data transfer process at a later time if the current circumstances are unfavorable. Conversely, an MA could remain stranded at a remote node, perhaps unable to return to the network's gateway upon encountering a situation that steered it into a deadlock state. An additional issue that can be used to argue against MA technology is that of security. To this regard, it is easy to see that an attacker could inject a malicious agent into a network to disrupt its normal operation (e.g., as a typical computer network virus). Conversely, one or more malicious device(s) could be used to disrupt an agent's normal operation or to embed a malicious code segment into it. As a result, using MAs can be deemed a safer option in closed networks where access is controlled. Additionally, well-known cryptographic methods, such as digital signatures, can be readily employed to reduce to some extent the inherent security risks, though some performance degradations would be inevitable. However, this would be highly detrimental for network tasks requiring near real-time response, or in networks formed by devices with limited hardware resources, given that processing digital signatures entails additional memory availability and processing capabilities that increases power consumption.

1.3   A Historical Perspective of MASs

A myriad of MA-based solutions ranging from the network to the application layer were proposed throughout the literature, mostly from the mid-1990s to the early 2000s when the first investigations into MASs and their potential applicability took place [7]. A great deal of research focused on the high-level application aspects of this technology (e.g., [8]), whereas other efforts were aimed at a subject widely known as active networking [9]. Several MASs were proposed, as per the wide range of possible applications that MAs could support. The majority of these systems were built to run on the Java virtual machine (JVM). In fact, some contemporary Java-based platforms such as JXTA natively support code mobility in the form of MAs [10]. In this section, we summarize the most important aspects of their deployment, instead of engaging in a detailed review of individual MASs.

JVM-based MASs were highly popular for applications that required portability and support to accomplish complex tasks. This provided a programming and execution platform with unmatched flexibility that enabled MAS deployment to support a wide variety of applications [11,12]. Nonetheless, performance issues and security vulnerabilities were important concerns in applications that employed MAS for cellular phones and personal digital assistants sporting lightweight versions of the JVM, as mentioned before [13]. In addition, their overall effectiveness was some-times compromised by distinct versions and flavors of the JVM installed in personal devices. This was not the problem of custom-built MAS, which provided a more homogeneous platform for implementing agent-based applications. However, these systems were less portable and were built for specific types of applications. It is also worth noting that some MA investigations did not involve any particular MAS and instead focused on other important aspects, such as migration strategy [14,15]. In fact, some early work advanced alternative MA schemes for wireless and mobile networks management without actually promoting a particular system [16]. In addition, some agent research targeted web-based applications for enhanced service discovery and composition (i.e., the combination of two or more services to form one single application) [17], though subsequent years saw a significant decrease in MA and MAS research activity. Nevertheless, enough interest remained on the subject to motivate sporadic research efforts on distinct networking technol-ogies. In our case, the benefits of employing MA technology in wireless networks applications are apparent because it has the potential to significantly reduce (1) bandwidth consumption incurred by network management overhead and (2) overall power consumption to help extend battery lifetime, as explained in Section 1.2.

One particular technology that exemplifies the benefits introduced by using MAS is WSNs. In brief, using MAs in WSNs may facilitate application programmability (also known as retasking) and collaborative signal and data processing. The MAS approach has a good potential to decrease bandwidth use (and its associated battery consumption), contrary to conventional WSN operations that rely heavily on the client–server communications model. WSNs have been the focus of much attention in the research community for nearly a decade [18–20], which is driven in part by a large number of theoretical and practical challenges. WSNs are intended to support specialized applications. However, it is tempting to try and employ a single WSN deployment to implement multiple applications due to the high cost of acquiring hundreds or even thousands of sensor nodes, if so necessitated by the application, or to cover a wide geographical area as proposed in Refs. [21,22]. The problem with this approach is that storing a multifunctional program to support diverse applications incurs significant memory utilization, which could be alleviated by employing the MAS approach. The advantage of using MAS here is that it enables the deployment of different types of agents to accomplish various tasks without the need to reprogram the WSN's nodes. It could be argued that the MAS approach is not much different from a multifunctional program for WSN applications. However, the multifunctional program approach will always be limited to the specific applications it has been built to support. However, the MAS approach provides the same functional value of a virtual machine, thus allowing MA deployment for applications that might not have been considered. In other words, it enables adaptation to unforeseen circumstances, which can be considered an inherent trait of environments monitored by WSN hardware.

Even though MASs were extensively studied by prominent researchers, to a certain extent it failed to fulfill the high expectations that many had placed on it [23]. Nowadays, MA research is still well positioned to enable contributions with a significant value, particularly in an area commonly known as *smart spaces* that has drawn considerable interest as of late [24–26]. This term is used by *pervasive computing* researchers when referring to intelligent environments enabled by consumer electronics and appliances with embedded devices whose behavior can vary as a result of their context awareness capabilities. Smart space applications are in turn enabled by *ambient intelligence*—a group of technologies assembled to provide an automated, personalized service or experience to one or more persons [27–29]. To this end, advances in electronics miniaturization technology enable the deployment of sensors and data processing devices with limited capabilities to create abstract representations of the surrounding environment, along with other devices that can be used to provide a personalized, context-aware service. In other words, a smart space can be envisaged as a complex, interactive system that enacts one or more actions by using one or more of the surrounding devices as outputs, in accordance to a series of inputs provided by intelligently networked sensors. This is a relatively new technology with both growing interest in the research community and a vast potential for commercialization. However, a great deal of research needs to be conducted before experimental devices implementing this technology leave the industry and university labs to become consumer devices available to the general public. It is not hard to see that a smart space is actually a hybrid system formed by both hardware and software deployed in and around people in a distributed fashion. Therefore, we envision using MA technology as a prime candidate supporting complex, mobile Ambient Intelligence systems.

1.4 Applications of MAs in Wireless and Mobile Networks

As mentioned before, this chapter describes our latest MA technology advances in WSN and in mobile computing environments that employ radio frequency identification (RFID) technology. In Section 2, we look into the design issues encountered when engineering both MASs and applications in WSNs. We survey the particular example of video sensor networks (VSNs) as a WSN application with unique traits that can be favored by employing MAs. Interest in VSNs stems from the commercial application of video surveillance in deployment settings where intrusions are extremely rare, there is no supporting infrastructure (i.e., electricity), and there is no personnel to monitor the operation of the system in a permanent basis [30,31]. As a result, MAs can be employed to provide an autonomous, low-power mode of operation. We dissect the MAS design functionality into the following components: architecture, MA itinerary planning, middleware system design, and agent cooperation methodology. This classification spans low- and high-priority design issues and assists in the creation of an MAS that can be useful in an ample range of applications. We argue that flexible trade-offs between energy and delay can be reached, depending on the specific requirements set by the application.

In Section 3, we present the results of our investigation after putting theory into practice through *Wiseman*: a middleware system developed for the deployment and execution of compact MA scripts in WSNs. The architecture of Wiseman was designed as a simplified version of a much older agent system originally devised for the effective coordination of active networking processes (e.g., routing performed by mobile programs, instead of using hard-coded protocols and algorithms). To this end, we developed a simpler but effective interpreter of codes for embedding in WSN devices characterized by having severe hardware constraints. Here, we detail the groundwork of our approach and its unique language constructs that minimize its operating cost. Wiseman was coded in the NesC language to produce a TinyOS ver. 1.x [32] binary image that spans 19KB of code and 3KB of SRAM. In addition, we elaborate on the distinct agent migration methodologies that the interpreter supports and present some performance evaluations regarding consumed bandwidth and internode hopping delay.

In Section 4, we advance a novel idea that relies on RFID technology as an enabler of diverse ambient intelligence applications. Given their small size and low cost characteristics, RFID tags can be easily embedded into consumer electronics devices in support of smart spaces. To this effect, RFID tags would readily enable the immediate identification of persons and objects to rapidly retrieve prestored, smart space configurations from a database and enact system personalization actions. However, there are problems that need to be sorted out with regard to the personalization of services and system configuration when person moves from one ambient intelligence environment into another. One of the major impediments for achieving this functionality is the way in which existing RFID systems function, which complicates their straightforward adaptation into real-world dynamics so as to fulfill application-specific requirements. We refer to this as identification-centric RFID system (IRS), which stores and forwards simple ID values that are referenced during a simple database lookup process to retrieve relevant information about the object that carries the corresponding ID tag. To address this problem, we promote advancing IRS into CRS—a code-centric RFID system, whereby actions are dynamically encoded and stored in RFID tags that possess improved memory capabilities. We argue that this innovative approach facilitates the operation of the implementing system to enact actions on demand in environments comprised by distinct objects, and under varying circumstances to achieve improved scalability. We present an E-healthcare management application that exemplifies the potential of our proposed CRS approach, and its importance in a smart space scenario. In Section 5, we conclude this chapter by summarizing our experiences using MA technology to solve distinct tasks in wireless networks and discussing possible improvements and areas of future research.

2. Architecting MA Applications and Systems for WSN

Recent innovations in the field of very large system integration (VLSI) facilitate the mass production of sensor devices that can be networked to enable the implementation of many distributed applications, which we introduced as a WSN. To this effect, energy efficiency becomes one of the core design principles for all research done in this area, given that these WSN devices are generally powered by batteries. Moreover, many commercial WSN platforms are comprised by devices with severe memory and processing power limitations. These and other circumstances motivate research of flexible and improved schemes that allow WSNs to be reprogrammed when a new data collection/dissemination methodology is needed. At the same time, it is important to determine whether these new schemes are practicable from an engineering point of view to ensure that neither performance nor data integrity is compromised. Given that the primary role of WSNs is data collection, it follows that environmental monitoring and people/object surveillance comprise a good portion of their intended applications. In this section, we explore the intricacies that WSN researchers and engineers encounter when architecting an MA-based solution aimed at monitoring and surveillance applications. In particular, we study VSNs and target tracking (TT) applications, both of which provide a prime example of how MA technology can be employed.

2.1   Using WSNs for Image Retrieval

One of the most challenging tasks that can be observed in WSNs is image retrieval. To this end, both heavy image preprocessing load and high bandwidth usage have adverse consequences in the battery lifetime of sensor devices. In addition to this, such amount of data has the potential to clog the wireless link (s) when being forwarded to the VSN gateway for subsequent processing, as discussed in Section 1. As a result, a number of approaches have been promoted in the literature to retrieve images or video from WSNs [33, 34]. Some of the latest advancements in this area include Cyclops [35] and SensEye [36], among others, which are image processing testbeds especially developed for WSN use [37]. A quick survey of existing VSN schemes reveals that they rely on source coding and multipath forwarding schemes to achieve their task. Because of the bandwidth limitations encountered in commercial WSN platforms employing IEEE 802.15.4 radio technology that supports up to 250Kbits/s data rates, there will always be a hard threshold for the amount of data that these and other schemes will be able to transport from a sensor device to the gateway.

From the above discussion, we can see that MAs are well positioned as a plausible solution to leverage the performance of VSNs [38]. To this end, we recently proposed a solution whereby an agent is dispatched to the node that initially captures an image that needs to be analyzed and executes a preprocessing algorithm to obtain the picture's ROI, as depicted in Fig. 4. There, we can observe that the MA carries with it image segmentation and preanalysis codes to isolate a portion of the original image and perform a preliminary assessment procedure before forwarding the image

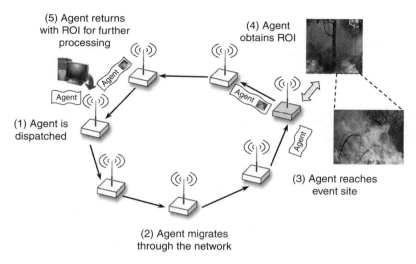

FIG. 4. Mobile agent-based image preprocessing in wireless sensor networks.

segment to the VSN's gateway. As a result, an otherwise large volume of image data originating at any region of the VSN can be significantly reduced to a much smaller, manageable one. The main feature introduced by the MA approach here is that if the conditions surrounding the monitored environment vary, then a new MA with an alternative image segmentation algorithm can be dispatched to the corresponding VSN devices to maintain the overall system's efficiency.

2.2   Target Tracking in WSNs

TT normally refers to the process whereby two or more devices work in conjunc-tion to estimate the location of an object. Although there are instances in which a single device can be used to track an object, we are interested in the case where multiple devices are employed to reduce uncertainty about the object's position. A traditional TT application focuses on the design and implementation of the corresponding algorithms as a signal processing problem. To this regard, the (distributed) system's operation is expected to remain unchanged. However, if the circumstances surrounding the object being tracked change, it is possible that the performance of the current (static) approach could be compromised to the point of becoming ineffective. However, an MA approach would enable system operators to deploy distinct TT algorithms on demand to adapt to the prevailing circumstances. It could be argued that a simple remote method invocation (RMI) mechanism meets the necessary requirements to implement this application, in which sensor nodes in the tracking region would maintain communications with a control unit outside of the WSN employed to orchestrate the task. However, it is clear that this approach would incur additional delay during the communications between the WSN control unit and the respective nodes.

Several solutions to the TT problem that employ MAs have been proposed in the literature. In Ref. [39], moving targets are tracked by MAs by employing a simple "trilateration" algorithm, and the result is periodically sent to a server that stores the targets' location. To achieve this, a node employs its own location measurement information and combines it with the readings obtained by two of its direct neighbors to produce a target location estimate. Figure 5A illustrates this approach, where the three-circled areas specify the possible positions of the target object based on the measurements taken by an equal number of MAs. One of these agents is referred to as the "mother agent," whereas the other two are referred to as "child agents" that are controlled by the mother agent to work cooperatively to obtain a better estimate of the target object's location. Figure 5A also shows that the mother agent temporarily stationed at node A dispatches the child agents to nodes B and C to help locate the target object. The child agent at B ends operations when the received signal strength at this node decays beyond a certain threshold, whereas node D receives a new child agent, as depicted in Fig. 5B. Later, the mother agent itself decides to migrate to node C to avoid losing track of the moving target. At this point, all child agents terminate, and new ones are dispatched to nodes D and E, as shown in Fig. 5C. From this example, it follows that multiple child agents can be deployed to track a moving object, and that their number can vary depending on the number of WSN nodes present in the monitored region. An alternative approach proposed in Ref. [40] also promotes dispatching an MA to track a moving object, as shown in Fig. 6. Upon migrating to a sensor node, the agent collects the necessary information to gradually

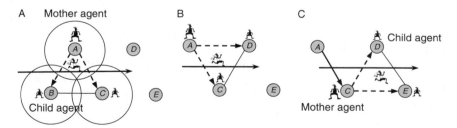

FIG. 5. Geographical target tracking using trilateration.

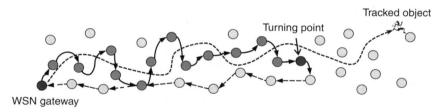

Fɪɢ. 6. Target tracking based on object recognition.

increase the accuracy with which an object is followed. When a certain threshold is met and the tracked object has been successfully recognized, the MA halts the tracking process and returns to the WSN gateway with the collected results.

2.3 Architecting Data Dissemination Schemes in WSN Using MAs

We classify the MA-based architectures as being either hierarchical or flat in accordance to the WSN's configuration. In a hierarchical architecture, the nodes' roles are different, whereas in a flat sensor network, the nodes' roles are either equal or very similar [41]. In this section, we will elaborate on each of these types of architectures and describe their pros and cons depending on the actual WSN application and configuration.

2.3.1 Hierarchical WSN Architecture

In general, the operation of an MA-based solution is simplified in hierarchical WSN deployments, such as in the clustered topology proposed in Ref. [42] that promotes intra- and intercluster hybrid methods. In the first case, every cluster head dispatches an MA that migrates to all cluster members collecting and combining data. Upon returning to its corresponding cluster-head, the MA sends the accrued data results back to the WSN's gateway for further processing. Conversely, the intercluster approach does not perform any MA operations inside the cluster. Instead, an MA follows an itinerary that takes it to all the cluster-heads, until the WSN gateway is reached. We can see that the intracluster method is intuitively favorable in cases where clusters are formed by many nodes, and the number of cluster-heads is reasonably small. On the contrary, the intercluster method is more efficient in clusters comprised by a smaller number of nodes. On the downside, network maintenance in hierarchical WSNs may involve significant signaling overhead. Evidently, this problem can be solved by resorting to a flat WSN configuration that may be appropriate for a broad variety of sensor applications.

2.3.2   Flat WSN Architecture

In Ref. [43], researchers introduced the MA-based distributed sensor network (MADSN) approach for using in both hierarchical and flat WSNs. Here, the WSN gateway dispatches a certain number of MAs that gather data in a target region. For this, it is assumed that source nodes are close to the WSN gateway; however, an MA can traverse a number of hops before reaching the first source node, if needed. One caveat is that dispatching MAs from the gateways to the source nodes can incur significant bandwidth, thus defeating the benefits obtained by using MAs. To address this side effect, we proposed a novel approach that we coin MA-based WSN or MAWSN [44]. In our approach, a single "mother" MA is dispatched by the WSN gateway to the target area and remains temporarily stationed at a designated node therein waiting for a trigger event or command. This MA carries the codes that perform the desired action within that region. When triggered, the mother MA dispatches one or more "child" agents that carry out one or more tasks. Child agents separately visit a set of data source nodes to collect and aggregate data. Then, the accrued data is either sent back to the mother MA or directly to the WSN gateway. Fresh batches of child MAs can be dispatched periodically by the mother MA in accordance to the strategy being implemented. In addition, several child MAs can also be concurrently launched by the mother MA to perform one or more tasks in parallel to reduce latency. From our description of MAWSN's operation, it follows that using MAs enables the reduction of data traffic at three levels. In the first level, unprocessed data can be reduced at the source node level as stipulated by child MAs, so that only digested information is sent to the WSN gateway. In the second level, data redundancy can be eliminated by having child MAs visit the source nodes that produced the highly correlated data. Finally, a mother MA can further aggregate data pooled by child MAs upon returning to the mother MA's location.

2.4   Agent Migration Itinerary Planning

The migration itinerary of an MA is defined as the path followed when hoping through the underlying network as it performs a given task. In our case, planning the itinerary of an MA involves two main steps that can be realized either by the WSN gateway or autonomously by the MA: (1) defining the subset of nodes to visit and (2) defining the actual path to follow to preserve bandwidth. This last aspect can have an important effect on the overall energy consumption of the WSN nodes involved. This is a well- and long-known problem in computer networks known as the traveling salesman problem [45]. It has also been shown that finding an optimal sequence for visiting the respective nodes of such a path is a nondeterministic task that can be solved in polynomial time of the factorial of the number of nodes to visit; that is, it is an NP-complete problem. If the visiting path is fixed, then the MA migration itinerary is determined by the WSN gateway before dispatching the MA. Conversely, if the visiting path is dynamic (variable), then the MA autonomously decides what WSN nodes to visit, depending on the current network conditions or on its task execution progress. However, it is also possible to implement a hybrid approach, whereby a preliminary WSN node-visiting path is decided by the gateway, whereas last minute changes can also be performed appropriate by the MA as deemed suitable. We now elaborate on the particularities of these approaches.

2.4.1   Planning a Static MA Itinerary

This approach relies on current global network information to derive a possible migration path before an MA is dispatched. Two methods that address this problem were presented in Ref. [46]: local closest first (LCF) and global closest first (GCF), both of which assume that out of the nodes to be visited, the executing one is the closest to the gateway. For this reason, LCF first searches for the node that is closest to the current node, whereas GCF does so for the node closest to the gateway. Alternative solutions also exist. For instance, a genetic algorithm is presented in Ref. [47] to devise MA itineraries for WSNs, which assumes that each sensor node can be visited only once to reduce the search space. This solution achieves global optimization, though it is a computationally heavy one whose actual suitability in resource-constrained nodes is debatable.

2.4.2   Planning a Dynamic MA Itinerary

Our previous descriptions of static MA itinerary planning solutions reveal that they may be unsuitable for WSNs that experience varying conditions if the global information stored at the gateway becomes outdated in the presence of continuous changes in the underlying environment. On the contrary, dynamic itinerary planning enables MAs to determine which node to visit as it hops through its migration path. To achieve this, trade-offs between the migration plan change costs and possible efficiency degradations should be taken into account. For instance, researchers in Ref. [40] promote a dynamic planning method that achieves progressive fusion accuracy without incurring excessive costs. To this end, the dynamic itinerary planning approach ensures that the visited sensor nodes (1) have enough battery power energy, (2) require minimum energy consumption for the MAs migration, and (3) yield significant information gain. As discussed before, one of the objectives of the MA should be visiting sensor nodes that reduce uncertainty to shorten the migration path, reduce bandwidth usage, and decrease task completion delay.

2.4.3 Planning a Hybrid MA Itinerary

This approach selects a static set of sensor nodes that should be visited, leaving the migration sequence open to changes. A hybrid itinerary planning scheme coined as mobile agent-based directed diffusion (MADD) is proposed in Ref. [38]. In it, exploratory packets are sent to the WSN's gateway as soon as sources in a certain region detect an event of interest. Then, the gateway defines a cost-effective migration path for the MA as it visits a WSN node subset.

2.5   Middleware Layer Design

MASs are frequently implemented as middleware that bonds the underlying operating system with high-level software components, which in our case has to take into account significant limitations and technical challenges inherent to WSNs. MAS middleware (MASM) provides a platform that enables MAs to realize application-specific tasks and rapid application development in WSNs. However, a trade-off arises by the need to produce a drastically simple system that consumes the least possible amount of resources, without sacrificing functionalities that are key to ensuring a successful WSN deployment. One way to achieve this is by creating a custom programming language with the necessary high-level constructs that embody repetitive sequences of low-level tasks that are routinely encountered. This approach reduces agent codes' size, simplifies the structure of the MA interpreter, and promotes using local function libraries at the sensor nodes. As a result, programmers relieve MAs from having to carry the codes to perform low-level tasks and reduce programs' sizes. The degree to which this approach can actually be implemented depends on several factors. For instance, if WSN nodes are resource constrained, then the number of library functions locally available might be limited too.

The previous discussion evidences the need to create custom MASMs whose architecture depends on the applications they are intended to support, as well as on the underlying hardware and the environment being monitored. An MASM could be designed to support either coarse- (high-level) or fine-grained (low-level) MAs employed for distributed task coordination or local data processing. For instance, SensorWare [48] employs high-level language constructs, whereby a single expression realizes multiple low-level tasks in WSNs. Conversely, Agilla [49] resorts to low-level codes that resemble assembly programming mnemonics. In general, fine-grained constructs yield lengthier programs that control task execution in greater detail, thereby requiring a more intricate MASM that consumes more memory at the local sensor nodes. However, an MASM architected under the coarse-grain approach yields shorter MAs that resemble Macroprograms—condensed instructions mapped to a lengthier sequence of detailed commands—that promote using the nodes' local function library. Consequently, the complexity of the MASM is reduced along with the MA's size. On the downside, this approach sacrifices detailed task control.

2.6   Multiple Agent Cooperation

MAs can be deployed to operate independently or collaboratively to realize one or more tasks. In fact, previous research has shown that active agent collaboration can decrease energy consumption in the WSN as a whole [39,48,49]. The reason for this is that parallelism is exploited more efficiently by sharing information that other agents can employ to reduce task execution delay and bandwidth due to repeated hoping through the network during the data collection process. Thus, it follows that fewer MA hops in its migration path leads to a reduced battery consumption rate in a shorter time frame, as agents finish their task quicker. The type of information that agents exchange can be simple or abstract. In addition, these data can be continuously modified by other agents in a time-decoupled manner until a certain outcome is found, which can be subsequently used in other decision processes, including, but not restricted to, the course of the current WSN task. To this effect, the tuple-space mechanism remains widely popular, whereby MAs communicate indirectly by saving typified data at the respective WSN nodes, contrary to directing messages to each other, as shown in the example of Fig. 7. Here, we see that *Agent 1* visits *Node n* to change the contents of a tuple-space entry, which is later updated by another MA. For this communications mechanism to work, it is necessary that all agents know how to access and store data in the corresponding tuple-space, so that no information is corrupted. Therefore, the semantic meaning of the tuple-space needs to be predefined. It is straightforward to see that this approach favors applications with loose timing requirements in which the significance of the information stored at the WSN nodes deteriorates slowly in comparison to the occurrence rate of the events being

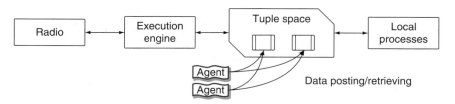

Fig. 7. Multiple agent cooperation using tuple-spaces.

monitored. Alternatively, direct agent communications might be the best solution under a tight timing requirement, as in the case of applications that require real-time information processing. An instance of this could be a WSN used for intrusion detection based on partial image evaluation, as explained before. Here, the WSN gateway could deploy agents that seek evidence of a certain event as captured by a sensor camera. Upon finding the piece of evidence sought for, agents could directly send signals indicating the current outcome, which would serve as an indication to the other agents to either continue or halt the process. However, it is always possible to employ more than one communications mechanism to accomplish a certain task.

2.7   Summary

An effective MAS design is crucial for overcoming the limitations found in alternative methods to solve diverse WSNs problems, where bandwidth and batter power conservation are fundamental. This section introduced important aspects that are relevant to MAS deployment in WSNs. Applications, system architecture, migration itinerary planning, middleware design, and MA cooperation issues were discussed. We stressed the notion that important bandwidth savings can be achieved by locally processing sensor data as specified by the codes carried by an MA. However, performing efficient MASM design is imperative to support the intended WSN application to solve a particular kind of problem. Thus, it is important that the MASM includes custom features to provide enhanced efficiency. We also discussed aspects directly related to MA cooperation and the corresponding communications mechanisms, which are ultimately a direct influence of the intended objective to achieve maximum performance. Consequently, the benefits that can be obtained by applying MA technology in a WSN, or even in other types of networks, also depend to a good extent on the skill of the programmer that creates the respective codes. Finally, there is an important qualitative aspect of using MAS: they provide an effective means to deploying alternative solutions for dealing with unexpected problems or unforeseen situations, which are much harder to tackle when message-passing schemes are used. In Section 3, we will present our original work in the area of MASMs, which takes into account all the provisions and discussions that we have presented.

3.   Programmable Tasking of WSN

3.1   Agents in WSN

In the previous section, we described the importance of providing WSNs with the ability to be seamlessly retasked as required by the underlying conditions of the environment being monitored. We mentioned the shortcomings encountered by employing classical message-passing schemes and vied for using the MASM approach to solve this issue. In recent years, researchers designed and implemented programmable-tasking schemes in WSNs by embedding virtual machines that systematically process and forward highly compact codes between nodes. This reduces packet transmissions and enables WSN nodes to effectively switch from one mode of operation into another. Virtual machines entered the WSN realm recently after WSNs became a popular research topic. The first systems proposed were Maté [50], Impala [51], and Deluge [52] and were promptly followed by SensorWare [48], SmartMessages [53], and Agilla [49]. Initial approaches were specifically designed to work on devices with severe resource constraints, as explained before, whereas the latter approaches introduced architectures for inter-pretable codes with more functionalities than their predecessors.

Prior to these advances, extensive investigations had already taken place in the late 1990s and early 2000s to gauge the advantages of deploying mobile codes in WSNs, contrary to implementing traditional message-passing protocols [6]. An important finding was that MASs indeed are able to produce better performance results than their conventional message-passing counterpart in WSNs, subject to the migration strategy employed to reducing the distributed data processing delay. In addition, execution and forwarding overhead, which depend to a good extent on the MAS' architecture, also play an important role. Consequently, we argue that MASM design is crucial for efficiently supporting the agents' operation. In other words, whereas MASs for WSN need to incorporate the necessary mechanisms that minimize bandwidth and power consumption, they warrant a design for dealing with the peculiarities of each individual WSN application, contrary to creating general-purpose solutions.

3.2   The *Wiseman* Approach

Unlike existing schemes that promote general-purpose approaches, we advance an MASM that implements specific network-level features for simplifying distributed task coordination in WSNs. Our proposed MASM, wireless sensors employing mobile agents (*Wiseman*), is characterized by the following features: (1) its architecture supports distinct migration strategies and provides a flexible code execution flow; (2) it follows a text-based, code scripting scheme, whereby compact MAs can be efficiently deployed to implement a number of actions, or to perform WSN maintenance tasks as needed; and (3) it implements an execution model whereby self-depleting text strings can be progressively eliminated to expedite their processing time and reduce the incurred transmission bandwidth and forwarding delay.

The ingenuity of embedded software engineers has been put to the test to create MASM that is amenable to hardware-constrained WSN devices to achieve the desired balance between system functionality and performance. To this end, there are two paradigms that can be followed. One promotes a fine-grained approach, whereby simple, mnemonic-like language constructs resembling assembly programming codes are used to specify a detailed flow of operations that an MA will perform (e.g., $<CLR\ REG0>$, $<JMPTO\ 0x04>$, etc.). The other paradigm follows a macroprogramming scheme, whereby course-grained constructs describing compound operations are employed to describe the order in which task will be executed (e.g., $<Run\ Task\ X>$, $<Run\ Task\ Y>$, $<IfSuccess\ END,\ Else\ Run\ Task\ Z>$). Evidently, there are both advantages and disadvantages to using one or the other. For the first, the MAS interpreter would deal with more compact agents invoking locally available libraries at the nodes (e.g., *Run Task X/Y/Z*) but would also encounter limited execution thread flexibility. In the other approach, a detailed operation flow sequence is possible at the expense of larger programs, even if a byte-code scheme is implemented to reduce their size. Ultimately, MASM engineers need to define the right degree of granularity required for implementing MAs, as dictated by the intended WSN application(s). However, it is apparent that the prevailing conditions of WSN hardware favor the implementation of coarse-grained approaches, combined with limited fine-grained functionalities that allow MAs to test for certain conditions to veer the flow of the current process as needed. In addition to this, a WSN is expected to operate in the same manner for a certain period of time after it has been (re)tasked, meaning that a number of subtasks execute repetitively until the WSN is reprogrammed into a different operation mode. In fact, contemporary WSN devices provide some limited memory space intended for logging sensor data, which can be conceivably partitioned to store additional data-processing algorithms, or "dormant" MAs that can be activated on demand. Regardless of this, the incentive behind employing MAs weakens if the tasks they are meant to perform become deterministic in relation to the WSN's operations. However, WSNs deployed in environments where a higher degree of uncertainty prevails benefit more from using MASM that enables flexible programmability, which enables them to adapt to unforeseen circumstances.

A caveat of the previous rationale is that, because WSN technology is still deemed as being relatively recent, it becomes tempting to assume that contemporary MASMs need to be designed from the ground up, and that older systems designs are altogether inappropriate (e.g., those based on the JVM). However, we make note of the existence of one particular system that dates back to the mid-1980s, whose design was based on the premise of deploying mobile codes in a time where message passing was a vastly predominant communications mechanism. The *wave* system [54,55] promoted one of the earliest code mobility paradigms in wired computer networks specifically conceived for the efficient coordination of distributed tasks [56].

It could be argued that looking into the past for earlier technologies that could be adapted to contemporary needs is counterintuitive. However, we note that limitations found in earlier computer network systems (e.g., processing power and bandwidth) still exist in some contemporary systems. This clearly is the case of WSNs formed by devices possessing 8-bit microprocessors with 128 KB of RAM that communicate at 250 Kbits/s. Therefore, we considered worthwhile revisiting previously explored concepts and technologies to understand how these issues were originally addressed, and whether they could be adapted to solve current WSN issues (i.e., contrary to attempting to reinvent a solution for a reasonably comparable problem). After a careful analysis, we observed that the wave's language constructs originally devised for bandwidth-constrained network systems could be adapted for WSN use. Consequently, Wiseman inherits many of the traits already seen in wave:

1. The MAs' primary task is geared toward distributed process coordination of a WSN by decoupling the data processing element, and instead promoting the execution of local algorithms, as explained before.
2. The size of MAs' scripts can be shortened by defining the language constructs that adequately describe the process coordination methodology that a WSN operator/engineer wishes to deploy.
3. As a result of the two previous aspects, Wiseman's interpreter architecture can be further simplified, yielding a smaller memory footprint that is amenable to WSN hardware.
4. MA forwarding delays are reduced by transmitting compact MAs' codes, which also promotes bandwidth conservation.

3.3   Architecture and Code Processing Flow of Wiseman MAs

Wiseman was designed to minimize program memory footprint. Therefore, it implements only four components: an incoming MA queue, a parser, a processor, and an MA dispatcher (see Fig. 8). In addition, the Engine and Session Warden blocks are incorporated to assist the other components. The incoming queue temporarily stores agents after being received from the wireless interface and are subsequently parsed for immediate processing once the currently executing MA finishes. It is also possible to inject agents that are stored in the node's local library, as explained before. In this case, an MA arriving from another node instructs the interpreter to fetch a particular MA for immediate queuing and processing. (Because of the processing limitations prevalent in WSN hardware, Wiseman is not designed to execute in a multithreaded manner.) Once an MA is removed from the incoming queue, the parser tokenizes individual MA codes by dividing them into two parts

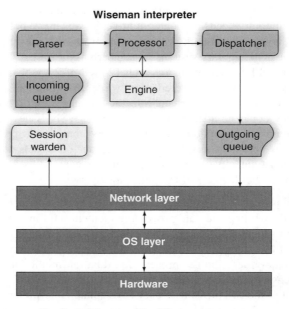

FIG. 8. Architecture of the Wiseman interpreter.

that we refer to as *head* and *tail*. The head is simply an indivisible code segment that cannot be further split, which is sent to the processor for immediate execution. The tail, however, is made of the rest of the MA's codes, which are also tokenized for subsequent processing, as needed. The processor almost always relies on the Engine as a helper block that performs certain simple tasks, including the transformation and/or adaptation of data.

The parser regains control of the MA's processing task as soon as the head finishes executing, at which point the tail is subsequently tokenized to obtain the next indivisible segment that becomes the new head, whereas the remaining codes become the new (shrunk) tail. At this point, the new head is passed onto the processor for immediate execution as before. Figure 9 illustrates the MA execution sequence of the Wiseman interpreter. We note that the processor may stop executing an MA if (1) the current code segment's outcome is unsuccessful, (2) the MA requires being forwarded to another node as indicated by the current instruction, or (3) an explicit MA termination is specified. The first case implies that the remainder of the MA being executed must be discarded if the current condition being evaluated results in a FALSE outcome. The second case implies that a hop operation was found, and so the tail of the MA is immediately passed onto the

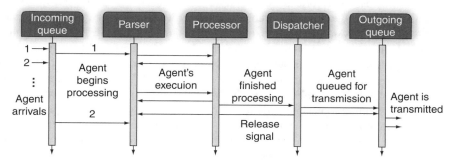

Fig. 9. Execution sequence of Wiseman agents.

dispatcher for its transmission to another WSN node. Finally, the third case is usually incorporated by the MA programmer as a fail-safe provision to avoid further propagation. Aspects pertaining to the Session Warden of the interpreter will be detailed later in this section. Figure 8 illustrates Wiseman's interpreter architecture.

3.4   Wiseman's Instruction Set and Language Constructs

Most of Wiseman's language constructs are derived directly from wave, although they have been further condensed to reduce program size and forwarding delay. Unlike other MASM approaches for WSNs that resort to bytecode-type agents, Wiseman agents are written as text scripts, making it flexible to dynamically incorporate modifications to their program structure. Therefore, Wiseman MAs can morph dynamically after they have been dispatched from the WSN's gateway. Wiseman's language constructs are made of variables, rules, operators, and delimiters, as explained next.

3.4.1   Variables

Wiseman requires that enough processor memory be reserved to store floating point type variables, known as *numeric*. The memory content of this type of variable is accessible through the letter N (e.g., $N0$, $N4$, etc.). Similarly, *character* variables require that memory be reserved to store single characters that can be referenced by the letter C (e.g., $C3$, $C5$, etc.). Access to these variable types is public, implying that all MAs that reach the local node have read/write privileges on them. Unlike Agilla, Wiseman does not implement the functionalities to perform operations on remote nodes' variables. Therefore, local operations on numeric and character variables have no effect on other nodes' variables. However, it is straightforward in Wiseman to spawn a simple MA that can hop to a neighboring node to update a local variable, if needed. In addition to numeric variables, MAs may carry with them *mobile* variables, whose purpose is analogous to that of private variables in object-oriented programming, and so they are inaccessible to other MAs. The contents for each of these variables is accessible through the letter *M* (e.g., *M7*, *M8*, etc.), which are semantically similar to private variables in object-oriented programming. All nodes reserve enough memory to store the contents of mobile variables when an MA is fetched from the incoming queue for immediate execution. When an MA finishes executing and is either dispatched or terminated, the reserved memory space is overwritten to store mobile variables carried by another MA being brought into execution. The WSN engineer must then ensure that the semantic meaning of all three variable types is kept throughout the network. For instance, the contents of variable *N1* at node *m* should have the same meaning as that of variable *N1* at node *n*. The *clipboard* variable is also provided by the interpreter to temporarily store data for diverse operations, and its contents can be accessed through the letter *B*. Finally, the interpreter defines three additional *environmental* variables that store data regarding the executing environment. The first of these is a read-only variable that holds the local node's identification number (ID) (i.e., 1, 2, etc.) and is defined as the *identity* variable *I*. The next is the *predecessor* variable *P*, which is populated with the identity number of the node that an MA arrived from as it is loaded into the parser for processing. The third and last of the environmental variables are designated as the *link* variable *L*, which is similar to *P* but is used to store a virtual label identifier of the link that the MA employed for hopping into the local node, as discussed later in the text. It follows that the contents of both the predecessor and the link variables are overwritten with every MA that enters the execution space, and that each MA carries this information that is provided by the node that last dispatched it.

3.4.2 *Operators*

Wiseman implements a number of operators that are available to the programmer. The first type is the arithmetic operator type (i.e., +, −, *, /, and =) that is used to update the contents of numeric and mobile variables. It follows that arithmetic operations are not applicable to character variables. Other general-purpose operators are also available to evaluate different conditions (i.e., <, <=, ==, =>, >, and !=). However, Wiseman defines other system-specific operators that are unique to our approach. The *hop* operator # is employed to indicate that an MA's tail is to be forwarded to a node with the ID specified on the right-hand side of the character (e.g., *#5* indicates a hop to node 5). Alternatively, a virtual link identifier (i.e., a label) can be employed to refer to a subset of neighboring nodes to which an MA can be multicast. For example, a virtual link labeled as *d* can be assigned to odd-numbered nodes in the node set [1 . . . 5] (i.e., 1, 3, 5), and a label *e* can be assigned to even-numbered nodes (i.e., 2, 4). In such case, multicast hopping is instructed by placing the corresponding label on the left-hand side of the operator (e.g., *d#*). Here, the Wiseman interpreter automatically clones the agent to forward a copy to each node in the corresponding subset. Then, agents resume executing at the code that follows the hop operation immediately after reaching the destination node. This simplistic form of strong mobility eliminates the need for forwarding a program counter and execution state variables with the MA. Alternatively, the *broadcast* operator @ can be used to forward a short agent to all neighboring nodes. Wiseman also provides the *query* operator *?* that allows an MA to check whether a given label has already been defined at the local node by an agent that visited the node earlier in the process (e.g., *e?*). As mentioned before, MAs can inject locally stored codes retrieved from the local library by employing the *code injection* operator ∧. To this effect, the MA programmer must know in advance the identifier needed to reference the respective agent's codes. For example, the code ∧*7* fetches a local agent labeled with the number 7 for immediate insertion into the incoming queue block and subsequent execution. Similar to this is the *execution* operator *$*, through which an MA invokes a local function or algorithm that is not in the form of an MA. One operand is used to indicate which function is being called, and the other operand represents a single parameter being passed to the functions, which appear in the left- and right-hand side of the operator, respectively. To date, functionalities to switch on/off LEDs are available, to retrieve temperature/light sensors readings, and to retune the frequency channels of the local radio circuit. Finally, the *halt* operator *!* is employed to indicate explicit termination of the MA currently executing.

3.4.3   Rules

Wiseman implements three methods to control the execution flow of MAs' codes. The first and most often used is the *repeat* rule *R*. This rule is provided as a simple loop, and so the interpreter executes the codes embraced by curly brackets cyclically. To this end, the codes inside the repeat rule are copied and reinserted before the whole construct (i.e., *R{...}* yields *...;R{...}*). Consequently, the codes within the *repeat* rule execute until a certain condition evaluation fails. In addition to this, the *And*/*Or* rules control an MA's execution flow by verifying the outcome of the delimited codes within square brackets. For example, an Or rule construct *O [<code1>;<code2>;<code3>]* executes until the outcome of one of these segments yields a TRUE outcome. However, if the last code to be evaluated (e.g.,

$<code3>$) yields a FALSE outcome, then the MA terminates. It follows that the "And" rule operates under a similar premise, though all the delimited codes must return TRUE if the agent is to continue executing.

3.5   Wiseman's Agent Migration Methodologies

3.5.1   Explicit Path Hopping

One intrinsic feature of existing MASM approaches is that they all provide the means for explicitly defining the migration path of MAs through the WSN. There are two implications here. The first is that either the WSN gateway or a server/ coordinator beyond the gateway must have knowledge of the network's topology for defining the corresponding hopping sequence, and the second is that the node-visiting sequence for the MA cannot/should not be revised once defined. Though this migration method is the easiest to implement, it hinders the ability of an MA to dynamically react to changes that occur rapidly or unpredictably in the WSN. As a result, an MA might visit a node that is no longer a relevant part of a subset of nodes that observed a certain event or, worse yet, an MA might be unable to follow the initial migration plan. Therefore, this approach is most useful if it is anticipated that the conditions of the underlying environment being monitored by the WSN will remain stable [38]. The hop operator available in Wiseman enables explicit path migration by specifically indicating the destination node on the right-hand side of the operator. Therefore, a sequence of hop operators with their respective destination creates the explicit sequence of nodes to visit (e.g., *#3;...;#7;...;#4;...;#8;...*). To this effect, it becomes the responsibility of the WSN engineer to ensure that the MA will perform the required task at each respective node.

3.5.2   Variable-Target Hopping

Wiseman provides the means to implement a migration scheme whereby the MA's path can be modified as needed after it has been dispatched from the gateway. In this case, either mobile or numeric variables holding the identity of target node can be specified on the right-hand side of the hop operator. Therefore, changing the contents of the corresponding variable has a direct effect on the outcome of the hop operation. For example, the operation *#N4* specifies that an MA will hop to the node the ID of which has been previously stored in *N4*. It follows that there must be a separate process, either carried out by another MA or executed by a local function that is in charge of updating the contents of *N4*. However, if the hop operation employs a mobile variable (e.g., *#M7*), then it becomes the task of the corresponding MA that carries this variable to update its contents accordingly as it migrates between WSN nodes. To this effect, either direct assignment or regular arithmetic operations can be employed. For instance, if the variable *N4* holds the number 2, then the operation *N4+1* reassigns the number 3 to *N4*, and so *#N4* would forward the MA to node 3. An identical process applies to mobile variables used as operands.

3.5.3 Labeled Path Hopping

A disadvantage of the previous agent migration methods is that they are unable to forward multiple copies of an MA to different nodes as specified in a single hop operation so as to multicast the MA. Wiseman addresses this issue by assigning the ID numbers of one or more nodes to a letter that becomes a label, as explained previously. When the interpreter finds a character on the left-hand side of the hop operation, it forwards a copy of the MA to each node that belongs to the subset assigned to the corresponding label (e.g., *a#*). From this, we infer that (1) a separate process is needed to label such virtual links and (2) the node subset assigned to a specific label may differ from node to node. For instance, node *9* may have nodes *5* through *8* as neighbors, from which two labeled subsets need to be formed: one for the even-numbered nodes and one for the odd-numbered nodes. To achieve this, the codes *L=s;#6;#P;#8* and *L=g;#5;#P;#7* lead to the creation of the corresponding labeled paths assigned to letters *s* and *g*, respectively, by employing the environmental variables *L* and *P*. Then, any MA that subsequently traverses either of these paths can employ the codes *s#* or *g#* to reach at once nodes *6* and *8*, or *5* and *7*, respectively. From here, it can be inferred that MAs traversing these paths do not need to know in advance the IDs of the nodes they will visit—the sole use of a label suffices. Similarly, this hopping method can be implemented by explicitly defining labels or by assigning labels to character variables (e.g., *C1#*).

3.6 Middleware Implementation of Wiseman

We now describe the most important aspects of the implementation of the Wiseman interpreter in actual WSN devices. After its initial coding and verification in the OMNeT++ discrete event simulator [57], Wiseman was ported to the NesC language to create a binary image of the interpreter that runs on top of TinyOS ver. 1.x that we installed and tested on the Micaz sensor platform [58]. The Micaz sensor nodes remain widely popular in academia to evaluate a number of WSN schemes ranging from the MAC layer to the application layer, as they provide a perfect example of a resource-limited wireless sensor node with merely 128 KB of program memory and 4 KB of volatile SRAM memory. Wiseman's implementation follows the architecture shown in Fig. 8, whose program requires almost 2400 NesC lines that yield a 19-KB binary image, and consumes around 3 KB of SRAM space for holding MAs that span at most

170 bytes. Given the lack of a transport layer in TinyOS ver. 1.x, Wiseman implements a simple scheme for MA segmentation and reassembly implemented by the Session Warden module. To this end, MAs spanning more than the default 29-byte user space available in TinyOS packets are segmented into smaller pieces that are individually forwarded onto the next node as specified by a hop command. At the destination, the segmented MA is sequentially reassembled before being injected into the incoming agent queue. The header of a Wiseman agent has the following fields, some of which can be used to recover from any possible error that may occur in the wireless channel during an MA forwarding session:

1. *Segment number*: employed for identifying any given MA segment i out of a total n, whose value is gradually incremented for each segment being sent.
2. *Last segment*: used to indicate that the current segment is the last of a total of n.
3. *Source ID*: used by the destination node to populate the environmental variable P.
4. *Session number*: a pseudo-random number assigned to the current MA forwarding process.

An MA forwarding session initiates when the sender issues a *request-to-send* (RTS) packet to the destination node. This is done to ensure that this node is not involved in active communications with another node and that it is ready for being engaged with. If this is the case, the destination node sends a *clear-to-send* (CTS) packet to acknowledge the RTS signal back to the source node. At this point, segment numbers are employed in subsequent packets being transmitted so that any discrepancy of the expected segment number in the current session is dealt with accordingly. This is a well-known mechanism that is not natively implemented in TinyOS ver. 1.x when forwarding packets, and so the programmer needs to implement it to ensure that packets are correctly forwarded. When the last segment is successfully received, both the sender and the receiver nodes reset their current session values in preparation for a future forwarding session. Deadlocks are avoided by employing timeouts that trigger the corresponding event after 300 ms at the sender when no CTS acknowledgement is received from the destination. Similarly, a maximum of three retransmissions are attempted for any given MA segment. The maximum number of MAs that the incoming/outgoing queues support in the current Wiseman implementation is 3 and 5, respectively, which is a limitation of the Micaz SRAM memory space. However, a TelosB mote that possesses 10 KB of SRAM memory can support more and larger agents that can be held at the queues. It follows that a sensor mote will not issue a CTS signal back to the sender if the incoming queue is full. We also note that no routing service is implemented in the WSN. However, labeled paths can be readily created by MAs to accomplish the same result.

3.7   Case Study: Early Forest Fire Detection

3.7.1   Experiment's Rationale

We conducted experiments that exemplify the usefulness of employing MAs in an environment where the underlying conditions can change unexpectedly. In this case, we emulate Wiseman's support in a forest fire detection application, which has the following characteristics:

a. The underlying conditions of the deployment setting may change rapidly and unpredictably.
b. A WSN can be employed to assess the likelihood of one or more sectors of the monitored area experiencing an uncontrolled fire.
c. Given the vast area of the deployment setting, the WSN's will likely be comprised of several hundreds of sensor nodes, depending on the desired monitoring granularity.
d. Sensor node battery replacement and/or reprogramming would be highly impractical. Therefore, a reprogrammable, energy-efficient design becomes a top priority.
e. Only two sensor types are needed: one for humidity and one for temperature.

We focus on early fire prevention as the main WSN task, instead of fire tracking [59], even though this and other applications relevant to the deployment setting type can be readily implemented in Wiseman. Figure 10 illustrates an example of how a WSN can be deployed in a large forest area partitioned into three sectors (i.e., *A–C*). The early forest fire detection application is implemented in two steps. In the first step, MAs are dispatched from the WSN's gateway to collect temperature readings at the sectors being monitored. To simplify the process, cluster-head nodes can be

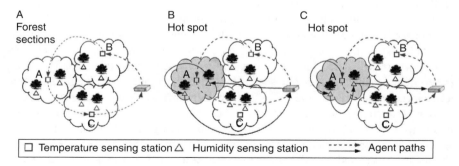

FIG. 10. A sample deployment setting for forest fire monitoring using Wiseman agents.

predesignated to pool temperature readings from individual sensor nodes dispersed in each sector. If an MA finds that temperature readings of one or more sensor nodes exceed a preset threshold, then the second step of the monitoring process collects humidity readings at the corresponding sector. If the MA deems that the humidity readings are below a preset threshold, then a warning signal is sent back to the monitoring center.

The previous rationale for this application indicates that MAs only have to migrate through a predefined path under normal circumstances, as illustrated in Fig. 10A. However, under adverse environmental circumstances, the secondary assessment process might be necessary, which can follow one of three possible approaches as shown in Fig. 10B and C:

1. *Approach A:* The MA returns to the WSN gateway immediately after the anomaly is found, which in turn dispatches another MA employed for obtaining humidity readings.
2. *Approach B:* A single MA is used for monitoring both temperature and humidity readings, implying that the MA implements both codes that realize two migration strategies.
3. *Approach C:* The MA operates as in the first approach; however, the secondary MA is dispatched from the respective cluster-head that coordinates the monitoring processes of the sector that observed the corresponding temperature anomaly, instead of from the gateway.

3.7.2   Case Study Setup

Our experiments implement four WSN topologies that emulate the deployment scenario explained in the previous section. Due to the limited number of sensor devices at hand, we programmed a few nodes to assume the role of cluster-heads, while a few others were programmed as regular sensor nodes assigned to a fictitious Sector 2, where the readings are made. In this sample setting, node 2 is the cluster-head of the forest area monitored by humidity sensor nodes 6–9, as seen in Fig. 11. The MA dispatched in experiments 1 and 2 migrates only through three cluster-heads, whereas in experiments 3 and 4, five cluster-heads are used. However, experiments 1 and 3 have four sensor nodes in the sensor node migration path, and experiments 2 and 4 employ six sensor nodes as part of Sector 2.

Table I illustrates the MA codes that implement approaches A, B, and C explained before for the forest monitoring application. The Micaz green LEDs are employed as visual aids to verify when the corresponding MA travels through the labeled paths (by means of the code "*l$n*" that toggles the corresponding LED—*l* for LED, and *n* for green), and the clipboard variable *B* holds the value 45 as the fictitious

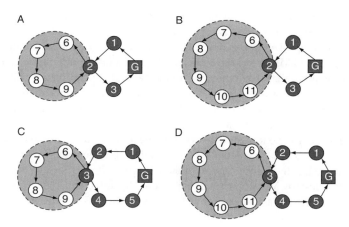

FIG. 11. WSN topology setup for the evaluation of Wiseman agents in a forest fire application.

TABLE I
WISEMAN AGENTS THAT IMPLEMENT APPROACHES A–C

Scheme	Agent	Script
A	1	1$n;M0=1;R{#M0;I!=0;M0+1;1$n;r$t;O[B>40;M1=I];O[M0<6;M0=0]}
	2	1$d;#1;#2;#3;M0=6;R{#M0;M0+1;1$d;I!=0;O[(I==9;M0=3);(I==5; M0=0);!1]; r$h;O[B<20;M1=I]}
B	1	a#;R{1$w;I!=0;O[(I<4;r$t;B>40;M2<1;M2=1;M0=I;b#);(I>3;r$h; B<20;M1=I;!0);a#;b#]}
C	1	R{a#;1$w;I!=0;O[(B>40;M0=I;2∧0);!1]}
	2	b#;R{1$d;I!=0;O[(I>5;r$h;B<20;M0=I;!0);a#;b#]}

threshold that is referenced to trigger the second stage of the process. A 59-byte-long MA that implements approach A visits the cluster-head route formed by nodes 1–3, as mentioned previously. It can be seen in that the variable-target migration method is used here, which does not rely on virtual links. Thus, mobile variable *M0* is incremented by one (*M0+1*) to reach the next destination node in the path made by nodes with sequential ID numbers (*#M0*). After hopping to the next node and toggling the LED, the MA obtains the latest temperature reading (*r$t*) and compares it against the maximum allowed temperature threshold (*B>40*). If the temperature reading exceeds the threshold, then the ID node is stored in mobile variable *M1* (*M1=I*), and it is delivered to the WSN gateway when the MA returns. To ensure that the MA reaches its final destination, variable *M0* is set to *0* just before the end of the migration itinerary. The second stage of the process initiates next by dispatching a second 85-byte-long MA, whose itinerary is preset to traverse the sensor node path of Sector 2. The second MA enters the corresponding humidity-sensing route, and verifies at each sensor node that the minimum humidity exceeds the predefined threshold. Mobile variable *M1* stores the ID of any node that returns a humidity reading below normal, as per the codes *r$h;O[B<20;M1=I]*. As mentioned before, approach *B* promotes a virtual path scheme, whereby MAs implementing the labeled-path hopping method visit the corresponding sensor nodes in the temperature-reading route assigned to the virtual path *a*, whereas letter *b* is assigned to the humidity-sensing route. The corresponding MA that carries out approach *B* spans 79 bytes of Wiseman codes. Finally, a 36-byte-long MA implements approach *C* by utilizing the local code injection operator (∧) to dispatch a 46-byte-long MA stored at the WSN nodes, which performs the second stage of the monitoring process after a 2-s delay (*2∧0*).

3.7.3   Case Study Results

We performed experiments to gauge Wiseman's generic performance, as well as its efficiency for the implementation of approaches A–C of the early forest fire detection application. The performance metrics that we consider are task completion delay and packet overhead. Table II shows the time it takes to run each Wiseman operation as averaged over 1000 runs in the Micaz sensor nodes, where it is evident that the hop operation incurs the shortest execution time, and the arithmetic operations incur the longest.

On the whole, average operation execution time lingers around 800 μs, which is higher than Agilla because Wiseman parses and tokenizes codes in the form of text strings. Nonetheless, the overall operation execution delay remains within acceptable boundaries. Table III shows the delay incurred by Wiseman MAs averaged over the course of 100 runs.

For these results, the MA's size in bytes is linearly increased to force a growing number of MAC layer segments for each consecutive experiment. When referenced in combination with the results presented in Table II, they yield a good approximation of the overall delay that the WSN operator can expect to see when deploying applications supported by Wiseman agents. Table IV illustrates the numerically calculated number of MAC packets containing the segmented MA for each of the three migration types through 40 hops. The outcome of these experiments further verifies that the labeled-path migration technique performs better than the other two. However, the bandwidth cost of implementing explicit hop migration can rival the one produced by labeled-path hopping if the number of hops that the MA performs is low.

TABLE II
OPERATION COMPLETION DELAY FOR WISEMAN OPERATIONS AND OPERATORS

Operation	Completion delay (μs)
Local broadcast (@)	543
Hop through label (a#)	603
Find label (a?)	613
No operation	732
Halt (!)	743
Hop to node (#1)	753
Insert local code ($\wedge$)	823
Execute ($)	843
Numeric comparisons	873
Add, subtract (+, −)	963
Assignment (=)	973
Multiply, divide (*, /)	1160

TABLE III
WISEMAN AGENT MIGRATION DELAY

MAC layer packets	Migration delay (s/hop)
1	0.235
2	0.250
3	0.264
4	0.278
5	0.294

TABLE IV
BANDWIDTH CONSUMPTION (NUMBER OF MAC LAYER PACKETS) OBSERVED FOR
EACH AGENT MIGRATION TYPE

Hops	Fixed path	Variable target	Labeled path
2	2	4	2
10	12	20	10
20	45	40	20
30	103	60	30
40	166	80	40

TABLE V
NUMBER OF MAC LAYER PACKETS INCURRED BY THE WISEMAN AGENTS IN EACH APPROACH

Approach	Topology 1	Topology 2	Topology 3	Topology 4
A	161	187	209	235
	[44(A1)+117(A2)]	[44(A1)+143(A2)]	[66(A1)+143(A2)]	[66(A1)+169(A2)]
B	135	165	165	195
C	99	117	126	144
	[36(A1)+63(A2)]	[36(A1)+81(A2)]	[54(A1)+72(A2)]	[54(A1)+90(A2)]

Finally, Table V illustrates the results of our experiments for approaches A–C. We can see that Topology 1 yields the shortest task duration. In contrast, Topology 4 yields the longest one, being that this parameter is proportional to the itinerary's path length. In addition to this, approach A always yields the longest task duration because two agents are employed to complete the task. However, approach C yields the shortest task duration, which is directly attributed to employing a single MA that injects another one locally (instead of dispatching it from the WSN gateway).

3.8   Summary

In this section, we have presented the design, implementation, and evaluation of the Wiseman system for supporting WSN applications. The design of our proposed system is based on a much earlier system targeted at supporting active networking in early local area networks. Several modifications had to be incorporated to make Wiseman amenable for WSN node deployment that is characterized by possessing severe hardware and communications bandwidth limitations. Our experiments corroborate that Wiseman can be effectively employed to support WSN applications, and that the efficiency of the MAs employed depends to a good extent on the type of migration technique employed. Specifically, we see that the explicit path migration technique reduces MA design complexity at the expense of higher bandwidth usage for the case of large WSNs, although good results can be obtained for the case of an MA hopping through a relatively small number of nodes before returning to the gateway. One important consideration when coding MAs that implement the labeled-path migration approach is that if the underlying conditions of the monitored environment change, then the semantic relationship expressed by the labeled paths becomes stale. In that case, a separate label maintenance process would need to be executed, thus incurring additional bandwidth. In this case, the gains introduced by the labeled-path hopping approach could be lost, whereas the variable-target hopping scheme might become the most efficient.

4. Embedding Agents in RFID Tags

4.1 Introduction to RFID Technology

RFID has been a crucial enabling technology for a myriad of commercial and industrial applications, including (but not restricted to): object tracking, inventory control, asset administration, supply chain management, and even an emerging field known as E-healthcare. RFID allows quick access to information assigned to an ID stored in an RFID device, also known as a tag. A RFID tag possesses a radio-frequency transmitter and an antenna to communicate with a special reader that retrieves the tag's ID number and uses it to retrieve the corresponding information from a database. Then, a handling procedure for the bearer object can be determined. This process presupposes a centralized scheme that controls the flow of events, and the actions that need to be taken for every object that has its RFID tag read. Consequently, multiple issues that are detrimental to the operation of the overall system and to its overall efficiency also arise. We refer to this approach as the Identification-centric RFID System, or IRS, whereby RFID tags store a simple alphanumeric string that identifies the bearer object. Though this approach has sufficed for a wide range of applications, one major problem is that updating the database from which any associated data is retrieved is not a straightforward process. This issue also raises a synchronization problem, in addition to possessing two significant disadvantages. First, the database entry for the corresponding object must be created and maintained prior to accessing it to retrieve any associated action. Second, this approach is not feasible for situations that require rapid processing of an object or an event, such as in emergency situations. It is also the case that the information stored in the corresponding database entry might become stale or even unreachable in case of network/system failures, which results in unwanted operation delays or interruptions.

In this section, we advance a CRS as an alternative solution to the problems found in traditional IRS, as previously reported in Chen et al. [60]. CRS employs MAs that are individually stored on demand in RFID tags in place of a regular alphanumeric code. These agents can later enact specific service directives as they are interpreted by the corresponding middleware system when the tag's contents are read. Because of recent memory enhancements in existing RFID tags (e.g., such as in the MB89R118 model by Fujitsu that provides 2 KB of memory [61]), we argue that the compactness of Wiseman agents makes them a good candidate for implementing

CRS applications. It is straightforward to see that CRS enables implementing a much more flexible scheme that promotes local decision making and process handling in response to specific situations. Additionally, full CRS-based solutions can be plausibly integrated with other technologies, such as WSNs, the IP backbone, and cellular networks that form scalable systems for implementing a number of user-driven applications. We believe that CRS has the potential to introduce the following benefits:

a. It enables a scalable and robust system that eliminates the need to access RFID-related information from a remote database.
b. It decreases system response time by implementing local processes.
c. It alleviates system complexity at the database side.
d. It introduces enhanced resilience to database and network failures.

In this section, we introduce the principles of our proposed MA-based system to implement an effective CRS. We also provide an overview of traditional RFID systems, and how they can evolve into CRS solutions. In addition, we provide a detailed rationale behind CRS based on our proposed middleware design. Finally, we describe and discuss preliminary results of an experimental testbed for CRS.

4.2   Review of Identification-Centric RFID Systems

As mentioned before, IRS applications are mostly designed to track or locate objects as they are moved from one place to another. For instance, RFID tags can be attached to chemical containers being transferred from one warehouse to another to provide close monitoring of potentially harmful material. However, RFID technology has become pervasive in supply chain management applications in which the IRS approach suffices by enabling real-time tracking. The same is true in other industrial sectors, such as manufacturing, warehouse storage, shipping and receiving, and purchase transactions. Figure 12 illustrates the product-tracking procedure

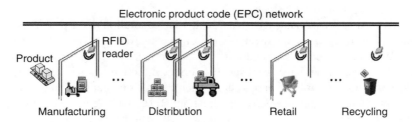

FIG. 12. Supply chain process using a classical IRS system.

through a whole supply chain process. We can see here that an RFID reader retrieves the data stored in a product carrying an RFID upon leaving a manufacturing plant. Then, the object's electronic product code (EPC) information is stored in a database server as soon as it is delivered to a distribution center or to a retailer. After the product is purchased and/or consumed, the RFID tag's information may be stored, for example, in a recycling center's database. In this scheme, the most important components of an IRS are

1. *Rule database:* This module maintains a list of rules associated to RFID code entries to which the corresponding actions can be readily mapped.
2. *Processing module:* This component is in charge of enacting actions/tasks immediately after retrieving the corresponding information from the rule database. Immediately following this, the processing module verifies that any required condition is satisfied.
3. *EPC network:* This subsystem comprises an object naming service (ONS), an EPC information service (EPCIS), and an EPC discovery service (EPCDS), all of which interact to ensure the seamless flow of RFID-related information.

A closer inspection into the operation of the IRS scheme reveals important shortcomings that need to be addressed:

a. The ID number that RFID tags hold does not provide any additional information on what type of service or handling the bearer object requires.
b. The type of service or handling instructions that the bearer object requires needs to be retrieved from a database, whose contents require manual updating.
c. Network and database scalability problems appear when the processing system is unable to handle a growing number of items carrying an RFID tag.
d. Database and/or network malfunctions negatively impact the system's performance.

In Section 4.3, we describe in detail the benefits introduced by the system that we advance to overcome the shortcomings just described for IRS.

4.3   Code-Centric RFID System

4.3.1   System Rationale

The primary goal of an IRS deployment is to help locate goods or objects, as seen in a typical supply chain scenario. Nonetheless, this approach has severe limitations when the service requirements of goods/objects change with time and/or location, in which case a dynamic approach that allows flexible object handling/servicing is needed. To address this issue, we advance the CRS, in which an MAS becomes the centerpiece of the improved RFID system architecture. In it, the object's handling/servicing directives are specified by MAs embedded into RFID tags in place of regular ID numbers. Our proposed CRS approach serves as a catalyst to harmoniously combine the prevalent environment circumstances and user's requirements. When the conditions surrounding the bearer object change, so can the MA codes embedded into the RFID tag as stored by the corresponding device that provides this context awareness service.

4.3.2 System Architecture

Our proposed CRS is divided in two main parts: the RFID tag, and the code-processing equipment that reads the tags contents (the MA) and executes the necessary actions. To achieve this objective, we introduce an extended message format used for storing information in RFID tags, as illustrated in Fig. 13. In essence, this change stipulates that enough room needs to exist in the RFID tags' memory to store an MA encoded in plain text, in addition to other information embedded into the RFID's memory space. Our proposed CRS approach comprises five principal components: a passive information manager, a middleware subsystem, a codes' information manager, a context awareness subsystem, and a service response system. The passive information manager is employed for retrieving the information stored in the RFID tag, which can be forwarded to the EPC network to generate a backup record. The retrieved MA is then sent to the code information manager, and then onto the middleware subsystem that interprets the MA codes. The context awareness subsystem provides the necessary environmental parameters and information that the middleware subsystem needs to make decisions and execute the appropriate actions. Finally, the commands that enact these actions are forwarded to the service response system, which realizes the commanded tasks that the object requires. The architecture of our proposed CRS is illustrated in Fig. 14.

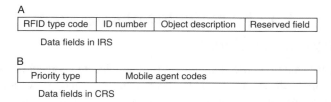

FIG. 13. Extended message format for CRS.

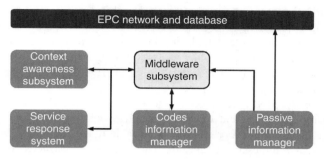

FIG. 14. Principal components of a CRS.

While all the modules mentioned above are indispensible for its operation, we note that the middleware subsystem is what gives CRS its distinctive feature. The middleware subsystem is in charge of interpreting the agent's commands that are eventually enacted by the rest of the infrastructure. MAs may receive limited input to make a decision, which is provided by the context awareness subsystem (e.g., in the form of geographical position, or as environmental information—humidity, temperature, etc.). However, other information relating to the overall system's internals can also be employed. Similarly, different action types can be enacted by the corresponding infrastructure devices after processing the MA, such as interacting with a video surveillance system, updating certain information in the tags of other objects, issuing an alarm signal, etc. Consequently, our proposed system becomes "code-centric."

4.3.3 Updating Mobile Codes

We note the importance of providing the CRS with the means to update MAs on demand, which ultimately makes it possible to provide enhanced quality of service (QoS). To this end, we propose the implementation of three code updating methods: passive, active, and hybrid:

a. *Passive mode:* In this method, the RFID tag has to be updated by a reader device located somewhere in the deployment setting (e.g., along a conveyor in an automatic assembly line). In such case, the handling operations on the product have to be performed one at a time. When the operation associated to the current code being executed finishes, the tags' codes are updated *in situ*. As more MA operations complete, it is expected that the size of the MA codes will shrink as the codes that indicate object handling/servicing actions gradually deplete. For the case when the object needs multiple processing/ handling steps, the RFID tag would have to be replenished with new codes that will be later read, interpreted, and enacted by other devices in a different location (e.g., when the object passes through multiple assembly lines). It follows that the MA's size stored in the RFID tag varies during the bearer object's handling/servicing process.

b. *Active mode:* If the bearer is a person, then the MA's codes possess the necessary directives that indicate specialized treatment or service for him/ her. In this case, the user employs a portable device equipped with an RFID reader that seamlessly updates the tag's codes as instructed by a software application. Therefore, the users' interactions with the portable device may lead to the RFID tag's update without his/her knowledge.

c. *Hybrid mode:* This mode of operation combines both passive and active updates. Therefore, a person might have his/her RFID tag updated by a portable device through a software application, or an RFID reader might update the codes after a service has been provided.

For objects and miscellaneous goods, it is expected that the embedded MA will define the actions that need to be carried out, whether to the bearer, or to the surrounding environment, as needed.

4.3.4 Design Issues for CRS

In this section, we introduce the necessary requirements for designing efficient language constructs that can be employed to code an MA for use in CRS. The first step is to determine all the actions that the CRS is intended to support, whether as a service or as a handling. A second, but also important consideration is to determine the memory space that the RFID tags will have. It is easy to see that an efficient language construct design will have a direct impact on the second consideration. An inadequate MA description language design will lead to large RFID tag memory requirements that directly translate into more expensive tags. Therefore, a deployment that spans thousands or even millions of tags would see its associated costs increased by a wide margin. However, RFID's memory capacity and tag type (i.e., active or passive) have a direct impact on its physical size. Therefore, a memory cap might have to be imposed for applications where size restrictions apply, which would evidently pose a constraint for the engineers designing MA language constructs. For the case where RFID tags have more memory, action script constructs with a fine granularity level can be implemented. Conversely, limited memory availability requires that the language constructs' granularity be coarser, as seen in Fig. 15, which shall be meticulously devised. Moreover, from the perspective of the

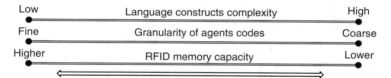

FIG. 15. Language design trade-off impact in RFID memory size.

middleware's design, more complex language constructs require greater processing capabilities and memory space for the interpreter, whereas simpler constructs are needed for hardware devices with limited capabilities.

4.4   An E-Healthcare Application Based on CRS

4.4.1   System Operation's Rationale

In this section, we advance an E-healthcare application based on our proposed CRS, as originally reported in Ref. [62]. In this approach, patients' health conditions are monitored at home, and information is collected and stored at a remote database after being forwarded using a cellular network, a WiFi connection, etc., depending on where the patient resides. To this end, any health-related anomalies not requiring immediate attention are immediately logged into a database, as determined by the patients' ambulatory monitoring devices. At the same time, these conditions are encoded and stored in an RFID tag that the patient carries. The advantage of this scheme is that any critical health information always travels with the patient, which can be retrieved at any location. For example, a patient with a chronic heart condition might decide to take a vacation at a remote place, where his/her condition suddenly worsens. When this happens, the patient's ambulatory monitoring system contacts his/her home healthcare provider, which in turn contacts the local health-care provider where the patient is currently visiting. If necessary, the RFID's tag information can be encoded in a format that is employed by the remote healthcare provider, which may include instructions on the type of treatment that the patient needs. As a result, a remote healthcare practitioner would not have to establish neither a verbal communication with the patient's home doctor nor a database connection with his/her healthcare provider's computer to obtain this information. Moreover, in case of emergency, medics administering care can readily obtain critical information and the required actions from his RFID tag, which could also encode actions to have the remote equipment directly contact the patient's home doctor. After arriving at a hospital, the local doctor can obtain the patient's relevant health records and prescription drug history. Similarly, the doctor at the remote location can have his own equipment to update the contents of the RFID tag. This type of enhanced services would be very hard to achieve employing a classical IRS. In addition to this, it is straightforward to see that this application enables a number of enhanced services:

a. A patient facing a health emergency while away from home or a hospital can still be able to receive adequate care by any medical practitioner that has an RFID reader to retrieve critical information. For instance, a person walking by a patient that has collapsed due to an emergency can use his/her cell phone as a gateway, whereby an embedded RFID reader obtains the required information and forwards it to the pertinent healthcare provider. It is here where we can see the benefits of employing an MA that encodes the necessary commands that instruct the RFID reader what to do with the information it just retrieved, such as giving indications to an ambulance's medics of how to deal with the patient.

b. Where feasible, the MA can instruct medical personnel to administer enhanced healthcare services as covered by the patient's medical insurance policy. For instance, the patient might be assigned a private hospital room.

c. The flow of actions that need to be taken according to the situation and/or place can be dictated by the MA, including how to contact the patient's immediate family in case of an emergency, or whether a life/death condition that requires immediate action can be performed as long as the family has encoded a preclearance code in the form of a digital signature that can be validated by the corresponding system.

4.4.2   Infrastructure Architecture

The architecture of the proposed CRS-based E-healthcare system is illustrated in Fig. 16, which employs existing telecommunications technologies and systems as detailed next:

a. *RFID Tag:* As mentioned before, RFID tags can indicate the service level and specific treatment priorities for the patient. In addition, the patient's RFID tag can be programmed to request access to certain areas of a hospital once inside. For example, after being admitted, RFID readers carefully placed in the hospital's gates and corridors can help determine whether a patient is in the correct place. This would help streamline the administration of the required care and prevent errors. Consequently, the contents of a patient's RFID tag can be dynamically updated depending on the healthcare stage where he/she currently is. Therefore, a direct database connection is not needed, in contrast to IRS, given that the RFID tag already encodes an MA that instructs

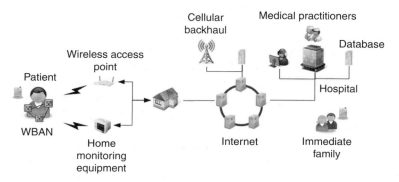

FIG. 16. An E-healthcare scheme based on a code-centric RFID system.

automated gates to grant access in accordance to a previously embedded access code or password.

b. *WBAN:* Physiological signals, such as temperature, heart rate, and muscle tension, provide vital information that can be sensed, collected, and forwarded by a WBAN to a remote healthcare facility for diagnosing the current health of a patient. These signals are collected by small sensors adhered to the patient's skin as strategically placed throughout his/her body. These sensors create wireless links to form a wireless body area network (WBAN) by means of ultra low-power radio technology, such as the one specified by the IEEE 802.15.4 standard [63].

c. *Gateway:* Another element that is crucial for the effectiveness of the proposed CRS-based, E-healthcare system is the communications gateway. This device enables the WBAN to forward collected data to an off-site healthcare provider for remote monitoring, condition assessment, and diagnosis by qualified medical personnel. Different types of communications interfaces can be used here: a cellular phone, a WiFi AP, or a WiMax modem. This implies that the communications gateway will probably be equipped with two radios: one for communications with the low-power WBAN and the other for external communications, possibly making it one of the most expensive devices that a user has to carry.

d. *Database:* In contrast to a classical IRS where a database is key to its operation in a CRS, this element takes on the role of a backup system. As explained previously, the database keeps medical records of patients and other pertinent information that needs to be maintained. In addition, the database needs to be always available for doctors to access directly, as needed. As mentioned before, the contents or corresponding patient's entry can be specifically encoded and stored in patients' RFID tags.

4.5   Summary

In this section, we have advanced an innovative concept that we call Code-Centric RFID System, or CRS. We discussed the potential benefits that our proposed CRS scheme can introduce in a number of applications and deployment settings. Among the most important contributions that CRS provides is: enhanced scalability, distributed information storage and availability, automated processing of goods, and enhanced access control schemes and service for people. We contend that these contributions can be readily achieved by means of RFID tags that possess larger memory to store a combination of carefully encoded information, along with compact MAs that can be interpreted and processed by the corresponding subsystems to enact specific actions. Whereas these type of RFID tags are already commercially available, their high cost precludes their widespread use for handling all kinds of goods. Therefore, the applications where CRS can be conceivably employed are those concerning high-value objects, or people. We believe that CRS would be a key enabler of enhanced IT systems currently being employed in the provision of E-healthcare. As per existing forecasts made for the current aging population, novel and improved systems need to be incorporated to help improve or replace altogether aging technologies that will be unable to cope with future requirements. Our proposed CRS solution employs MAs to provide unmatched flexibility for enhanced services, as clearly exemplified in our E-healthcare application.

5.   Final Summary and Conclusion

We have provided an account of our latest advancements in MA technology applied to wireless networks and mobile computing systems. In Section 1, we introduced the reader to basic concepts and particularities of employing mobile codes, and we discussed their potential advantages and disadvantages. We explained that although this technology has the potential to introduce significant bandwidth and process completion delay savings, the degree to which these features become a reality depends on several factors, including the type of MAS employed, the application, and the way in which agents are coded to solve the problem. To this regard, the scheme applied can become inefficient if the number and/or size of MAs deployed to solve a particular problem exceeds the one produced by employing message passing or any other communications mechanism for that matter. Therefore, a trade-off analysis might be necessary to ensure that the MA approach has a good chance of yielding better performance than the current solution. We also provided a brief historical review of this technology and stressed the importance of revisiting early MAS developed for computer networks that possessed severe bandwidth and power processing constraints, as seen in contemporary WSNs.

In Section 2, we discussed important aspects for architecting MAS from the perspective of WSNs. In particular, we discussed the advantages of employing MAs for image retrieval and TT. Both of these WSN applications are prime examples that show how MAs can be deployed in an attempt to achieve significant bandwidth savings (in the case of image retrieval), or flexibility in the WSN operations (in the case of TT applications). In the first case, one or more MAs can be dispatched from a WSN gateway to examine image data at the location where it was captured, instead of sending raw images for remote processing. For the second case, the MA approach enables WSN operators to deploy distinct types of tracking algorithms on demand to adapt to possible changes in the type or motion characteristics of the object being tracked, thereby providing a much more flexible solution than message passing. We also noted that the WSN might have to be virtually partitioned in a hierarchical fashion to be serviced by multiple MAs when a classical, flat approach results inconvenient. By the same token, we discussed the advantages and disadvantages of employing static, dynamic, and hybrid MA migration itinerary schemes. Though static MA itineraries are more straightforward to implement, they might be insufficient to cope with rapidly changing circumstances as observed by WSN devices, thus raising the need to support dynamic itinerary changes. Alternatively, a hybrid approach might be beneficial, at the expense of increased complexity in the MAS' architecture. Multiple MA cooperation was also discussed, which is an essential trait that MAS designers have to take into account to ensure that agents can operate effectively and efficiently.

In Section 3, we introduced our own MAS for enabling programmable tasking of WSNs. Wiseman's architecture was discussed, along with its instruction set and unique language constructs and code processing flow features. The agent migration methodologies that Wiseman supports were explained in detail, along with examples and design premises for employing one scheme or another. Wiseman's ability to support distinct MA migration techniques is one of its most important features, as it enables static, dynamic, and hybrid schemes. We implemented Wiseman as a proof-of-concept prototype for commercially available WSN devices that possess severe hardware limitations. To this end, we presented both generic performance evaluations and case study results for an early forest fire detection application. In it, we provided examples to show how this WSN application can be effectively implemented through MA technology.

Finally, in Section 4, we advanced a scheme whereby MAs are embedded in RFID Tags to streamline a number of processes and operations. First, we provided a review of IRS that handle simple alphanumeric numbers employed for referencing database entries that store specific object handling instructions, if any. Then, we introduced what we call the Code-centric RFID System, or CRS. Here, agents are embedded in RFID tags possessing enhanced memory capabilities. This approach enables systems to apply object handling instructions or service directives for people carrying the tag. These actions are obtained directly from the agent, instead of a database. In addition, agents can be updated on demand, and *in situ* without the need to explicitly interact with any off-site system. Agent mobility occurs in two forms. First, actual physical mobility is inherited from the tag's movement with the carrier object. Second, an agent retrieved from a RFID tag can be injected into a network and can be forwarded to distinct system blocks to enact certain actions as specified by its code. As an example of this, we elaborated on an E-Healthcare application that employs our proposed CRS for providing enhanced services to ambulatory patients as they travel. In the coming years, we foresee a renewed interest in MA technology to deal with intricacies of resource-constrained systems where ambient intelligence capabilities are a key requirement. To this end, personalization and customization needs provide the clearest motivation for employing MAs that operate based on the prevailing circumstances, and/or the parameters of the deployment setting.

ACKNOWLEDGMENTS

This work was supported by the National Sciences and Engineering Research Council of the Canadian Government under grants STPGP 322208-05 and 365208-08. In addition, this work was supported in part by NAP of Korea Research Council of Fundamental Science & Technology.

REFERENCES

[1] S. Franklin, A. Graesser, Is it an agent, or just a program? A taxonomy for autonomous agents, in: J.G. Carbonell, J. Siekmann (Eds.), Proceedings Third International Workshop on Agent Theories, Architectures, and Languages, Lecture Notes in Computer Science (LNCS), vol. 1193, Springer-Verlag, New York, 1996.
[2] D.B. Lange, M. Oshima, Seven good reasons for mobile agents, Commun. ACM 42 (3) (1999) 88–89.
[3] P. Braun, W. Rossak, Mobile Agents - Basic Concepts, Mobility Models, and the Tracy Toolkit, Elsevier, The Netherlands, 2005.
[4] N. Borselius, Mobile agent security, Electron. Commun. Eng. J. 5 (14) (2002) 211–218.
[5] W. Jansen, T. Karygiannis, "Mobile Agent Security", NIST special publication 800-19 (Technical Report), National Institute of Standards and Technology (NIST), Computer Security Division, Gaithersburg, Maryland, United States, 2000.
[6] H. Qi, S.S. Iyengar, K. Chakrabarty, Multiresolution data integration using mobile agents in distributed sensor networks, IEEE Trans. Syst. Man Cybern. C Appl. Rev. 31 (3) (2001) 383–391.
[7] D. Milojicic, Mobile agent applications, IEEE Concurrency 7 (3) (1999) 80–90.
[8] M. Ma, Agents in E-commerce, Commun. ACM 42 (3) (1999) 78–80.

[9] W.S.E. Chen, C.L. Hu, A mobile agent-based active network architecture for intelligent network control, Inf. Sci. 141 (1/2) (2002) 3–35, Elsevier.

[10] H. Wang, Z. Deng, Research on JXTA architecture based on mobile agent, in: Proceedings of the Third International Conference on Genetic and Evolutionary Computing, 2009, pp. 758–761, Guilin, China, October, 14–17.

[11] A.R. Tripathi, N.M. Karnik, T. Ahmed, R.D. Singh, A. Prakash, V. Kakani, et al., Design of the Ajanta system for mobile agent programming, J. Syst. Softw. 62 (2) (2002) 123–140.

[12] D. Horvat, D. Cvetkovic, V. Milutinovic, P. Mocovoc, Mobile agents and Java mobile agents toolkits, Telecommun. Syst. 18 (1–3) (2001) 271–287.

[13] G.M.W. Al-Saadoon, A flexible and reliable architecture for mobile agent security, J. Comput. Sci. 5 (4) (2009) 270–274, Science Publications.

[14] S. González-Valenzuela, S.T. Vuong, et al., Evaluation of migration strategies for mobile agents in network routing, in: Proceedings of Mobile Agents for Telecommunication Applications, LNCS, vol. 2521, Springer, Berlin, 2002, pp. 141–150.

[15] Y. Xu, H. Qi, Dynamic mobile agent migration in wireless sensor networks, Int. J. Ad Hoc Ubiquitous Comput. 2 (1/2) (2007) 73–82.

[16] N. Minar, K.H. Kramer, P. Maes, Cooperating mobile agents for mapping networks, in: Proceedings of the First Hungarian National Conference on Agent Based Computation, 1998, Hungary.

[17] J. Raoa, P. Küngasa, M. Matskin, Composition of Semantic Web services using Linear Logic theorem proving, Inf. Syst. 31 (4–5) (2006) 340–360.

[18] S. Arnon, Collaborative network of wireless microsensors, IEEE Electron. Lett. 36 (2) (2000) 186–187, IET Journals.

[19] I.F. Akyildiz, W. Su, Y. Sankarasubramaniam, E. Cayirc, Wireless sensor networks: A survey, Comput. Netw. 38 (4) (2002) 393–422.

[20] S. Misra, M. Reisslein, X. Guoliang, A survey of multimedia streaming in wireless sensor networks, IEEE Commun. Surv. Tutorials 10 (4) (2008) 18–39, IEEE Journals.

[21] M. Cortez, J. Sánchez, Wireless communication system for a wide area sensor network, Wirel Sensor Actor Netw, IFIP 248 (2007) 59–69.

[22] A. Sharma, K. Yoon, D. Vanhorn, M. Dube, V. McKenna, M.S. Bauer, ScoutNode: A multimodal sensor node for wide area sensor networks, in: Proceedings of 18th International Conference on Computer Communications and Networks, 2009, pp. 1–6, San Francisco, USA, August.

[23] G. Vigna, Mobile agents: Ten reasons for failure, in: Proceedings of the IEEE International Conference on Mobile Data Management (MDM), 2004, Berkeley, California, USA, , Juanuary, 19–22.

[24] N. Dimakis, J.K. Soldatos, L. Polymenakos, P. Fleury, J. Curín, J. Kleindienst, Integrated development of context-aware applications in smart spaces, IEEE Pervasive Comput. 7 (4) (2008) 71–79.

[25] R. Bose, Sensor networks motes, smart spaces, and beyond, IEEE Pervasive Comput. 8 (3) (2009) 84–90.

[26] I. Marsa-Maestre, M.A. Lopez-Carmona, J.R. Velasco, A. Navarro, Mobile agents for service personalization in smart environments, J. Netw. 3 (5) (2008) 30–41.

[27] G. Bosch, C. Barrue, Managing ambient intelligence sensor network systems, an agent based approach, in: Bio-Inspired Systems: Computational and Ambient Intelligence, LNCS, vol. 5517, Springer, Berlin, 2009, pp. 1121–1128, June.

[28] W. Weber, J. Rabaey, E.H.L. Aarts (Eds.), Ambient Intelligence, Springer, Berlin, 2005.

[29] J. Delsing, P. Lindgren, Sensor communication technology towards ambient intelligence, Meas. Sci. Technol. 16 (4) (2005) 37–46.

[30] T. He, S. Krishnamurthy, J.A. Stankovic, T. Abdelzaher, L. Luo, R. Stoleru, et al., Energy-efficient surveillance system using wireless sensor networks, in: Proceedings of the 2nd International Conference on Mobile Systems, Applications, and Services, 2004, pp. 270–283, Boston, USA, June 6–9.

[31] A.B. Mahmood Ali, M. Jonsson, Wireless sensor networks for surveillance applications? A comparative survey of MAC protocols, in: Proceedings of the Fourth International Conference on Wireless and Mobile Communications, 2008, pp. 399–403, July 27–August 1.

[32] TinyOS for deeply embedded Wireless Sensor Networks, http://www.tinyos.net.

[33] A. Fallahi, E. Hossain, QoS provisioning in wireless video sensor networks: A dynamic power management framework, IEEE Wirel. Commun. 14 (6) (2007) 40–49.

[34] Y. Gu, Y. Tian, E. Ekici, Real-time multimedia processing in video sensor networks, Image Commun. 22 (3) (2007) 237–251.

[35] M. Rahimi, R. Baer, O.I. Iroezi, J.C. Garcia, J. Warrior, D. Estrin, et al., Cyclops: In situ image sensing and interpretation in wireless sensor networks, in: Proceedings of the 3rd International Conference on Embedded Networked Sensor Systems, 2005, San Diego, USA, November 02–04.

[36] P. Kulkarni, D. Ganesan, P. Shenoy, Q. Lu, SensEye: A multitier camera sensor network, in: Proceedings of the 13th Annual ACM International Conference on Multimedia, 2005, Singapore, 6–11 November.

[37] I.F. Akyildiz, T. Melodia, K.R. Chowdhury, Wireless multimedia sensor networks: Applications and testbeds, Proc. IEEE 96 (10) (2008) 1588–1605.

[38] M. Chen, T. Kwon, Y. Yuan, Y. Choi, V.C.M. Leung, Mobile agent-based directed diffusion in wireless sensor networks, EURASIP J. Appl. Signal Process. 2007 (1) (2007) 219.

[39] Y.-C. Tseng, S.-P. Kuo, H.-W. Lee, C.-F. Huang, Location tracking in a wireless sensor network by mobile agents and its data fusion strategies, Comput. J. 47 (4) (2004) 448–460.

[40] Y. Xu, H. Qi, Mobile agent migration modeling and design for target tracking in wireless sensor networks, Ad Hoc Netw. 6 (1) (2007) 1–16.

[41] R. MacRuairi, M.T. Keane, G. Coleman, A wireless sensor network application requirements taxonomy, in: Proceedings of the Second International Conference on Sensor Technologies and Applications, 2008, SENSORCOMM, Cap Esterel, France, 25–31 August.

[42] Y. Xu, H. Qi, Distributed computing paradigms for collaborative signal and information processing in sensor networks, Int. J. Parallel Distrib. Comput. 64 (8) (2004) 945–959.

[43] H. Qi, Y. Xu, X. Wang, Mobile-agent-based collaborative signal and information processing in sensor networks, Proc. IEEE 91 (8) (2003) 1172–1183.

[44] M. Chen, T. Kwon, Y. Yuan, V.C.M. Leung, Mobile agent based wireless sensor networks, J. Comput. 1 (1) (2006) 14–21.

[45] D.L. Applegate, R.E. Bixby, V. Chvatal, W.J. Cook, The Traveling Salesman Problem: A Computational Study, Princeton University Press, New Jersey, USA, 2006.

[46] H. Qi, F. Wang, Optimal itinerary analysis for mobile agents in ad-hoc wireless sensor networks, in: Proceedings of the 13th International Conference on Wireless Communications, vol. 1, 2001, pp. 147–153, Calgary, Canada, July.

[47] Q. Wu, N.S.V. Rao, J. Barhen, S.S. Iyengar, V.K. Vaishnavi, H. Qi, et al., On computing mobile agent routes for data fusion in distributed sensor networks, IEEE Trans. Knowl. Data Eng. 16 (6) (2004) 740–753.

[48] A. Boulis, C.-C. Han, M. Srivastava, Design and implementation of a framework for efficient and programmable sensor networks, in: Proceedings of the First International ACM Conference on Mobile Systems, Applications and Services, 2003, San Francisco, USA, May.

[49] C.-L. Fok, G.-C. Roman, C. Lu, Rapid development and flexible deployment of adaptive wireless sensor network applications, in: Proceedings of the 24th International Conference on Distributed Computing Systems (ICDCS), 2005, Columbus, USA, June.

[50] P. Levis, D. Culler, Maté: A tiny virtual machine for sensor networks, in: Proceedings of the 10th International Conference on Architectural Support for Programming Languages and Operating Systems, 2002, San Jose, USA, October.

[51] T. Liu, M. Martonosi, Impala: A middleware system for managing autonomic, parallel sensor systems, in: Proceedings of ACM SIGPLAN: Symposium on Principles and Practice of Parallel Programming, 2003, San Diego, USA, June.

[52] J. Hui, D. Culler, The dynamic behavior of a data dissemination protocol for network programming at scale, in: Proceedings of the 2nd International Conference on Embedded Networked Sensor Systems, 2004, Baltimore, USA, November.

[53] P. Kang, C. Borcea, G. Xu, A. Saxena, U. Kremer, L. Iftode, Smart messages: A distributed computing platform for networks of embedded systems, Comput. J. 47 (4) (2004) 475–494, Special Issue on Mobile and Pervasive Computing, Oxford Journals.

[54] P. Sapaty, Mobile Processing in Distributed and Open Environments, Willey, New York, 2000.

[55] P. Sapaty, Ruling Distributed Dynamic Worlds, Wiley-Interscience, New York, 2005.

[56] P. Sapaty, A wave language for parallel processing of semantic networks, Comput. Artif. Intell. 5 (4) (1986) 289–314.

[57] The OMNeT++ Discrete Event Simulator. http://www.omnetpp.org.

[58] Micaz Sensor Nodes by Crossbow Technology. http://www.xbow.com.

[59] C.-L. Fok, G.-C. Roman, C. Lu, Mobile agent middleware for sensor networks: An application case study, in: Proceedings of the 4th International Symposium on Information Processing in Sensor Networks, 2005, pp. 382–387, Los Angeles, USA, April, 25–27.

[60] M. Chen, S. Gonzalez, Q. Zhang, V. Leung, Software agent-based intelligence for code-centric RFID systems, IEEE Intell. Syst. 25 (2) (2010) 12–19, 12–19, March/April.

[61] FRAM Embedded, High-speed RFID tag MB89R118 by Fujitsu. http://www.fujitsu.com.

[62] M. Chen, S. Gonzalez, Q. Zhang, M. Li, V. Leung, A 2G-RFID based E-healthcare system, IEEE Wireless Commun. Mag. 17 (1) (2010) 37–43.

[63] H. Cao, V.C.M. Leung, C. Chow, H.C.B. Chan, Enabling technologies for wireless body area networks: A survey and outlook, IEEE Commun. Mag. 47 (12) (2009) 84–93.

Virtual Graphics for Broadcast Production

GRAHAM THOMAS

BBC Research & Development, Centre House, London, United Kingdom

Abstract

This chapter looks at the technology involved in the mixing of 3D graphics with broadcast video in real time. This is essentially the application of augmented reality techniques in the context of TV production. Examples of the use of this technology include virtual graphics used for presenting election results, and graphics overlaid on a sports pitch to indicate distances. Whilst similar techniques are commonly used in films, these often require extensive post-production; this chapter focuses specifically on approaches that can be used live, which is a common requirement for TV, particularly in news and sport.

Following a brief review of the history of virtual graphics in TV, the technology used in each stage of the production process is examined, starting with the camera and lens. Some of the important characteristics of broadcast video are discussed, and the need for lens calibration is explained. To maintain accurate alignment of the virtual graphics and the real scene, the motion of the camera must be tracked accurately, and methods for achieving this are reviewed. The requirements for high-quality rendering of graphics are then discussed, looking particularly at the differences from rendering for applications such as computer games. The process of keying graphics into an image using chroma-key is then examined in detail. It can be difficult for actors or presenters to work with virtual objects in a studio, unless there is some way for them to see what is going on, so methods of providing visual feedback are presented. Some specific issues related to the use of virtual graphics for sports are then discussed, including methods for tracking camera motion and keying graphics onto areas such as grass or sand. The chapter concludes with a short discussion of an alternative approach to combining graphics and live action, in which graphical representations of real objects and people are created from live video, and placed into a 3D model, allowing the scene to be rendered from a viewpoint that is not tied to the location of the camera.

ADVANCES IN COMPUTERS, VOL. 82
ISSN: 0065-2458/DOI: 10.1016/B978-0-12-385512-1.00005-0

1. Introduction

Virtual graphics, defined here as computer-generated graphics that appear to be a part of a real scene, are now a common sight in TV programs. They are essentially an application of augmented reality to TV production. From the humble weather map inserted behind the presenter using a blue screen, to sophisticated 3D virtual graphics showing distances and off-side markings on live sports coverage, they provide a useful tool for the program maker to present information in an easy-to-understand and visually appealing manner. Furthermore, they can be used as a creative tool around which new kinds of programs can be based, or can reduce the cost of producing conventional programs by replacing all or parts of the scenery with computer-generated backgrounds. New developments promise to further extend the reach of real-time 3D graphics into new areas, and to help the development of crossplatform content, as 3D graphics are already a mainstay of computer-based entertainment.

Although much of the underlying technology used for adding virtual graphics to TV is the same as that used for effects in the film industry, its application in TV usually differs in two important aspects: speed of production and level of perfection of the result. While films generally take a long time to make, and have production budgets that can support many months of both computer-intensive and labor-intensive postproduction, TV production budgets rarely support this level of postproduction, nor need to produce content with the high spatial resolution or production values demanded by the film industry. Also, many kinds of programs that can benefit most from virtual graphics, such as news and sport, need to be broadcast live, or at least within an hour or so of being recorded. Any program that relies on a significant level of interaction between real and virtual content also needs to have that content inserted into the image in real time during the recording, so that the cameraman can frame the shots appropriately, and those taking part in the program can see how they are interacting with the virtual content. The focus of this chapter is thus on the use of real-time virtual graphics for TV production, rather than techniques relying on extensive postproduction.

After presenting a brief history of virtual graphics in TV production, this chapter examines the main elements needed in a program production system that incorporates virtual graphics, namely the camera and lens, the tracking system to estimate the motion of the camera relative to the object with which the graphics are to be registered, the real-time graphics rendering system, and the keying system. Methods of providing real-time visual feedback to actors are then discussed. Some specific issues concerned with the production of virtual graphics for sports are then presented. Following that, an alternative approach to mixing real and virtual images, where 3D models are created from real-world images, is briefly described.

2. A Short History of Virtual and Augmented Reality in TV Production

Electronic graphics have been used in live TV program production for many years, with chroma-key being used in applications such as placing a virtual weather map behind a presenter. The presenter stands in front of a brightly colored background (usually green or blue), and any parts of the image having this color are automatically switched to show another image, such as a weather map.

Chroma-key was used in films from the very early days—certainly before any electronic processing was around. The term "traveling matte," still sometimes used in the industry, refers to the use of a second reel of film, with transparent areas of the negative showing the areas that should be keyed in, derived from placing a blue filter over the film while making a copy. This masked out the background blue screen area when the film was being copied. An inverted version of this was run on top of the desired background footage, and exposed onto the copy, thereby placing a background behind the keyed-out foreground. It was first used in the 1940 film *Thief of Bagdad*, long before electronic image processing.

With the advent of electronic image capture and thus the arrival of the age of television, it became possible to implement the keying process in real time. One of the first uses was by the BBC in 1959 [1] in a contribution to a live program. This was before the dawn of color TV, so the key signal for the blue background was obtained from a monochrome camera sensor with a blue filter in front, while the foreground signal was obtained from a camera sensor with a yellow filter. A beam splitter was used to allow both cameras to look through the same lens. The composite shot of a singer against a pictorial background was successfully broadcast live.

With a normal chroma key setup, it is important to keep the camera stationary, as any movement will affect the foreground objects while the keyed-in background remains static. There were some early attempts to allow camera movement; for example, the BBC used a system called Scene-sync for the 1980 *Doctor Who* story *Meglos*. This system moved a second camera viewing a model by the same amount as the main camera, so that the model could be keyed into the background of the main camera. However, this approach was restricted to using background images shot using a motion-controlled camera.

It was not until the 1990s that graphics hardware became powerful enough to render high-quality graphics at video frame rate, allowing virtual backgrounds to be used. This allowed camera movement, since 3D virtual objects or backgrounds could then be re-rendered for each TV field (50 or 60 times each second), to match the current camera view. The freedom to move the camera allowed virtual objects or backgrounds to be used in a much wider range of programs, and the term "virtual studio" was used to distinguish these new systems from simple chroma-keying techniques. Early virtual studio systems relied on high-end graphics supercomputers such as the SGI Onyx; an example of this was the ELSET system [2], demonstrated in 1994 at IBC in Amsterdam.

Since the early days of virtual studios, the technology has developed significantly. Camera tracking systems need no longer rely on mechanical sensors on the camera mounting to measure the camera movement, and graphics can be rendered on a conventional PC rather than needing specialized graphics systems. The way in which the technology is used has also developed: the initial enthusiasm for replacing the entirety of a real set with a virtual background (as in the example in Fig. 1) has to some extent given way to the addition of virtual objects into a real environment, so that only those elements of the set that cannot be easily created for real are synthesized. Examples include virtual video walls and graphics for news, and overlaid graphics for sports analysis.

The technology has also enabled the production of innovative programs where the virtual elements are the central part, such as the childrens' game show BAM-ZOOKi [3] (see Fig. 2).

FIG. 1. An example of a virtual studio being used to present election graphics by the BBC for the 2005 UK General Election. The presenter is standing in front of a blue screen, which has been replaced with a virtual background.

FIG. 2. The BBC program BAMZOOKi, in which virtual creatures designed by children compete live in the studio.

3. Elements of a TV Production System Incorporating Virtual Graphics

3.1 System Overview

The main elements of a studio-based system for inserting virtual graphics are shown in Fig. 3. The figure shows the system for a single camera (often referred to as a "camera channel"); in a multicamera studio, each camera generally has its own system.

The TV camera is equipped with a zoom lens that incorporates a sensor to measure the zoom and focus settings. The camera is fixed to a tracking system to measure its position and orientation. The lens sensor and tracking system send information at video rate (generally 50 or 60 Hz) to a graphics rendering system, which usually consists of a high-end PC with a powerful graphics card. The PC renders the virtual elements of the scene with camera parameters (position, orientation, and field-of-view) matching those measured by the sensors on the real camera. The graphics output is converted to broadcast video format usually via a serial digital interface (SDI). It often consists of two signals: the graphics themselves, plus a "key" signal that indicates the areas of the image occupied by the graphics that should appear in front of any real elements. Meanwhile, the video signal from the camera is passed through a delay to compensate for the processing time of the tracking system, renderer and video

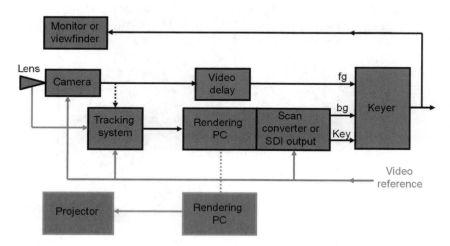

FIG. 3. The main elements of a virtual graphics system.

format conversion. This delay is typically of the order of a few video frames. A keyer combines the video and graphics, using the key signal generated by the renderer and/ or an internally generated key signal from a chroma keyer to determine whether graphics or camera video should appear in each part of the image. In some systems, the keyer may be implemented in software and run on the same PC as the renderer. If the tracking system works by analyzing the camera video to track the motion of the camera, it too may run on the same PC, leading to a very compact system.

The following sections discuss the elements of the system in more detail, focusing on those aspects that are particularly relevant when attempting to insert virtual graphics into the camera image.

3.2   Camera and Lens

Before considering specific aspects of a TV camera lens, it is worth summarizing the way in which a camera and lens are usually represented in computer vision and computer graphics.

3.2.1   Lens Model

A camera is usually modeled as a *pinhole camera*, where all light passes through a point which is in front of the image sensor by a distance corresponding to the focal length of the lens. This model provides a straightforward way of calculating the location in the image where a given point in the world would appear, using simple geometry. It ignores lens distortion; this can be accounted for by applying a suitable transformation to the "ideal" image coordinates from the pinhole model.

It is often convenient to think of the image sensor being *in front* of the pinhole, rather than *behind* it, to avoid the image being inverted. The camera model used in this chapter is shown in Fig. 4. The coordinate system of the camera is chosen to match that of a camera in OpenGL, with x pointing to the right, y pointing up, and the camera looking in the negative z direction. The origin of the camera reference frame is at the location of the pinhole. The image plane is a distance f (the focal length) in front of the camera center. The point on the image sensor that lies on the z-axis is known as the *principal point*. This is the point where a ray from a world point to the camera center is at right angles to the image sensor. Note that this point is not necessarily at the middle pixel in the image, as the center of the sensor may not be exactly in line with the center line of the lens, or the portion of the image read from the sensor may not be exactly central. In the case of an analog camera, a shift can also be introduced by the presence of a slight timing offset in the horizontal synchronizing signal relative to the video before being digitized.

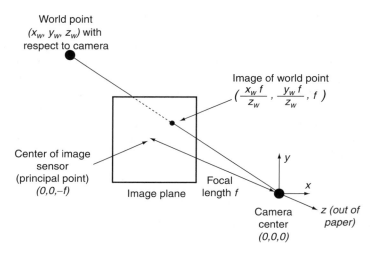

World point
(x_w, y_w, z_w) with
respect to camera

Image of world point
$(\frac{x_w f}{z_w}, \frac{y_w f}{z_w}, f)$

Center of image
sensor
(principal point)
$(0,0,-f)$

Image plane

Focal
length f

y

x

Camera
center
$(0,0,0)$

z (out of
paper)

Fɪɢ. 4. Pinhole camera model.

In order to establish the relationship between the 3D position of a point in the
world and its 2D position in the image, it is necessary to know the *intrinsic*
parameters of the camera and lens (focal length, pixel spacing, coordinates of the
principal point in the image, and any lens distortion parameters) and the *extrinsic*
parameters (orientation of the camera and the position of the camera center in the
world).

3.2.2 Lens Calibration

There are many well-known methods of estimating the intrinsic parameters for a
camera with a fixed-focal-length lens, for example, see Ref. [4]. These typically
involve capturing multiple images of a calibration object (such as a flat chart marked
with squares of known dimensions), and using an optimization process to find the set
of intrinsic parameters that give the best match between predicted and observed
locations of the calibration markings. The focus setting of the lens will usually be
fixed to a chosen value before calibration, as changes of focus usually also affect the
focal length.

Whereas many film and digital cinematography cameras use a fixed focal length
(or "prime") lens, a typical TV camera is fitted with a zoom lens, so it is necessary to
calibrate the focal length of the lens as a function of the setting of the zoom control.
The focus control can also have a significant effect on the focal length, so it is

necessary to measure the settings of both zoom and focus. The distortion introduced by the lens will vary with zoom (and possibly with focus) as well. Furthermore, the location of the nodal point (effectively where the "pinhole" is) varies as well, moving along the axis through the center of the lens. For some lenses, its effective position can even be behind the back of the camera for a tight zoom. The movement of the nodal point position with zoom and focus is often referred to as "nodal shift."

Some lenses (sometimes referred to as "digital lenses") now include built-in zoom and focus sensors, which send out data specifying the settings via a serial interface. For lenses without this interface, a separate sensor needs to be fitted. To be useful in virtual graphics applications, the repeatability and resolution of the sensors needs to be at least 14–16 bits. Figure 5 shows a typical lens, with a sensor for zoom and focus, fitted to a broadcast camera. The lens sensor has two cog wheels that mesh with the "teeth" around the zoom and focus control rings. This particular sensor has no "absolute" reference points (it just counts up or down from where it was when power was first applied), so to get an absolute measurement of the position of the zoom and focus rings, they must be turned to one end when powered up. The system remembers the maximum value it sees, and subtracts this from the current value, to produce an absolute measurement.

Calibration of a zoom lens typically involves calibrating the lens at a range of different zoom and focus settings, and either using a lookup table to interpolate values for focal length, or fitting a polynomial to the data.

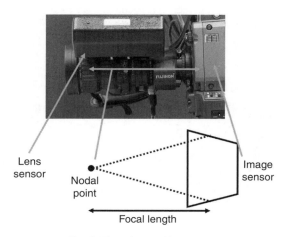

FIG. 5. Zoom lens and lens sensor.

Although chart-based calibration can be used at wide lens angles, this method is unsuitable at narrow lens angles. This is because it is very difficult to have a sufficient range of depths of the chart visible in a captured image to tell the difference between the chart being near the camera with a given field-of-view and the chart being further away with a smaller field-of-view: the method relies on perspective variation with distance to determine how far away the chart is. Furthermore, to determine the position of the nodal point, it is necessary to measure the position of a reference point on the camera with respect to the calibration chart, so that the position of the nodal point with respect to the camera body can be determined. Another problem is that when changing the focus setting to gather data on different combinations of zoom and focus, the calibration chart may go out of focus so much that the relevant features on the chart (such as corners of squares) can no longer be seen clearly in the image.

Given these problems with chart-based calibration, alternative methods are often used when calibrating zoom lenses. If a camera mount with pan and tilt sensors is available, then one approach is to point the camera at one or more reference points, and measure the image coordinates at which the point appears as a function of the camera pan angle. By repeating the measurement process with different known distances between camera and reference points, the position of the nodal point can be estimated at the same time as the focal length and lens distortion. The reference point can be as simple as a single point light source, the center of which is easy to determine even in an out-of-focus image.

Figure 6 shows an example of polynomials estimated for the focal length and nodal shift as a function of the 16-bit zoom sensor output for a Fuji HA16 × 6.3 lens. Note the small but significant effect that focus has on focal length, particularly for long focal lengths (i.e., narrow angles of view).

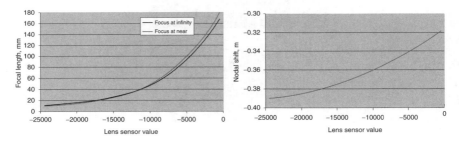

FIG. 6. Example of focal length and nodal shift variation for a Fuji HA16 × 6.3 zoom lens.

3.2.3   Broadcast Camera Image Characteristics

The area of virtual graphics, by definition, involves the seamless integration of captured video images and computer-rendered graphics. This section looks at some of the characteristics of broadcast cameras and the ways in which the image is sampled that need to be understood in order to ensure that the two image sources are as closely matched as possible. More in-depth information relating to broadcast video standards can be found in textbooks such as Poynton [5].

3.2.3.1   Integration Time.   Cameras usually have adjustable integration time. This can have a significant effect on the registration of virtual content: if the camera tracking system does not operate "through the lens" by tracking visible features (and thereby inherently matching the apparent motion in the image), then it ideally needs to be configured to measure the camera parameters at a time halfway through the integration period. For a through-the-lens system, feature positions are likely to be measured to be roughly in the middle of the blurred region, thereby roughly compensating for the effective time delay caused by the camera integration. However, significant motion blur may make feature-based tracking unreliable. In many cases, it is simplest to use a short integration time, giving a well-defined image capture time, not requiring motion blur to be added to graphics to achieve a convincing match with the real image, and easing feature detection in image-based tracking approaches. However, very short integration times result in significantly reduced camera sensitivity (needing increased gain which introduces noise), and unnatural motion in areas of the image that the viewer's eye is not tracking (e.g., a waterfall will appear as a succession of sharp water droplets rather than giving the appearance of continuous flow). In practice, an integration time of around 1/100th of a second gives a good compromise. Whilst cameras using CCD sensors sample the whole image at the same time, it is worth noting that cameras with CMOS sensors generally have a 'rolling shutter' (sampling the bottom of the image later than the top); this can make it difficult or impossible to achieve perfect alignment of real and virtual parts of the scene during rapid camera motion.

3.2.3.2   Sampling and Aspect Ratio.   Once the image is captured, it is digitized according to the relevant standard (ITU-R Recommendation BT.601 for standard definition images, BT.709 for high definition). It is worth looking at some aspects of these standards, since they have some idiosyncrasies (particularly at standard definition) that a developer of a virtual graphics system should be aware of.

All TV production now uses widescreen (16:9) images (for 4:3 images replace "16/9" with "4/3" in the explanation below). Use of the correct aspect ratio when inserting virtual graphics is vital in order to avoid the graphics losing registration as the camera is panned.

A widescreen 16:9 image in its standard definition digital form, as specified by ITU-R Recommendation BT.601 and shown in Fig. 7, actually has an aspect ratio wider than 16:9, due to the presence of "nonactive" pixels. The nonactive pixels are there principally because the edge pixels could be corrupted by ringing in the analog to digital conversion process, and because it is difficult to guarantee that exactly the right part of the signal is captured by the digitizer. These make the aspect ratio of the whole image slightly wider than 16:9. The choice of 13.5 MHz for the sampling frequency, which determines the pixel aspect ratio, was the result of an international standardization process which considered many factors including finding a value that gave a whole number of samples per line for existing analog TV systems. An interesting account of the process is given by Wood and Baron [6]. The figure of 702 active pixels comes from the "active" portion of the 625-line "PAL" (European TV format) analog signal being 52 μs, and $52 \times 13.5 = 702$. Using the figures of 702×576 corresponding to a 16:9 image, we can calculate the aspect ratio of a pixel (W/H) as follows:

$$702 \times W = 16/9 \times 576 \times H,$$

therefore $W/H = (16 \times 576)/(9 \times 702) = 1.458689.$

For "NTSC" (American TV format) images at 59.94 Hz, there are only 480 active lines, and 704 pixels are "active," although there are still 720 pixels per full line. The pixel aspect ratio is therefore 1.21212. Note also that when two fields are "paired up" to store as a frame, the first field occupies the lower set of lines, rather than the upper set as in "PAL" (European standard TV).

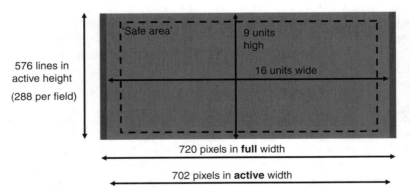

FIG. 7. A standard-definition 16:9 "625 line" 50 Hz image.

Images should be composed under the assumption that the whole image is unlikely to be displayed, with all important information lying in the so-called "safe area." Historically this is because it is difficult to set up the image on a cathode ray tube (CRT) to exactly fill the display—even with careful setting-up, poor regulation of the high voltage supply tends to make the displayed picture size change as the average image brightness varies. Rather than shrink the image so it is guaranteed to be all visible, and thus end up with a black border round the image (as was common with CRT monitors used in PCs), CRT TVs usually slightly overfill the display ("overscanning"), so the outer part may not be visible on all displays. Thus, important picture content (such as captions) should not be placed so close to the edge that it may not be visible on some displays. Ironically, many modern flat screen displays also overscan, because broadcasters sometimes do not fully fill the active part of the image as they do not expect the outermost edges to be displayed! There are actually two "safe areas": one for "action" and the other for graphics, with the graphics safe area being smaller. Details can be found in EBU Recommendation R95 [7].

Some rationalization has happened in the standardization of HDTV. The image format is 16:9, contains 1920×1080 pixels, and has no "nonactive" pixels. The pixels are square. However, interlace will still be common for the short to medium term, except for material originated on film or designed to mimic film, where instead of 50 Hz interlaced, the standard supports 24 Hz (and 23.98 Hz) progressive. At least, all interlaced formats (50 and 59.94 Hz) have the top field first. Unfortunately, some HDTV displays still overscan, hence the continued need for the concept of a safe area. For a discussion of overscan in the context of flat-panel displays, see EBU [8].

3.2.3.3 *Chrominance Sampling.* Although computer-based image processing usually deals with *RGB* signals, the majority of broadcast video signal routing, recording, and coding operates on luminance and color-difference signals. Fundamentally this is because the human visual system is less sensitive to resolution loss in the chrominance channels, so the best use of the available bandwidth can be made by having more resolution in luminance than in chrominance.

There are a variety of ways of subsampling the chrominance channels, which have potentially misleading names. Some of the more common formats are as follows:

- 4:2:2 format subsamples the color difference signals horizontally by a factor of 2. This is the format used in digital video signals according to ITU Rec. 601 (for standard definition) or 709 (for high definition) and is the format most commonly encountered in TV production.

- Some lower quality cameras (e.g., DVC Pro) produce "4:1:1," with color difference signals subsampled horizontally by a factor of 4.
- Some compression systems (e.g., broadcast MPEG-2) convey "4:2:0," where the color difference signals are subsampled both horizontally and vertically by a factor of 2.
- Some high-end production systems handle "4:4:4" *YUV* or *RGB*, which sample both the luminance and chrominance (or the signals in their original *RGB* format) at the same resolution. These tend to be used primarily for electronic film production, or high-end postproduction. The use of full-bandwidth chrominance is particularly valuable in processing such as chroma keying, where any reduction in the bandwidth of the chrominance channels can affect the luminance channel and thus become more visible.

3.2.3.4 Black and White Levels.
In the world of computer graphics, 8-bit signal levels range from 0 (black) to 255 (white). Digital broadcast-standard video defines black level as 16 and white level as 235, allowing headroom for undershoots and overshoots due to filtering.

3.2.3.5 Gamma.
Video signals are generally "gamma corrected," that is, they are not linearly related to actual light levels, as shown in Fig. 8. Perhaps surprisingly, this does not generally create problems with image processing or compositing, but it is something to be aware of. Almost all cameras (except some designed for tasks such as machine vision) will generate gamma-corrected signals, and displays (CRT or otherwise) have a power law response.

The value of gamma assumed for a display varies (2.8 in Europe, 2.2 in the United States), although in practice the actual value varies according to the setting of black level (brightness) and gain (contrast). Cameras typically do not implement an exact power law, as this would give infinite gain at black: the slope at black is often limited to around 4. In practice, the operator of the camera control unit (CCU; often

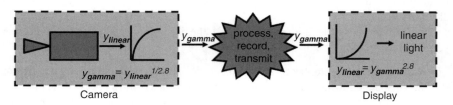

Fig. 8. Gamma correction in the broadcast chain.

referred to as the "racks operator") will adjust the gamma value to produce a subjectively pleasing result when viewing the image on a "grade 1" professional monitor in a dim environment. The best results are generally obtained with an overall "system" gamma greater than 1 (i.e., the gamma value assumed at the production end is less than that of the display), and the dimmer the viewing environment, the greater the overall system gamma should be (see Appendix A of EBU [8] for a discussion of this).

Figure 9 shows four CCUs that one operator in an outside-broadcast truck would operate. The job of the operator is to adjust the controls (including iris, black level, gamma, white balance, detail) to produce correctly exposed and subjectively pleasing images, with matching brightness and color across all the cameras. Note that a "grade 1" CRT monitor (rather than an LCD monitor) is available to make quality judgments, as the performance of LCD monitors is not yet good enough for them to be used as reference monitors. This photo was taken during the setting up of a stereoscopic broadcast, which is why the iris controls on pairs of control units are ganged together; this allows the operator to adjust a pair of cameras at the same time.

It is worth noting that although gamma correction was initially required due to the inherently nonlinear response of CRT displays, and has thus found its way into the standards for digital video, it actually performs a useful function independent of the need to compensate for display response. Applying more gain to the signal at lower brightness at the camera means that the noise introduced by subsequent processing and transmission stages (including quantization noise from digital sampling) is proportionately less in dark areas. The response of the eye to light is logarithmic, so the overall effect of gamma correction at the camera and display, combined with the response of the eye, is to make noise appear more uniformly distributed across all brightness values. With a fully linear transmission and display system, noise from processes such as quantization would be more visible in dark areas.

3.2.3.6   Detail Enhancement.

3.2.3.6   Detail Enhancement.   Most cameras include a control for detail enhancement. This allows the high frequencies in the image to be boosted, making edges appear sharper. It is sometimes referred to as "aperture correction," as one purpose of boosting the high frequencies is to compensate for the low-pass filtering effect of the finite size (or "aperture") of the capture and display sampling elements. In the days of tube cameras and CRT displays, this "aperture" corresponded to the area of the tube that the electron beam sampled (in the camera) or illuminated (in the display). With digital image sensors and flat-screen displays, the pixel sizes are generally smaller, so there is less inherent filtering and therefore less of a need for aperture correction as such. However, the CCU operator will still adjust the detail control to give a picture that looks subjectively pleasing on his display; this

FIG. 9. Four camera control units as used by a "racks operator" in an outside broadcast truck.

can result in "ringing" around edges (e.g., a black overshoot around a bright white area), as this makes pictures look shaper. This can present a problem with subsequent image processing (such as image-based tracking or keying), and may result in a different "look" between elements of the scene captured with a camera and virtual elements inserted using computer-generated graphics.

3.3   Camera Tracking System

To insert a virtual object into a real image from a TV camera, the position of the object must appear correct as the camera moves. This requires the camera position and orientation (referred to as the camera "pose") as well as its field-of-view to be measured at the same rate as the video signal (50 or 60 Hz), and with a stability sufficient to ensure negligible visible drift between the real and virtual elements.

3.3.1   Accuracy Requirements

Specifying the measurement accuracy required for a convincing result is difficult, as it depends on numerous factors including the field-of-view of the lens, the resolution of the TV system (standard or high definition), and the composition of the scene (where virtual and real objects appear close together). For example, if the virtual object was to drift by no more than one TV line in a standard-definition image of around 500 lines vertical resolution, at a lens angle of 5° (a fairly tight zoom), an angular accuracy of around 0.01° is needed. If the virtual object in this scene was at a distance of around 6 m, a camera movement of about 1 mm would correspond to one picture line, indicating that the spatial position needs to be measured to an accuracy of about 1 mm. Measurement inaccuracies may take various forms, such as random noise (which may have both low-frequency and high-frequency components, and may vary in amplitude depending on the speed of camera motion) and drift as a function of camera position. The influence of these inaccuracies will be different; for example, an error that varies smoothly with camera position will generally be much less of a problem than a rapid noise-like variation that is present even when the camera is still.

3.3.2   Types of Tracking System

In the early days of virtual studios, the only way of measuring camera movement was by fitting sensors to the camera mounting (e.g., to measure pan and tilt, plus motion along a track), or by using motion-control mounts that were already equipped with sensors. A range of different tracking systems that do not rely on mechanical mounts are now available, allowing the use of conventional camera mounts, including cranes and hand-held. Most of these nonmechanical systems are based on optical tracking technology, and can be classified as "outside-in" or "inside-out" systems.

3.3.2.1 *Optical Tracking Systems.*

An "outside-in" tracking system uses cameras mounted around the operating area (e.g., on the studio ceiling), and a set of passive or active markers on the camera. These systems can be expensive to scale up to large studios, as a large number of cameras may be needed. An example of such a system is Walkfinder [9], which claims to need 16 cameras to cover an area of 120 m².

An "inside-out" tracking system uses images from either the TV camera itself or an additional camera fixed to the camera being tracked. The camera views markers, patterns, or other easily identifiable features in the studio, whose 3D coordinates are known. By analyzing the image, the pose of the camera can be computed. Such systems were first developed for head-mounted augmented reality using active beacons [10], but have been developed to be suitable for large TV studios.

An example of such a system is the BBC-developed *free-d* system [11] which uses circular retroreflective bar-coded markers on the studio ceiling (Fig. 10). A small

FIG. 10. Circular bar-coded markers mounted on the ceiling of a TV studio.

upward-looking monochrome camera surrounded by a ring of LEDs is mounted on each studio camera to be tracked (Fig. 11). The retroreflective nature of the markers ensures that they appear very bright to the upward-looking camera, allowing them to be identified in the image using relatively simple image processing methods, and ensuring that they are not swamped by the studio lights. The camera is shuttered to around 1/1000th of a second, and the LEDs are pulsed during the exposure period. This ensures that the image of the markers suffers minimal motion blur, and that the LEDs do not appear overly bright if the camera operator was to look into them. Each marker carries a 12-bit circular bar code, allowing enough unique markers to cover the ceiling of very large studios. The camera needs to see a minimum of four markers in order for the system to compute a unique camera pose, but sufficient markers are usually installed to ensure that many more are visible, to improve the accuracy. The accuracy is also improved by having markers fitted at several different heights; this helps the system to distinguish between camera tilt and forward/backward translational motion because although both these kinds of motion will tend to move the markers across the image in the same way, translation will cause a parallax shift in the relative position of markers at different heights whereas tilting the camera will not. A processing unit analyzes the image from the camera, estimating the coordinates of the center of each marker to an accuracy of around 0.1 pixel, using the edges of the bar code rings. The processor then estimates the pose of the upward-looking camera, using the known positions of the markers in 3D, and the

FIG. 11. *free-d* tracking camera mounted on studio TV camera.

intrinsic parameters of the camera. It uses an iterative optimization process that adjusts the estimated pose so as to minimize the sum of the squared errors between the observed image coordinates of each marker, and the position at which each marker would be expected to appear. The pose of the TV camera is then computed, using knowledge of relative offset and orientation of the upward-looking camera. The data from the lens sensor is multiplexed into the video from the upward-looking camera and extracted by the processing unit. It is sent along with the computed pose information as an RS-422 data stream to the graphics rendering system.

3.3.2.2   *Inertial Hybrid Tracking Systems.*   It is also possible to use inertial sensors to track the movement of a camera. As such sensors inherently measure acceleration, it is necessary to double-integrate their output in order to obtain absolute position and angle data, and this makes the measurements very susceptible to long-term drift. To address the drift problem, other forms of sensor need to be incorporated to produce a hybrid tracking system. An example of inertial sensors being used with video is the InterSense IS-1200 system [12], which uses a camera viewing fiducial markers placed in the area of operation to correct the long-term drift. Other systems use ultrasonic transducers such as found in Foxlin et al. [13]. Further discussion of other commercially available tracking systems may be found in Wojdala [14].

3.3.2.3   *Optical Systems Using Natural Features.*   All the systems mentioned so far rely on some form of sensors or special markers in the environment in which the system is being used. A current topic of active research is the development of tracking systems that can use naturally occurring features in the scene. One example of a system that combines tracking of natural features and the use of inertial sensors is described in Chandaria et al. [15]. In applications such as sports outside broadcasting, there is a distinct advantage in being able to track the camera movement from the video image alone; some systems specifically tailored for these applications are described in Section 4.

3.4   Tracking Hand-Held Objects

There are applications where it is useful to be able to attach virtual graphics to small physical objects rather than fixing them in the world reference frame. This allows a presenter to pick up a virtual object, and can provide an interesting way to interact with such objects [16]. An example of the use of an image-based marker tracking system for TV production is shown in Fig. 12. Similar systems have been used for hand-held augmented reality using a PC and webcam [17], although for broadcast use the systems need to satisfy the high frame-rate and robustness

FIG. 12. Vision-based tracking of rectangular markers (top) used to produce hand-held 3D graphics (bottom).

requirements for TV. A potential problem with the use of such systems is that by the very nature of the close interaction between presenter and object, there is a risk of the presenter covering the marker, or placing a hand into the space that the virtual object should occupy. Careful rehearsal is usually required.

The system shown in Fig. 12 uses markers consisting of a rectangular colored rectangle, containing a simple 2D bar code sufficient to identify uniquely a small number of markers, and to allow their orientation to be determined. The use of a strong color allows the marker to be easily located in the image, using a chroma-key technique similar to that described in Section 3.6.3. The corners of the marker are located by fitting straight lines to the edges of the rectangle in the key signal, and from these the locations of the centers of the 2D bar code can be deduced and the bar code can be read. The 3D position and orientation of the marker with respect to the camera is then estimated, using an iterative optimization process. This processing can be carried out at full video rate on a standard PC.

It is theoretically possible to estimate the focal length of the camera in addition to the pose of the marker; however, this is an ill-posed problem in that there are generally many combinations of distance of marker from the camera and focal length of the lens that would provide a good fit to the observed corner positions. Therefore the system is usually used either with the focal length fixed to a known value or with a lens sensor fitted. It is worth noting that a small discrepancy between the actual and assumed camera focal length will not have a significant effect on the rendered graphics, as the estimated marker pose will always result in good alignment of the virtual graphics at the corners of the marker. If the virtual object is significantly larger than the marker, or extends a long way out of the plane of the marker, then errors such as incorrect perspective or uncertainty in marker orientation will become more apparent if the actual focal length is significantly different from that assumed.

3.5   Renderer

The tracking data is sent from the camera tracking system, via a link such as RS232, Ethernet, or USB, to a PC which runs a proprietary real-time rendering software application. This will typically allow preprepared animations to be triggered and will allow other changes to the 3D model to be made interactively such as changing lighting. Generally, it is necessary to generate an alpha channel (also known as key or mask signal) associated with the video to delineate objects that should be forced into the foreground by the keyer.

There are a range of software packages available commercially for the real-time rendering of graphics for mixed reality/virtual studio production. Most require high-end PC systems, equipped with broadcast-standard video capture and output cards. The continuing rise in performance of the graphics processing unit (GPU), driven by the needs of the gaming market, allows such systems to offer very rich 3D environments, including effects such as shadows, reflections, motion blur, and depth-of-field. The features that differentiate such systems from related gaming applications include:

- *Broadcast-standard video output*: This is usually achieved by using either a graphics card that supports serial digital video output, or a separate card that provides broadcast-standard output, in conjunction with software that copies the rendered image from the frame-buffer on the graphics card. An alternative is the use of a stand-alone scan converter connected to the video output of a conventional graphics card, although this makes frame synchronization impossible.

- *Genlock*: The output video signal needs to be locked to the video signal from the camera.

- *Consistent and stable high frame rate*: The image must be re-rendered exactly once per field, otherwise the motion of virtual objects will not match the smooth motion of the real camera. This is in contrast to applications such as games, where any frame rate above 20–30 frames per second may be considered good, and the higher the rate, the better.

- *Alpha (or key) output*: An additional video signal is often required to indicate those parts of the graphics that should always appear in the foreground.

- *Antialiasing*: While this is important in applications such as games, it is more important when the rendered images are being combined with video, as any differences in quality between the real and virtual parts tends to shatter the illusion that both are really present in the same scene.

The following subsections discuss some of these in more detail.

3.5.1 Genlocked Broadcast-Standard Video Output

If the graphics card has a hardware genlock, the rendered image can be taken directly out of the card, either via a broadcast-format output (if it has one) or via a scan converter fed by the VGA/DVI output. This has the advantage that conversion to interlace does not have to be handled by the renderer, but requires a specialized graphics card.

If the card has no genlock facility, the rendered image can be copied out of its frame-buffer and into a genlocked broadcast-standard video output card, over the PCI bus in the PC. The buffer swapping (to initiate redrawing of the graphics) should be initiated in software, triggered by a signal from the video output card. This approach has the advantage that there is no need for a special graphics card, although there will be some CPU or GPU overhead in copying the rendered video from the GPU memory. It is also necessary to consider how to handle interlace in the case of an interlaced broadcast output. Simply copying alternate lines from the rendered image will result in an unacceptable level of vertical aliasing. Rendering a half-height image (with an appropriate half-line offset to get the correct position for the lines for the field polarity) may result in an image that is too soft vertically, if the renderer has good antialiasing. A good approach is to render the full number of lines, and then average pairs of lines in order to generate lines of a field, as shown in Fig. 13. This is the same approach as used in some TV cameras, when generating an interlaced image from a sensor that is inherently progressive. This provides a gentle vertical prefilter, which removes the bulk of the vertical frequencies that would cause unacceptable "line twitter" on an interlaced display, while gaining some additional vertical resolution over that which a single field can convey. It can be implemented as a "shader" on the GPU.

3.5.2 Antialiasing

When assessing the quality of the processing applied to an image, in particular where any sampling or filtering is involved, a useful test pattern is a zone plate [18] such as those incorporated in the test pattern shown in Fig. 14. This test image includes three hyperbolic zoneplates for luminance (top right) and the two color-difference signals (bottom left and right). It also includes a set of color patches that have transitions between all the primary and secondary colors.

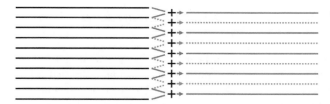

FIG. 13. Generation of two interlaced fields (shown in solid and dotted lines) from a progressive signal by averaging pairs of lines.

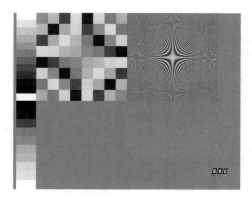

FIG. 14. A test pattern useful incorporating luminance and color-difference hyperbolic zone plates.

By using such an image as a texture in a 3D model being rendered, it is possible to assess how well the renderer resamples the image during the rendering process, and to judge the benefits from features such as oversampling and mip-mapping that the graphics card may provide.

Figure 15 shows an image of a virtual art gallery rendered on an SGI Octane. One of the pictures has been replaced by the test pattern in Fig. 14, allowing the effect of imperfections in the prefiltering and resampling of the Octane's texture mapping to be seen. Note that the main problem with aliasing in this scene is visible on the polygon edges (particularly on the two pictures on the left) which do not appear to have been rendered with any antialiasing at all. Although most modern 3D graphics cards support much better antialiasing on polygon edges than this old Octane supports, it is still generally a good idea to use textures in place of geometry wherever possible to achieve the best visual appearance.

3.6   Keyer

3.6.1   Simple Keying

At simplest, "keying" refers to switching or cross-fading between two images based on a key signal, as shown in Fig. 16.

The output of this simple keyer is

$$out = (k \times bg) + ((1 - k) \times fg),$$

where fg and bg are the foreground and background images, respectively; the key signal $k = 0$ indicates fully opaque foreground, $k = 1$ indicates fully transparent.

Fig. 15. A rendered image of a 3D scene incorporating a zone plate test pattern.

This approach for combining foreground and background is fine for simple graphics overlay, where the presence of foreground always reduces the visibility of the background, such as superimposing captions. Shadows can be represented by considering the shadow of a foreground object as being black with partial transparency. However, reflective or transparent objects, such as reflections from glass, light scattered from smoke, or emitted by a flame, contribute to image but cause little or no reduction in the contribution from background. Figure 17 shows that a candle flame is almost completely transparent. An approach to dealing with such cases is discussed in the following section.

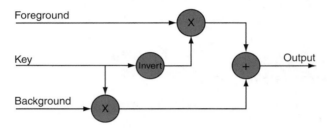

FIG. 16. A simple keyer, using an externally supplied key signal.

FIG. 17. A candle and its shadow, showing that the flame is transparent.

3.6.2   Handling Partial Transparency with Additive Keying

To handle partial transparency, instead of performing a cross-fade between foreground and background, the key signal (representing the transparency of the foreground) is only used to attenuate the background, and a separate process is used to remove any unwanted background that was captured with the foreground image (such as the blue screen). The foreground image with the unwanted background set to black is referred to as the "suppressed foreground" or "premultiplied foreground" (implying that no multiplication by the key signal is needed). The operation of the keyer then becomes:

$$\text{out} = (k \times \text{bg}) + (\text{suppressed fg}).$$

The process of generating suppressed foreground is usually combined with the generation of the key, as both require the detection of the key color in the foreground image. Figure 18 shows a block diagram of a chroma-keyer that uses this principle. The key generator generates a signal proportional to the amount of key color in the background. This is used to suppress (set to black) the background areas. The key signal is processed by adding user-adjustable lift and gain in order to produce a

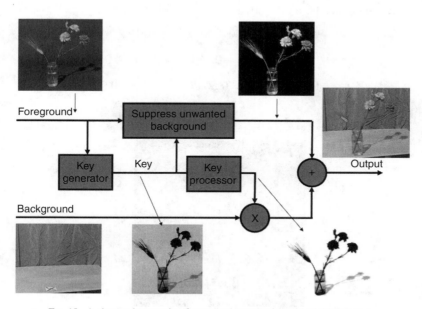

Fig. 18. A chroma-keyer using foreground suppression and additive keying.

signal that varies from 0 in foreground areas to 1 in the background areas. The background is multiplied by this signal (a process that can be thought of as cutting holes in the background corresponding to the degree to which the foreground object obscures the background), and finally the suppressed foreground is added to produce the final composite image.

3.6.3   Key Generation from a Chroma-Key Background

A good way of looking at the behavior of a chroma-keyer is to look at the color space represented in terms of the two color-difference signals $(B-Y)$ and $(R-Y)$, known as U and V in the context of analog PAL TV, or Cb and Cr in digital video. Figure 19 shows the colors corresponding to the possible values of Cb and Cr (those where R, G, and B are in their allowable range), with the luminance value chosen to be as high as possible. The image shows that saturated blue lies at a point on the far right, saturated red at the point nearest the top, and saturated green at the point nearest the bottom left-hand corner. The colors vary smoothly across the image, with white at the center, where the color difference signals are zero.

The relationship between, RGB and $YCbCr$ for standard-definition TV according to ITU-R Recommendation BT.601 is

$$Y = 0.299R + 0.587G + 0.114B,$$

$$Cb = 0.564(B-Y) = -0.169R - 0.331G + 0.500B,$$

$$Cr = 0.713(R-Y) = 0.500R - 0.419G - 0.081B,$$

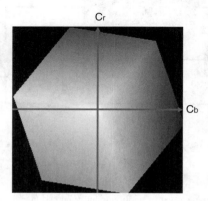

FIG. 19. *RGB* space mapped into color difference space.

where Y, R, G, and B are in the range [0,1] and Cr and Cb are in the range $[-0.5, 0.5]$. Note that for HDTV, as specified in ITU-R Recommendation BT.709, the coefficients are different.

An easy-to-implement method for a key color around blue, if working in *RGB* space, is to derive the key using

$$K = B - \mathrm{Max}(R, G).$$

This is the basis of method originally patented by Petro Vlachos in 1969 [19], which is still used in the Ultimatte™ range of image composition systems. The shape of the area can be "fine-tuned" by scaling R and/or G before processing. Red or green can be used as key colors in a similar manner.

If working in *YCbCr* color space, then a similar approach can be used, for example,

$$K = \mathrm{Cb} - |\mathrm{Cr}| \text{ (clipped to } 0 \ldots 1),$$

which has a response greater than zero in the 90° quadrant centered on the Cb axis where $\mathrm{Cb} > 0$. Figure 20 shows the key signal generated by these two methods when applied to the image of UV space in Fig. 19. A gain of 4 has been applied in each case, with the key signal clipped at $+1$.

The following paragraphs look in more detail at implementing a keyer in *YCbCr* space, following the approach in Devereux [20].

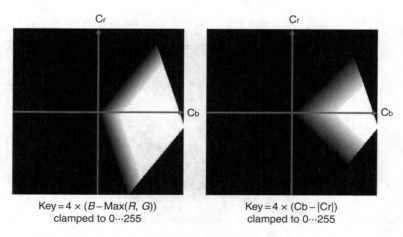

Key = 4 × (*B* − Max(*R*, *G*))
clamped to 0⋯255

Key = 4 × (Cb − |Cr|)
clamped to 0⋯255

FIG. 20. Key signals generated with simple formulae in *RGB* and *YUV* space.

The key color and the range of colors can be varied by first rotating the Cb–Cr plane to a new pair of axes, here called X and Z, where X aligns with the desired key color with a hue angle of h, as shown in Fig. 21:

$$X = \mathrm{Cb} \cos h + \mathrm{Cr} \sin h,$$

$$Z = \mathrm{Cr} \cos h - \mathrm{Cb} \sin h,$$

$$K = X - a|Z|,$$

where acceptance parameter $a = 1/\tan(\mathrm{acceptAngle}/2)$.

The acceptance angle (the angle of the wedge in which the key colors lie) can be reduced by multiplying Z by a number greater than 1 when computing the key, or increased by multiplying by a number less than 1. With the acceptance scaling parameter $a = 1$, the acceptance angle is 90° as before; when $a = 0$ it becomes 180°.

Figure 22 shows a scene containing difficult material including fine detail, partial transparency, and shadows against a blue background, and the distribution of the hue of the image in CbCr space. Note how the blue background is concentrated in a relatively small part of this space. The blue background has a range of brightness values (shown by the variation in luminance of samples in the blue area), but these all have a similar hue. This shows an advantage of defining the key color in terms of its hue angle rather than a small region in *RGB* space: brightness changes do not have a large effect on the key signal generated.

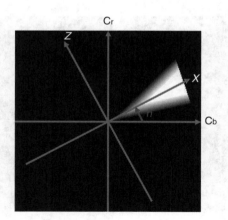

FIG. 21. Key signal generated for a chosen hue angle.

A key signal for this test image is shown in Fig. 23. This was generated by adjusting the hue and acceptance parameters (*a* and *h*) to maximize the key signal in the background, and then applying lift and gain to the key signal in the key processor shown in Fig. 18 to produce an acceptable result, where the unshadowed background is fully transparent. A good process to follow is:

- With a narrow acceptance angle, adjust the hue to give maximum key in the background area;

FIG. 22. Image with a blue screen background and its color distribution.

FIG. 23. Key generated from the test image of Fig. 22.

- Increase the acceptance angle until parts of wanted foreground start to appear in the key signal, then back off a little;
- Adjust the key gain until the background has a solid key signal, but leave the shadows.

3.6.4 Suppression of Unwanted Background

An image of the foreground needs to be generated with the unwanted background suppressed to black, so we can add it to the virtual background after cutting a hole for it using the key signal.

For any pixels where the key signal is greater than 0, the amplitude of the hue signal is reduced such that colors on (or near) the key color axis X have their chrominance set to (nearly) zero:

$$Cb_{sup} = Cb - K \cos h,$$

$$Cr_{sup} = Cr - K \sin h.$$

Note that these equations only completely suppress hues exactly at the specified angle; in practice a range of hues close to this value should also be suppressed, as explained in Devereux [20].

Luminance is similarly suppressed by subtracting from it the key signal amplitude multiplied by a user-specified amount Ys:

$$Y_{sup} = Y - KYs,$$

Ys is chosen to bring the background down to black, but to leave any wanted highlights, for example, from reflections (Fig. 24).

The suppressed foreground image shown in Fig. 25 was generated by adjusting the hue and acceptance angles as before, and then adjusting the luminance suppression parameter to set the background to black. Note that a few highlights have been left in the background where light is reflecting from or refracting through the glass.

The background image, multiplied by the key signal, is then added to the suppressed foreground image to form the final output image. The image on the left of Fig. 26 shows the result with the key signal shown in Fig. 23, where the key gain has been adjusted to leave the shadow visible. The presence of the shadow is important: the fact that the shadow, which our brain tells us must lie on a surface, meets the base of the jar, is a good visual clue that the base of the jar must also lie on this surface. The image on the right of Fig. 26 was generated with higher gain applied to the key, so that the shadow was clipped off. The reduced realism is clearly apparent.

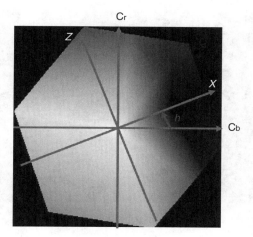

FIG. 24. Suppression of hue and luminance.

FIG. 25. Suppressed foreground image for the test image of Fig. 22.

Commercial chroma-keyers typically provide a number of other adjustments such as allowing the brightness and color of the foreground and background to be individually adjusted to help produce a good match. Another common feature is a "garbage matte" (an additional key signal that forces given areas of the foreground

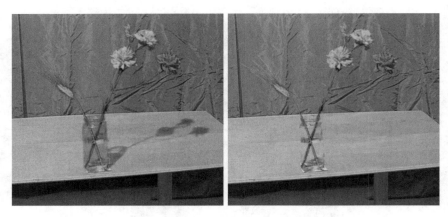

Fɪɢ. 26. Composite image, with and without a shadow.

image to be treated as background). Keyers often have an additional key (or alpha) input that can be used to force areas of the output to either foreground or background to force a virtual object to always appear in front of a real object, for example, the virtual creatures on the table in Fig. 2.

3.7   Feedback to Presenters and Crew

For any situation in which a presenter, actor, or other participant in a program need to interact with virtual content, it is important to provide some form of visualization for them. At simplest, this can be provided by positioning a TV monitor out-of-shot but visible to the presenter, showing the composite image. Sometimes, the auto-cue on the camera is used for this, often with the image reversed to simulate the behavior of a mirror.

In order to allow the presenter to maintain the correct eyeline while viewing the virtual content, a view of the virtual object can be projected into the scene, at the position where the virtual object will appear. It is important that this projected image does not appear in the final composite image. If a chroma-key background is being used, this can usually be achieved by projecting a low-brightness image that does not interfere with the keying process, and ideally using back projection so that the projected image does not fall on the presenter.

However, where the image needs to be projected onto real scene elements (e.g., if the presenter needs to see virtual objects that are to be placed on a real table), a low-brightness projection may be visible to the camera, particularly if the rendered virtual objects do not exactly obscure the projected image. A method of rendering such a projected image invisible to the camera is to blank the projector synchronously with the camera integration period (e.g., by reducing the shutter time on the camera so that it integrates for 1/100th of a second at a field rate of 50 Hz, and applying a similar but opposite-phase shutter on the projector). An early example of the use of this technique [21] used a specially designed liquid crystal shutter on the projector, but recent advances in DMD projectors, particularly those designed for time-sequential stereo such as Christie [22], mean that off-the-shelf projectors can now achieve the same results. Figure 27 shows an example of projection feedback being used to show virtual graphics on a table top for the BBC program BAMZOOKi shown in Fig. 2. The projector is positioned high above the table, projecting downward.

Even when a shuttered projection technique is used, it is advantageous to avoid projecting light directly onto a presenter, in order to avoid dazzling them. This can be achieved by generating a key signal for the presenter, using a camera located

Fig. 27. Projection feedback in use on the BBC show BAMZOOKi, to show the participants a view of the virtual elements projected from above onto a horizontal surface (the monitors on the right show the composite image and the original camera image).

Fɪɢ. 28. Projector with associated camera to generate key image to avoid projected light landing on presenter.

close to the projector, and using this to blank out the portion of the projected light that would otherwise fall on them. Figure 28 shows such a setup: the camera is surrounded by a ring of blue LEDs as a retroreflective cyclorama [23] is being used as a chroma-key background. Figure 29 shows the cyclorama with the projected image. One advantage of using a retroreflective cyclorama in this application is that it appears gray (rather than bright blue) to the presenter, making the projected image easier to see. The studio TV camera is also fitted with a blue LED ring, so that the cyclorama appears bright blue from its point of view. An example of a composite image obtained from this setup is shown in Fig. 30. Note how the presenter is able to see what he is pointing at.

The projection method described above works well for virtual objects that appear roughly coincident with surfaces (such as tables, walls, and floors) onto which images could be projected. However, in situations where a virtual object (such as a virtual actor) is standing freely in space, this relatively straightforward approach will not work. For example, if a top-down view of a virtual actor was projected onto the point on the floor at which he stands, the eyeline of a real actor will be wrong when looking at the head of the virtual character, as the presenter will be looking at the floor. This problem can be solved by using a view-dependant projection method [24], in which the 3D position of the presenter's head is tracked, and an image appropriate for their viewpoint is projected onto a wall.

FIG. 29. Projected image, showing blanked portion for presenter.

FIG. 30. Composite image as broadcast, with presenter using projected image to view virtual graphics.

4.   Virtual Graphics for Sports

In order to present analysis of sports events to TV viewers, a common requirement is to be able to overlay graphics on the image, which appear to be tied to the ground. It is also useful to be able to show markings at the correct absolute scale, such as distances from a player on a football pitch to the goal. As in the studio-based applications described earlier, this requires knowledge of the camera pose (position and orientation), as well as the focal length. The calibration data generally needs to be generated at full video rate (50 or 60 Hz). An example of some typical overlaid graphics is shown in Fig. 31.

One way in which camera calibration data can be derived is by performing an initial off-line calibration of the position of the camera mounting using surveying tools such as a theodolite or rangefinder, and mounting sensors on the camera and the lens to measure the pan, tilt, and zoom. Figure 32 shows an example of a camera head equipped with sensors. However, this is costly and not always practical, for example, if the cameras are installed and operated by another broadcaster and only the video feed itself is made available. The sensor data has to be carried through the program production chain, including the cabling from the camera to the outside broadcast truck, recording on tape or disk, and transmission to the studio. Also, any system that relies on sensor data cannot be used on archive recordings.

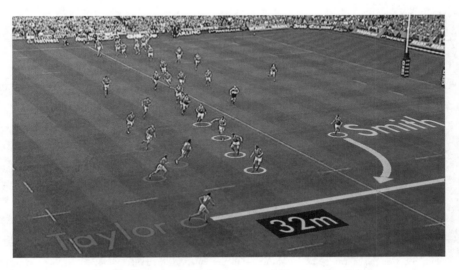

FIG. 31. Example of virtual graphics overlaid on a rugby pitch.

Fig. 32. A camera mounted on a pan/tilt head equipped with motion sensors.

A more attractive way of deriving calibration data is by analysis of the camera image. The lines on a sports pitch are usually in known positions, and these can be used to compute the camera pose. In some sports, such as football, the layout of some pitch markings (such as those around the goal) is fully specified, but the overall dimensions vary between grounds. It is thus necessary to obtain a measurement of the actual pitch. A minimum of four lines (which cannot all be parallel) must be visible to compute fully the camera pose, although fewer are needed if the camera position is already known.

Image processing methods based on identification of the pitch lines are now routinely used to derive camera tracking data for these kinds of sports application. An overview of one method used in commercial products for performing this task is given in Section 4.1. In some sports applications, there are insufficient lines visible for this approach to be used, so an approach based on tracking areas of rich texture or other details such as corners may be used, as described in Section 4.2.

4.1 Tracking Camera Movement Using Pitch Lines

The process of estimating the camera pose using lines on a sports pitch can be broken down into the steps of estimating the position of the camera mounting (which is assumed to remain fixed), starting the tracker given a view of the pitch, and tracking from one image to the next at full video rate (50 or 60 Hz). An overview of how these steps can be implemented is given in the following sections. A detailed description of this method is given in Ref. [25].

4.1.1 Estimating the Position of the Camera Mount

Most cameras covering events such as football generally remain in fixed positions during a match. Indeed, the positions can remain almost unchanged between different matches at the same ground, as the camera mounting points are often rigidly fixed to the stadium structure. It therefore makes sense to use this prior knowledge to compute an accurate camera position, which is then used as a constraint during the subsequent tracking process.

Estimating the position of a camera from a set of features in a single image can be a poorly constrained problem, particularly if focal length also needs to be estimated, as changes to the focal length have a very similar effect on the image to moving the camera along the direction of view. To improve the accuracy, multiple images can be used to solve for a common camera position value.

The pose computation method described in the following sections is used to compute the camera position, orientation and field-of-view, for a number of different camera orientations, covering a wide range of pan angles. The pose for all images is computed simultaneously, and the position is constrained to a common value for all the images. This significantly reduces the inherent ambiguity between the distance of the camera from the reference features and the focal length. By including views of features in a wide range of positions (e.g., views of both goal areas), the uncertainty lies along different directions, and solving for a common position allows this uncertainty to be significantly reduced. The "diamonds" in Fig. 33 show the positions computed from approximately 40 individual images for a camera viewing a football pitch, indicating the range of uncertainty that using individual images produces. The points tend to lie along lines from the true camera position to the main clusters of features on the pitch (the goals and the center circle). The "cross" shows the position optimized across all these images; note how this position is not simply the average of the individually measured positions.

Cameras usually cannot roll (i.e., rotate about their direction of view). However, this does not necessarily mean that the roll angle can be assumed to be zero. The camera may not necessarily be mounted flat on the pan/tilt head, or the head itself may not be aligned with the pan axis exactly vertical. Also, it is usually assumed that the plane of the pitch is essentially horizontal, but this may not be the case. Each of

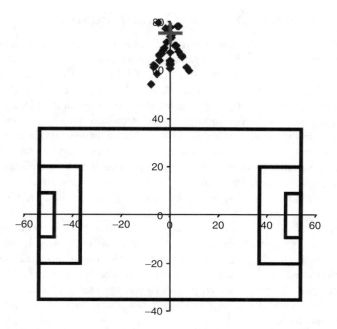

Fɪɢ. 33. Camera positions estimated from pitch lines in the image, using individual images.

these effects can give rise to what appears to be a small amount of camera roll, which could vary with pan or tilt, depending on the cause. One solution would be to compute camera roll for every image during the tracking process, but this introduces an additional degree of freedom, and therefore will increase the noise sensitivity and increase the minimum number of features needed for accurate pose computation. Another option would be to attempt to solve for each of these small misalignments separately. A simpler alternative is to solve for the apparent rotation of the pitch plane about the dominant direction of the camera view. This pitch rotation is computed during the global position computation process, giving a single value optimized for all the images used.

The process described above can be repeated using images from all the cameras into whose feeds the production team are likely to want to add virtual graphics. For football, this is likely to include the camera on the center line, the cameras in line with the two "18 yard" lines, and possibly the cameras behind the goals. The computed camera positions are then stored for future use.

4.1.2   Initialization of the Camera Pose

Before the tracker can be run at full video rate, it is necessary to initialize it by determining which of the precalibrated camera positions the camera is at, and roughly what its values of pan, tilt, and field-of-view are. This process needs to be carried out when the tracker is first started, and also whenever it loses track (e.g., if the camera briefly zooms in tightly to an area with no lines, or the video signal is cut between cameras). It is usually possible to track from a so-called "iso" feed (isolated signal from a single camera, rather than the output of the vision mixer that switches between cameras), so the tracker can maintain track even when the tracked camera is not on air. The challenge of the initialization process is to locate pitch lines in the image and deduce which lines on the pitch they correspond to. The only prior knowledge available is the list of known camera positions, and the dimensions of the pitch.

The Hough transform is a well-known way of finding lines in an image. It maps a line in the image to a point (or accumulator "bin") in Hough space, where the two axes represent the angle of the line and the shortest distance to the center of the image. If the camera pose is known roughly, it is possible to predict which peak in Hough space corresponds to which known line in the world, and hence to calibrate the camera. However, if the camera pose is unknown, the correspondence can be difficult to establish, as there may be many possible permutations of correspondences. Furthermore, if some lines are curved rather than straight, they will not give rise to a well-defined peak and are thus hard to identify. Figure 34 shows an example of a Hough transform of an image, operating on the output of the line detector described in the following section.

Rather than attempting to establish directly the correspondence between world lines and peaks in Hough space, the Hough transform can be used as a means to allow us to quickly establish a measure of how well the image matches the set of lines that would be expected to be visible from a given pose. A "match value" for a set of lines can be obtained by adding together the set of bins in Hough space that correspond to the locations of the lines we would expect for this pose. Thus, to test for the presence of a set of N lines, it is only necessary to add together N values from the Hough transform, rather than examining all the pixels in the image that we would expect the lines to lie upon. By representing a curved line as a series of line segments, curves can also contribute to the match, even if they do not give rise to local maxima in the Hough transform. Although specific forms of Hough transform exist for circle or ellipse detection, the line segment approach allows both curves and lines to be handled in a single process.

This approach can be used in an exhaustive search process, to establish the match value for each pose that we consider. For each predetermined camera position, and

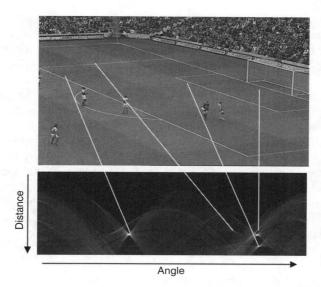

FIG. 34. Hough transform of lines as used for initialization of camera pose.

for the full range of plausible values of pan, tilt, and field-of-view, the match value can be calculated by summing the values in the bins in the Hough transform that correspond to the line positions that would be expected. The locations of the bins to sum can be precomputed by projecting the pitch line positions into the camera image for many thousands of possible camera poses, covering the full range of plausible values. The bin locations can be precomputed and stored, meaning that the process of adding the values in Hough space becomes no more than summing elements whose addresses are held in a look-up table. In practice, a slightly modified Hough transform can be used that takes greater account of the location of the line segment observed, to give greater discrimination between lines. The whole initialization process can take less than a second when implemented on a modern PC, testing around 700,000 possible combinations of pan, tilt, field-of-view for three different camera positions. Details may be found in Ref. [25].

4.1.3 Frame-to-Frame Tracking of the Camera Motion

The tracking process uses the pose estimate from the previous image (or from the initialization process), and searches a window of the image centered on each predicted line position for points likely to correspond to pitch lines. A straight line is fitted through each set of points, and an iterative minimization process is used to find the values of pan, tilt, and focal length that minimize the distance in the image between the ends of each observed line and the corresponding line in the model when projected into the camera image. These steps are described in more detail below.

Each line in the pitch model is projected into the camera image using the previous camera pose as an estimate of the current pose. A simple filter is applied to all pixels in a neighborhood around the predicted line position of each line. The filter uses knowledge of the predicted line width and orientation to produce a measure of the extent to which each pixel looks like it may be at the center of a pitch line. Pixels having a filter output above a given threshold are candidates for lying on the line. The pixels adjacent to each candidate are tested to see whether they have a color in the range expected for grass, to discard points in areas of the image such as the crowd or advertising hoardings. A hue-based chroma keyer, as described in Section 3.6, is used for this purpose.

For each line, a straight line is fitted through the set of detected pixels, weighting each point in accordance with the amplitude of the line detector output. Figure 35 shows an example of the lines fitted through the detected line pixels overlaid on the image. The detected lines lie virtually on top of the real lines. Note how several line segments have been used to represent the semicircle.

Once all of the lines that are expected to be visible have been processed, a least squares iterative optimization is performed, to compute the pan, tilt, and focal length values that minimize the sum of the squares of the distance (in image pixels) from

FIG. 35. Detected lines used for pose computation.

the end points of the observed lines to the lines in the pitch model projected into the camera image. For the purpose of computing the distance from an observed end-point to the projected pitch model line, the lines in the pitch model are assumed to be of infinite extent; this allows the distance to be computed in a straightforward manner. The minimization process is similar to the well-known Levenberg-Marquardt method [26], using the pose from the previous image as the initial estimate. It takes around 6 ms to implement this process for a standard-definition video field on a modern PC. Note that when this process is being applied in the initial position estimation stage, the minimization process also varies the camera position and pitch orientation, and is applied simultaneously across a number of images (see Section 4.1.1).

4.2   Camera Tracking Using Areas of Rich Texture

For sports such as athletics, the camera image will generally show limited numbers of well-defined lines, and those that are visible may be insufficient to allow the camera pose to be computed. For example, lines on a running track are generally all parallel and thus give no indication of the current distance along the track, making pose computation impossible from the lines alone. For events such as long jump, the main area of interest (the sand pit) has no lines in it at all. Thus, to accurately estimate the camera pose for the insertion of virtual graphics for these kinds of events, an alternative approach is needed. Figure 36 shows an example of virtual graphics being overlaid for long jump, which is typical of what is required.

Fig. 36. Virtual distance markings overlaid on a long jump pit.

The challenge is to be able to estimate the camera pose for these kinds of applications from the content of the image, without resorting to the use of mechanical sensors on the camera. This is a specific example of a problem known as SLAM (simultaneous location and mapping) [27], in which the pose of the camera and the 3D location of tracked image features are estimated as the camera moves. The general approach involves storing patches of image data centered on good feature points (such as corners), and matching these to the features seen in subsequent frames. From these observations, the pose of the camera and the 3D location of the features can be estimated using techniques such as an Extended Kalman Filter.

In this application we need to be able to cope with significant changes in camera focal length, but can make use of the constraint that the camera is generally mounted on a fixed point. This is in contrast to most implementations of SLAM, which assume a fixed focal length camera but allow full camera movement. We also need to be able to cope with a significant degree of motion blur, as motion speeds of 20–30 pixels per field period are not uncommon with tightly-zoomed-in cameras covering sports events. The approach described in Ref. [28] is designed to meet these requirements. It uses a combination of fixed reference features to prevent long-term drift (whose image texture is always that taken from the first frame in which the feature was seen), and temporary features to allow nonstatic scene elements (such as faces in the crowd) to play a useful part in the tracking process. The image features are assigned an arbitrary depth, as their depth cannot be determined from a fixed viewpoint. Figure 37 is an image from a hurdles race, showing the features that have been selected for tracking.

Fig. 37. Reference features selected for camera tracking on a hurdles event.

In order to obtain a calibration in a fixed world reference frame, the absolute positions of some features in a selection of views can be specified by an operator, and the system then refines the positions of all the fixed reference features to be consistent with these, before storing the features for future use. Figure 38 shows an operator carrying out this process, using a model of the layout of the hurdles and track to align the system.

In situations where some lines are visible, such as that shown Fig. 37, it is possible to use these in addition to the features centered on areas of image detail. Further details of the algorithms used in this system, including the approach taken to initialize the camera pose when tracking is first started, can be found in Ref. [28].

4.3   Keying Graphics onto the Background

Once the camera pose has been computed, the graphics rendering and keying processes for sports applications closely follow those described for studio-based programs in Sections 3.5 and 3.6. Perhaps surprisingly, a conventional chroma-keyer works remarkably well for keying graphics onto grass, as shown in Fig. 31. Grass-covered pitches are not uniformly green, and graphics will not be keyed well into areas such as mud. However, this gives the impression that the virtual graphics are painted onto the grass, and their absence in muddy areas can actually add to the realism. Athletics presents a greater challenge, with the need to generate a key signal corresponding to areas of a running track or a sand pit so that the graphics can appear

Fɪɢ. 38. Operator in outside broadcast van carrying out calibration process.

to be behind or underneath the athletes. Many tracks have distinct colors, but sand tends to have a color very close to skin color, and it can be a challenge to distinguish it from the arms or legs of the athlete. It is often necessary to define a much tighter area in *RGB* space than is possible just by specifying a range of hue angles. The example in Fig. 36 used a keyer configured to detect specific colors, which were specified by an operator manually selecting parts of the sand pit during an initial calibration process. One drawback of this keying method is that a good key may not be generated if there are significant lighting changes after the keyer is set up, so a method of automatically updating the keyer settings on a regular basis is useful, particularly for outdoor events.

5. Compositing Real Images into the 3D Model

The approach outlined so far in this chapter has been to insert virtual graphics into an image captured from the camera. The virtual elements are rendered from a viewpoint that matches the real camera, and the real and virtual elements are combined in the form of 2D images using a conventional keyer.

Although this is the approach most commonly used at present, there is an alternative: create a 3D model of the relevant parts of the real-world scene, and incorporate these into a 3D model of a virtual scene which is then rendered from an arbitrary viewpoint. This allows the viewpoint to be chosen independently from that of the real camera, for example, allowing a moving camera view to be simulated using a fixed camera, or a camera view simulated from a location where a real camera could not easily be placed.

This alternative approach is most commonly used at present in the so-called track-less virtual studio systems. For example, to produce a composite scene of a news-reader in a virtual set, the newsreader is captured in front of a conventional blue screen. Instead of rendering a view of the virtual set and keying it behind the newsreader, the image of the newsreader is instead texture-mapped onto a flat plane, which is placed in the 3D model of the set at a location corresponding to the point at which they are standing. A key signal is generated from the camera image and used as the alpha (transparency) channel for the texture. A view of the scene rendered from the point-of-view of the real camera will produce a result essentially identical to that which would have been produced by rendering the virtual background separately, and keying it behind the newsreader. However, it is possible to move the virtual camera, for example to simulate the camera flying into the studio. The range of camera movement is limited by the planar nature of the modeled image, meaning that the virtual viewpoint should not be very far away from that of the real camera. If the direction of view is more than about 10–20° away from that of the real camera, the flat nature of the modeled foreground becomes apparent and the illusion is broken. However, this approach can provide a cost-effective way of giving the appearance of real camera movement, without the need for a cameraman or any form of camera tracking system.

Figure 39 shows an example of a presenter being texture-mapped onto a flat plane. The image on the left is rendered from a viewpoint that closely matches that of the real camera, and shows correct perspective. Note how the occlusion of part of the presenter by a part of the set is handled as a natural part of the 3D rendering process. The image on the right shows the problem that arises when the virtual camera viewpoint is moved too far away from that of the real camera. This approach can be extended by using more sophisticated ways of modeling the foreground image. For example, Grau et al. [29] describes a method of inferring a rough 3D shape for a person from the outline of the key signal, which can allow a slightly wider range of viewpoints to be used.

To allow a wider range of virtual camera views, a full 3D model of the live action needs to be created. This is a challenging task, as the quality of the rendered model needs to be equivalent to that which a real camera would have captured. Grau et al. [24] describes research into a multicamera studio-based system, and the development of this approach for sports applications such as postmatch analysis for football is described in Grau et al. [30]. At present, such systems are not generally suitable for real time use, and a detailed description of them is beyond the scope of this chapter.

6. Conclusions

This chapter has reviewed the technology needed to generate 3D graphics in real time to insert into broadcast video, in a way that makes the virtual objects appear to be physically present in the scene. The methods described are in regular use in broadcast production today. Unlike their counterparts in film production, the systems described are designed for use in real-time applications, where there is generally no opportunity to use labor-intensive postproduction techniques.

Although the focus of this chapter has been on the technology, it is important to remember that the technology is there to support the program maker. It can provide them with ways to "tell a better story" to the viewer (e.g., in sports programs), or can enable new kinds of program that would not otherwise be possible (such as the BAMZOOKi childrens' game show). There should always be a good reason to use the technology; otherwise it can end up as "eye candy," not really adding any value to the production.

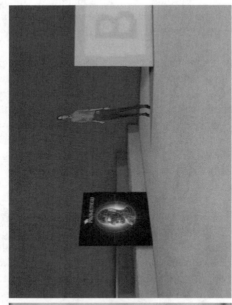

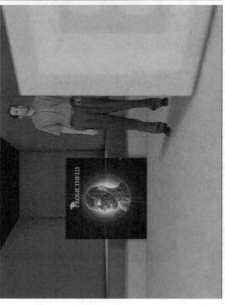

FIG. 39. Texture mapping a presenter onto a plane in a 3D model.

ACKNOWLEDGMENTS

The author would like to thank his colleagues at BBC R&D, in particular Oliver Grau, Paul Debenham, and Robert Dawes, for their help and contributions to the work described here. He would also like to thank Danny Popkin in BBC Studios & Post-Production, who was responsible for the virtual aspects of many of the studio-based productions mentioned in this chapter, and provided invaluable insights into the practical applications of the technology. Finally, he would like to thank the Piero team at Red Bee Media, who commercialized the sports graphics system used in the examples in this chapter, and gave many helpful suggestions and feedback on the image-based tracker.

REFERENCES

[1] R.C.H. Wright, R.E. Fletcher, Development of operational techniques using C.S.O. (chromakey) and technological developments that could effect a change in production methods, in: Proceedings of the International Broadcasting Convention, 1978, pp. 54–58.

[2] L. Blondé, et al., A virtual studio for live broadcasting: the Mona Lisa project, IEEE Multimedia 3 (2) (1996) 18–29.

[3] BBC, The BBC programme BAMZOOKi. 2010. www.bbc.co.uk/cbbc/bamzooki.

[4] R.Y. Tsai, An efficient and accurate camera calibration technique for 3D machine vision, in: Proceedings of IEEE Conference on Computer Vision and Pattern Recognition, Miami Beach, FL, 1986, pp. 364–374.

[5] C. Poynton, Digital Video and HDTV: Algorithms and Interfaces (The Morgan Kaufmann Series in Computer Graphics), first ed., Morgan Kaufmann, 2002, ISBN 1-55860-792-7.

[6] D. Wood, S. Baron, Rec. 601—the Origins of the 4:2:2 DTV standard, EBU Technical Review, October, 2005, http://www.ebu.ch/en/technical/trev/trev_304-rec601_wood.pdf.

[7] EBU, Safe Areas for 16:9 Television Production, EBU Recommendation R95, 2008, http://tech.ebu.ch/docs/r/r095.pdf.

[8] EBU, EBU Guidelines for Consumer Flat Panel Displays, EBU Technical Specification 3321, 2007, http://tech.ebu.ch/publications/tech3321.

[9] THOMA, 2009, http://www.thoma.de/en/produkte/walkfinder_tracking_system.html.

[10] M Ward, et al., A demonstrated optical tracker with scalable work area for head-mounted display systems, in: Proceedings of 1992 Symposium on Interactive 3D Graphics, Cambridge, MA, 29 March–1 April 1992, pp. 43–52.

[11] G.A. Thomas, J. Jin, T. Niblett, C. Urquhart, A Versatile Camera Position Measurement System for Virtual Reality TV Production, IBC, Amsterdam, 1995, IEE Conference Publication No. 447, pp. 284–289, http://www.bbc.co.uk/rd/pubs/papers/paper_05/paper_05.shtml.

[12] D. Wormell, E. Foxlin, P. Katzman, Advanced inertial-optical tracking system for wide area mixed and augmented reality systems, in: 10th International Immersive Projection Technologies Workshop (IPT)/13th Eurographics Workshop on Virtual Environments (EGVE), July15–18, 2007, Weimar, Germany, http://www.intersense.com/uploadedFiles/Products/White_Papers/IPT_EGVEShortPaper_AdvInertialOpticalTrackingSysFINAL.pdf.

[13] E. Foxlin, M. Harrington, G. Pfeiffer, Constellation^{TM}: a wide-range wireless motion-tracking system for augmented reality and virtual set applications, in: Siggraph 98, Orlando, FL, July 19–24, 1998, http://www.intersense.com/pages/44/114.

[14] A. Wojdala, Virtual studio in 2000 the state of the art, in: Virtual Studios and Virtual Production Conference, New York, 17–18 August 2000.

[15] J. Chandaria, et al., Real-Time Camera Tracking in the MATRIS Project, IBC, Amsterdam, 2006, pp. 321–328.

[16] V. Lalioti, A. Woolard, Mixed Reality Productions of the Future, IBC, Amsterdam, 2003, pp. 312–320. Available as BBC R&D White Paper 071 http://www.bbc.co.uk/rd/publications/whitepaper071.shtml.

[17] M. Billinghurst, H. Kato, I. Poupyrev, The MagicBook: a transitional AR interface, Comput. Graphics 25 (5) (2001) 745–753.

[18] J.O. Drewery, The Zone Plate as a Television Test Pattern, BBC Research Department Report No 1978/23, 1978, http://downloads.bbc.co.uk/rd/pubs/reports/1978-23.pdf.

[19] P. Vlachos, Electronic Composite Photography, US Patent 3,595,987, 1969.

[20] V.G. Devereux, Television Animation Store: Digital Chroma-Key and Mixer Units, BBC Research Department Report No. 1984/16, 1984, http://www.bbc.co.uk/rd/pubs/reports/1984-16.pdf.

[21] T. Fukaya, et al., An Effective Interaction Tool for Performance in the Virtual Studio—Invisible Light Projection System, IBC, Amsterdam, 2002, pp. 389–396.

[22] Christie, The Christie S+14K Projector, 2010, http://www.christiedigital.co.uk/emea/3D/products-and-solutions/projectors/Pages/mirage-S14K-3D-Stereoscopic-Projector.aspx.

[23] G.A. Thomas, Retro-reflective Flexible Material Sheet for Use as Background in Chroma-Keying Video Image Composition System, UK Patent GB2321565, 1998, http://www.bbc.co.uk/rd/projects/virtual/truematte/.

[24] O. Grau, T. Pullen, G.A. Thomas, A combined studio production system for 3D capturing of live action and immersive act or feedback, IEEE Trans. Circuits Sys. Video Technol. 14 (3) 2003, (Available as BBC R&D White Paper 086), http://www.bbc.co.uk/rd/publications/whitepaper086.shtml.

[25] G.A. Thomas, Real-time camera tracking using sports pitch markings, J. Real Time Image Process. 2 (2–3) (2008) 117–132, (Available as BBC R&D White Paper 168), http://www.bbc.co.uk/rd/publications/whitepaper168.shtml.

[26] K. Levenberg, A method for the solution of certain non-linear problems in least squares, The Quart. Appl. Math. 2 (1944) 164–168.

[27] A. Davison, I. Reid, N. Molton, O. Stasse, MonoSLAM: realtime single camera SLAM, IEEE Trans. Pattern Anal. Machine Intell. 29 (6) (2007) 1052–1067.

[28] R. Dawes, J. Chandaria, G.A. Thomas, Image-based camera tracking for athletics, in: Proceedings of the IEEE International Symposium on Broadband Multimedia Systems and Broadcasting (BMSB 2009), Bilbao, May 13–15, 2009, (Available as BBC R&D White Paper 181), http://www.bbc.co.uk/rd/publications/whitepaper181.shtml.

[29] O. Grau, M. Price, G.A. Thomas, Use of 3-D techniques for virtual production, in: SPIE Conference on Videometrics and Optical Methods for 3D Shape Measurement, 22–23 January 2001, San Jose, USA, 2001, (Available as BBC R&D White Paper 033), http://www.bbc.co.uk/rd/publications/whitepaper033.shtml.

[30] O. Grau, G.A. Thomas, A. Hilton, J. Kilner, J. Starck, A robust free-viewpoint video system for sport scenes, in: Proceeding of 3DTV Conference 2007, Kos, Greece, 2007, (Available as BBC R&D White Paper 149), http://www.bbc.co.uk/rd/publications/whitepaper149.shtml.

Advanced Applications of Virtual Reality

JÜRGEN P. SCHULZE

Calit2, UC San Diego, La Jolla, California, USA

HAN SUK KIM

Department of Computer Science and Engineering, UC San Diego, La Jolla, California, USA

PHILIP WEBER

Calit2, UC San Diego, La Jolla, California, USA

ANDREW PRUDHOMME

Calit2, UC San Diego, La Jolla, California, USA

ROGER E. BOHN

IR/PS, UC San Diego, La Jolla, California, USA

MAURIZIO SERACINI

CISA3, UC San Diego, La Jolla, California, USA

THOMAS A. DEFANTI

Calit2, UC San Diego, La Jolla, California, USA

ADVANCES IN COMPUTERS, VOL. 82
ISSN: 0065-2458/DOI: 10.1016/B978-0-12-385512-1.00006-2

217

Abstract

In the first 5 years of virtual reality application research at the California Institute for Telecommunications and Information Technology (Calit2), we created numerous software applications for virtual environments. Calit2 has one of the most advanced virtual reality laboratories with the five-walled StarCAVE and the world's first passive stereo, LCD panel-based immersive virtual reality system, the NexCAVE. The combination of cutting edge hardware, direct access to world class researchers on the campus of UCSD, and Calit2's mission to bring the first two together to make new advances at the intersection of these disciplines enabled us to research the future of scientific virtual reality applications. This chapter reports on some of the most notable applications we developed.

1. Introduction

The term virtual reality (VR) first made it to the mainstream about 25 years ago, when Scott Fisher's group at the NASA Ames Research Center presented the virtual interface environment workstation (VIEW) system, a head-mounted display with headphones and gloves [1]. However, at the time, technology was not advanced enough for VR to be economical for real-world applications, and even the video game industry gave up on it after several attempts in the 1990s at bringing the technology into video game arcades, for instance, the Trocadero in London.

Today's VR systems consist, at a minimum, of the following components:

- Graphics rendering units: The computer hardware to compute the virtual scene and render it to a frame buffer, ready to be sent to a display device. This is typically a high-end graphics PC.
- 3D stereo display units: Serve as the interface from the computer to the user. These used to be projectors and screens, but with the advent of 3D flat panel LCD or plasma displays these are more and more common.
- Tracking system: Serves as the interface from the user to the computer.

VR made a comeback in the past decade, when consumer graphics computers became powerful enough to compete with high-end, specialized graphics mainframes. This development brought the cost for graphics rendering down by more than one order of magnitude, while increasing image fidelity at the same time. Today, graphics mainframes are no longer being manufactured; they have been replaced by professional versions of computer gaming hardware, which are based on their consumer counterparts and thus only marginally more expensive than consumer solutions.

Similar developments have been happening with display and tracking technology. Tracking systems used to be either wireless and very expensive, or tethered and still expensive. Today, wireless optical tracking systems are available at a cost similar to a high-end PC. And with the advent of consumer 3D TVs, VR displays have finally made it to the consumer market. It remains to be seen if 3D is going to survive in the consumer market, and if the trend toward making VR feasible in the home is going to continue.

1.1   VR Hardware at Calit2

At Calit2, we built a number of novel 3D VR display systems over the past 5 years. The most notable ones are the StarCAVE, the NexCAVE, and the AESOP wall. The StarCAVE [2], as seen in Fig. 1, is a room-sized immersive VR system with about 10 ft diameter. The user wears polarized glasses and stands in the center of an array of 15 screens, each driven by two projectors for passive stereo. A cluster of 18 high-end graphics PCs renders 3D images on 34 HD (high definition) projectors (1920×1080 pixels each) with Nvidia Quadro 5600 graphics cards. We use passive stereo, so the user has to wear glasses with polarizing filters. In order to give

Fɪɢ. 1. The StarCAVE with two users looking at a protein structure.

a 360 viewing angle, the screens are rear projected. For head and hand tracking, we use a wireless, optical tracking system with four infrared cameras, mounted at the top of the StarCAVE. For surround sound output, we have a 5.1 channel surround sound system.

The NexCAVE [3], shown in Fig. 2, is the first tiled, immersive VR system based on flat panel displays. The LCD displays use micropolarization to create a stereo image viewable with polarizing glasses. The system consists of ten 46 in. HD displays, six high-end graphics PCs, and a two-camera optical tracking system. A Yamaha 5.1 channel digital sound bar can deliver spatialized sound. The displays are mounted with overlapping bezels, to minimize the space the bezels cover.

The AESOP wall, shown in Fig. 3, is a monoscopic tiled display wall, consisting of a 4×4 array of LCD displays, driven by a cluster of five high-end graphics PCs. The screens have ultrathin bezels, with only about 7 mm bezel space between two displays. This allows the system to run applications which do not need to worry about significant parts of the screen not permitting to display pixels, as it is the case with previous tiled display walls. The AESOP wall also features a two-camera optical tracking system and a 5.1 channel digital sound bar.

Fig. 2. NexCAVE: 10 overlapping passive stereo LCD displays.

1.2   VR Software Applications

This chapter is not going to focus on VR hardware, but instead at our recent developments in VR software. At the Calit2 center of UCSD, we have been researching and developing VR software since 2005. The VR center at Calit2 is in a unique position, as it was created, like many other laboratories at Calit2, to be a shared resource for researchers on the entire UCSD campus to allow them to utilize VR approaches without having to make the investment in expensive VR hardware themselves.

The software framework we use in all our VR systems is called COVISE [4]; its VR renderer is called OpenCOVER [5]. VR applications are written in C++ as COVISE plugins, multiple of which can run at the same time. COVISE abstracts the fact that the application is running in parallel over many machines and multiple OpenGL contexts, and automatically handles things such as stereo perspective calculations and OpenGL context management so that the application developer does not need to worry about them.

The Calit2 VR group has been working with researchers from a variety of disciplines at UCSD, but it has also conducted its own independent research into VR software applications, especially real-time immersive rendering and 3D user interfaces. In this line of work, we have been focusing on getting away from the

FIG. 3. AESOP Wall: 16 large, monoscopic narrow-bezel LCD displays with tracking and sound.

traditional mouse and keyboard interface, toward intuitive, immersive 3D interfaces. To us, good VR software applications use surround visualization and immerse the user in the data; 3D objects can be found at all possible distances from the user, from an arm's length to infinity; and user interaction does not just mean navigation of a static scene, but it means to interact directly with individual objects in the 3D scene with as much direct, object-oriented interaction as possible, without using menus or similar abstract constructs.

This chapter reports on some of the most innovative VR software applications we have created at Calit2. We are going to present one application from each of the following five topic areas:

- VR technology: Orthogonal developments of algorithms which do not stand alone, but are used in conjunction with other applications.

- Scientific visualization: The visualization of data sets which have inherent 3D structure, so that the mapping of data to the three spatial dimensions and sometimes also time is given.

- Real-time data visualization: The real-time visualization of data acquired by sensors and sent over networks.

- Information visualization: The visualization of data sets which do not have inherent 3D structure, where the mapping of data to the three spatial dimensions and time has to be created artificially and sometimes dynamically by the user.
- Cultural heritage: Applications aiming at preserving or investigating objects and places of a country's cultural heritage.

2. Virtual Reality Technology

In this section, we report on a project in which we created software infrastructure which can be used by other VR applications. The project enables high-resolution video display in multiscreen VR environments. The video can coexist with other 3D data, so that it can be mapped on other geometry such as virtual screens or buildings.

2.1 High-Resolution Video Playback in Immersive Virtual Environments

Today, most new feature films, TV shows and documentaries, and a rapidly growing number of home and professional videos are shot in HD. The most popular HD resolutions are 720 pixel (1280×720 pixels) and 1080 pixel (1920×1080 pixels). In addition to HD, there is the new digital cinema standard, called "4K," which describes resolutions from exactly four times HD (3840×2160 pixels) up to 4096×2400 pixels. While no cameras exist for even higher resolution video, it can be created by stitching together video from lower resolution cameras, or it can be rendered in the computer.

Real-time graphics applications, such as computer games and VR applications, often embed video in their virtual worlds. Examples could be a computer game which intends to realistically visualize Times Square in New York City with its video screens, or an architectural walk-through of a 3D model of a movie theater with a movie playing (see Fig. 4), or a surveillance system with many camera feeds. Integrating video into 3D applications can increase the level of realism, and it can bring important information into the virtual world.

Because of the large data rate of high-resolution video, easily exceeding hard disk throughput rates, it is not straightforward to display high-resolution video in real time. Playing back HD video is already CPU and GPU intensive for today's computers, even when it is displayed on a 2D monitor with software like Windows Media Player or Apple QuickTime. While these video players benefit from hard-wired, optimized circuits on the graphics card and special operating system routines,

FIG. 4. The video playback plugin embedded into a virtual theater VR application. Users can navigate into the theater and watch high-resolution videos. The virtual theater application renders 201,688 polygons.

3D applications which display video in a virtual 3D world cannot benefit from these optimizations because the video is not aligned with the screen.

Our approach limits the video source to prerecorded material, because we apply a non-real-time preprocessing step to the data. Our algorithm can display HD and 4K video, and even higher resolutions as well in a 3D virtual environment, where the video's projection on the screen is not rectangular, but a general quadrangle whose shape depends on the viewing angle and the orientation of the virtual screen plane with respect to the physical display. Shape and location of this quadrangle change as the tracked user moves around. Our algorithm is based on mipmapping [6] and tiling (clip mapping [7]) of the video frames, on top of which we add several optimizations to maintain a constant frame rate. Mipmapping means that we render the video at as low a resolution as possible, matching or slightly exceeding the physical display resolution. This minimizes the data bandwidth during playback. Predictive prefetching of data further enhances the performance of our system. Our approach is entirely software-based and only assumes a more recent graphics card. Our demonstration algorithm is based on the VR framework COVISE and OpenSceneGraph [8]. Besides high resolutions, our algorithm supports the simultaneous rendering of multiple video streams, each of which can be independently positioned within the virtual world.

2.1.1   Related Work

Tiling and mipmapping have often been combined [9–14]. An important variable in mipmapping is how the appropriate mipmap level is selected. Two approaches are commonly used: one that matches the screen resolution as closely as possible across the entire screen and one that uses a point of interest to use higher resolution around the point of interest. LaMar et al. [9] constructed a spatial data structure, a quadtree, to store multiresolution data sets. The generation of a proper level-of-detail is determined by two factors: (1) the distance from view point p to a tile and (2) the area a tile covers in projected space. Given point p, a tile is selected if the distance from the center of the tile to p is greater than the length of the diagonal of the tile. As the projection transformation matrix transforms objects closer to p to appear larger and those further from p smaller, data points closest to the view point have the highest resolution.

Blockbuster [15] is a movie player for high-resolution videos, which runs on tiled display walls under the DMX (Distributed Xinerama) window manager. It plays movies in Lawrence Livermore National Labs' SM format, which supports tiled images, multiple levels of detail, and several types of intraframe image compression. The main difference to our approach is that Blockbuster assumes a flat display wall and renders the video parallel to the screens.

2.1.2   System Overview

DVDs are meant to be played at a constant frame rate: 60 interlaced frames per second in the NTSC standard. The frame rate for digital cinema is typically 24 frames per second. We refer to these frame rates as the *video frame rate*, with every frame being a *video frame*. We assume the video frame rate to be constant and only to vary between different video clips.

In interactive computer graphics applications, each frame, which we call an *image frame*, typically takes differently long to render, depending on how complex the scene is. This *image frame rate* is not variable.

Our video display algorithm needs to solve the problem of rendering a video at a variable image frame rate. Our strategy is that if rendering an image frame takes longer than the duration of a video frame, we skip video frames as needed to play the video at a constant pace, which is a requirement for synchronization with audio, and it keeps natural motions at their natural pace. If rendering an image is faster than the duration of a video frame, we display the same video frame again in the next image frame.

2.1.2.1   Bandwidth Considerations.   An uncompressed 4K video clip of 10 min at 24 frames per second uses more than 400 GB of disk space. The bandwidth required to load the entire video easily exceeds the

performance limit of even today's high-end PCs. However, our VR display systems rarely need to render the entire video at full resolution, because the video extends across multiple screens and the physical resolution of an individual screen is often much lower than 8 megapixels. Our approach optimizes the loading bandwidth by loading only those mipmap tiles which are actually going to be rendered.

2.1.2.2 Multiple Instances.
One goal we had for our algorithm is the ability to display multiple video streams concurrently and also to display 3D geometry along with the videos. For instance, we want to be able to display a virtual surveillance center with a control room which displays a multitude of videos. This requires that our algorithm uses a reduced amount of memory for each video stream, depending on how many streams there are and how much bandwidth they require, so that it can coexist with the other video streams, as well as the rendering of the 3D geometry.

2.1.3 Software Design

Figure 5 shows the main components of our system. The *video playback renderer* cooperates with three other components: *frame manager*, *mipmapped tile manager*, and *LOD mesh generator*. *Frame manager* controls which image frame has to be rendered at a given time to synchronize with the video frame rate. *Mipmapped tile manager* manages a large number of tiles. It first loads metainformation for all tiles, and whenever the renderer requests a tile for metadata or texture data, it returns all the necessary data to the renderer. Due to the typically large size of these videos, it is

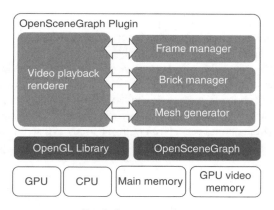

Fig. 5. System overview.

impossible to load all data into main memory at once. Thus, the *mipmapped tile manager* swaps requested tiles into main memory and then texture memory and removes the expired tiles. The decision about cache eviction is also made here. *Mesh generator* computes the best possible LOD for each region of the playback screen so that the smallest possible amount of data is copied into the texture, which utilizes memory resources and bandwidth more efficiently. We integrated the renderer and its accompanying three components into an OpenSceneGraph plugin for the COV-ISE software.

2.1.4   Rendering Algorithm

The rendering algorithm for a video stream consists of four steps: (1) mesh generation, (2) data loading, (3) prefetching, and (4) tile rendering. This routine is called once for every image frame, and it gets as its input the image frame to render from the frame manager. The mesh generation algorithm is presented in Section 2.1.6, and data loading and prefetching are discussed in Section 2.1.7. Once the algorithm completes mesh generation and data loading, it is ready for rendering the tiles. The final step is to iterate over the tiles which have to be rendered in the current image frame to draw them with their corresponding texture data.

2.1.5   Mipmap Generation and Tiling

In our approach, we preprocess the video frames in an off-line step. First, we extract the frames from the video clip. Then we downsample these frames to a set of consecutively smaller images by downsizing by 50% at every step, until the size is smaller or equal to an empirically determined tile size.

Figure 6 shows the layout of the tiles, which are stored in separate TIFF files. An image is divided into a 2D grid, and the origin of the grid is shown at the bottom left. Tiles at the rightmost column and at the topmost row are padded with zeros so that all tiles have a uniform size. Using a uniform size simplifies the rendering process.

2.1.6   Mesh Generation

The first step of rendering is to subdivide the playback screen into a set of tiles, which we call the mesh. The mesh comprises multiple tiles of different mipmap levels. The goal of subdividing the screen is to allocate the best possible mipmap level to each region with a limited number of tiles overall, because the number of tiles determines the amount of data to be loaded from disk or network.

We render areas closer to the viewer at higher resolution than those farther away. Rendering at lower resolution does not hurt the overall image quality because, after

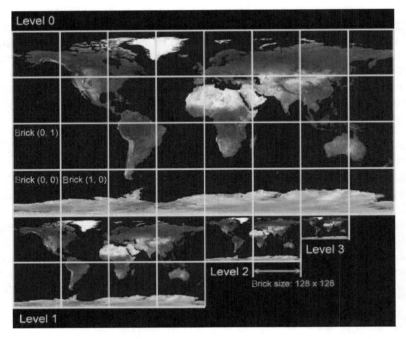

Fɪɢ. 6. Layout of tiles at multiple mipmap levels. The image is from NASA's Blue Marble data set [16].

perspective projection, the tiles farther from the viewer occupy fewer pixels on the screen, and the downsampled mipmap texture is still detailed enough to render this tile correctly without a noticeable change of the image quality. Our algorithm is based on quadtree traversal. Starting from the root node, which is the maximum mipmap level of the image, the algorithm checks whether or not the tile visited can be subdivided further. The area, *area(b)*, of tile *b* after transformations, that is, model view, perspective projection and viewport transformation, is used in the decision rule for the subdivision. Let *tileSize* denote the size of a tile. Then, if one tile of a certain mipmap level occupies about *tileSize* × *tileSize* pixels on viewport screen, the subdivision of this tile cannot further improve the image quality of the region. In virtual environments, the decision rule can be relaxed by adding a constant value α as follows:

$$area(b) > \alpha \times tileSize \times tileSize \qquad (1)$$

where α can be any float value larger than 1. The algorithm subdivides a tile if Predicate 1 is true and stops if false. The constant α controls how detailed the image is rendered. If α is 1, the texel to pixel ratio of the rendered tiles is near 1. However, a large α makes the mesh algorithm stop the subdivision even if 1 texel of each tile maps to more than 1 pixel, which creates an image of lower resolution. α is introduced to control the system between high frame rate and the best image quality.

Another variable, *tileLimit*, controls the number of tiles to be rendered on a physical display screen. Tiles in the output list grow exponentially along the traversal of the quadtree. However, *tileLimit* guarantees that the rendering system does not have excessively many tiles on the rendering list. The ideal number for *tileLimit* is different from hardware configurations, and a realistic number often used is around 40×128^2 tiles. That is, 40 tiles on one display screen correspond to $40 \times 128 \times 128$ texels, which is about 640K texels.

With *tileLimit*, not all tiles can have the most desired mipmap level. Some tiles still can be subdivided into four smaller tiles to have higher resolution. Our algorithm, therefore, has to rank all tiles so that it can choose one tile among multiple possible choices of tiles given the bounded *tileLimit* value. In order to give priorities to each tile, a cost function is employed as follows:

$$cost(b) = \frac{area(b)}{distance(e, b)} \qquad (2)$$

cost(b) denotes the cost for tile *b* and *distance(e, b)* measures the distance between the viewer's location and the center of tile *b*. The viewer's location is given by the tracking position in the VE. Intuitively, tiles occupying a large area on screen have higher priorities so that no large tiles of low resolution are left on the list. The denominator, *distance(e, b)*, gives higher priority to tiles closer to the viewer. Namely, this term provides a point of interest mechanism; as the viewer walks toward a specific part of the playback screen, the region around the viewer is set to higher resolution.

Figure 7 shows an example of a mesh generated by our rendering algorithm. The image plane is tilted in such a way that the bottom right corner of the plane is closer to the viewer. Tiles around the bottom right corner have a smaller size, which results in a higher resolution.

Due to the viewer's constant movement registered by the head tracker, *distance (e, b)* returns updated and normally different values than in the last image frame. This generally does not allow reusing the mesh generated for the previous frame, so we have to recompute the mesh for every image frame. Our view frustum culling test reduces the cost of the quadtree traversal by removing offscreen mesh cells. The quadtree optimizes this process by culling a culled parent's child nodes along with it.

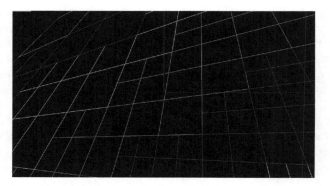

Fɪɢ. 7. Dynamically generated multiresolution tiled 2D volume.

Therefore, when the video is very large and spans multiple physical displays, a large portion of the quadtree is getting culled. As the video gets smaller, the traversal does not need to go down the quadtree as far anymore. This approach keeps the number of tiles rendered relatively constant.

2.1.7   Data Loading and Prefetching

The next step is to load the texture data from disk. Loading several megabytes of video data from disk as well as transferring them to texture memory for every frame slows down the rendering process as the bandwidth for data reads from hard disk is much lower than others in the system. We implemented three optimization methods to mitigate the disk bottleneck: prefetching, asynchronous disk I/O, and DXT compression.

2.1.7.1   Prefetching.   When videos are displayed in the StarCAVE, users either walk around the scene without paying particular attention to the videos, or they stop to watch a video clip. Even if they stop, there is always a slight change of the viewer position due to head tracking, but it is much smaller than when the user walks around. Therefore, our algorithm optimizes for a stationary viewer, for whom we found that mipmap meshes differ only by about four tiles.

Another issue is to predict the video frame from which the tiles are to be prefetched. After rendering video frame n, with n being the index of the video frame on disk, we calculate the next video frame to be displayed to be $(n+k)$. This means that we skip video frames $(n+1)$ to $(n+k-1)$. At every rendering step, k has to be estimated as correctly as possible, or the system will prefetch unnecessary tiles.

Again, we adopted a simple, computationally light scheme based on reinforcement learning [17]. We estimate the next frame by looking at the history of image frame durations. If the system has been skipping, for instance, every other video frame, we estimate that in the next image frame we are going to skip a video frame again. More formally, let A_n denote the current estimate of how many frames the system will skip and a_n be the current observation of the skip. Then, the next estimation of A_{n+1} is the weighted average between A_n and a_n.

$$A_{n+1} = \alpha a_n + (1 - \alpha)A_n$$

where α is a parameter representing how fast the algorithm adapts to new information a_n as opposed to the history A_n. We use the rounded values of A_n for the estimation of how many steps to skip. In order to further improve the accuracy, the $(n+k-1)$th and $(n+k+1)$th frames are also prefetched. The number of tiles prefetched is conservatively kept low, from one to four tiles, to prevent prefetching from generating too much load for the entire system and to utilize only the idle time of the I/O thread without delaying immediate requests from the rendering process even in the case of misprediction.

2.1.7.2 *Asynchronous Disk I/O.* In order to accelerate data transfers between main memory and texture memory, a separate thread is dedicated to asynchronous disk read operations. Every disk read request is sent to the I/O thread via a message queue and the I/O thread reads data whenever it finds a message in the queue. There are two queues: a tile request queue and a prefetch request queue. The tile request queue contains the request from the main thread, which is for texture data of a tile that is needed to render the current frame. The prefetch request queue contains requests for texture data of a tile which will be needed in the near future. The messages from the tile request queue always have a priority over the messages from the prefetch request queue. In addition, the request for data loading is made as soon as the main thread finds a tile which will be needed for rendering. By posting disk read requests as early as possible, the parallelism between the rendering process and disk operations can be maximized. Another message used for communication between the main thread and the disk read thread forwards the current frame number.

2.1.7.3 *DXT Compression.* DXT is a lossy compression standard which allows us to reduce the data rate by a factor of four, without a noticeable loss of image quality. This compression method works well for video because, due to the quick frame updates, it is hard for the eye to perceive the compression artifacts.

2.1.8   Synchronization

The time for rendering an image frame varies between frames, mostly depending on the number of tiles loaded for each frame. This causes two types of synchronization problems: synchronization (1) between frames and (2) between StarCAVE nodes. The first problem is that, without a synchronization scheme, the video frame rate changes depending on how many tiles are rendered for the frame, which varies depending on the viewer's location.

The second synchronization problem occurs because in a multinode virtual environment all nodes generally have different workloads and cause an imbalance in rendering times. For those display nodes that do not render much data, the rendering time is short, whereas other nodes might need more time for an image frame update than the video frame rate allows for, so that video frames have to be skipped. In our StarCAVE system, which consists of 17 rendering nodes, we update the images on all nodes at the same time, so that the update rate is equal to the image frame rate of the slowest node.

Our software provides a synchronized time which is the same on all nodes. Using this clock, we measure the time passed since the start of rendering the first frame, t_{elapsed}. Then, the desired video frame number, d, can be easily computed with the following formula for a 24-frames per second video clip:

$$d = d_{\text{base}} + \left\lceil \frac{t_{\text{elapsed}}}{1/24} \right\rceil$$

d_{base} denotes the frame number of the first frame. d_{base} will change when a video stream is paused and later continued. This approach solves the two problems because the above formula enforces frames to change neither too fast nor too slow, which solves the first problem, and because t_{elapsed} is measured from the globally synchronized clock, which is the solution for the second synchronization problem.

2.1.9   Results

We tested three different videos in the StarCAVE. We distributed the entire video to the local hard disks of the rendering nodes to avoid network bottlenecks. We used three different video clips: (1) A 1200 frame 4K clip showing a tornado simulation created by the National Center for Supercomputing Applications (NCSA); (2) The same tornado clip at a quarter of its original resolution; (3) A set of 24 microscopy images (14914×10341 pixels) from the National Center for Microscopy and Imaging Research (NCMIR). We preprocessed each of the video clips with our tiling and mipmapping tool and used a tile size of 512×512 pixels. Each display panel has full HD 1080 pixel resolution. Figure 8 shows the tornado clip in the StarCAVE.

Fig. 8. The VR video playback application in the StarCAVE with creator Han Suk Kim.

Table I shows the frame rates for various settings. Because the StarCAVE displays stereoscopic images, the frame rate here is defined as the time to render two images. Note that right eye images are rendered faster than left eye images, because they are rendered second and can thus benefit from the cached tiles loaded for the left eye. All measurements were averaged over a full playback cycle of each clip.

2.1.10 Conclusion

We showed and discussed the design and implementation of high-resolution video textures in virtual environments. In order to achieve a constant video frame rate, we created multiple levels of detail and dynamically subdivide the video into a set of tiles with different levels of detail. For efficient disk read operations, we assume that the plane will not change too much between image frames and prefetch tiles for the next frame. This helps overlap rendering with texture copying. In addition, synchronization was considered to sync the speed of rendering image frames and the video frame rate. Our experiments showed that our system provides constant frame rates and usable video playback performance.

TABLE I
FRAME RATES FROM THREE DIFFERENT VIDEO SOURCES

Video clip	2K Video 1920 × 1080			4K Video 3840 × 2160			Microscopy 12,941 × 10,341		
Configuration	Opt	No opt	LOD	Opt	No opt	LOD	Opt	No opt	LOD
2 × 2 panels	23.7	7.5	44.2	9.4	2.7	26.0	8.9	2.8	26.7
Single panels	20.4	5.0	59.6	18.0	4.9	45.1	21.8	6.1	58.4

Frame rate (frames per second) is the reciprocal of the time to render two images (stereoscopic image from left and right eye) and is averaged over a full playback cycle of each clip. We tested video playback on four (2 × 2) panels and on a single panel.

3. Scientific Visualization

Scientific visualization is the general term for almost all of the visualization projects we do at Calit2. This section reports on a very typical, albeit particularly sophisticated application we developed in close collaboration with scientists at UCSD. It is also our most successful application in a sense of how many scientists have used it for real work.

3.1 ImmersivePDB: A Protein Browser

To offer a new way of looking at molecular structure, we created a VR application to view data sets of the Protein Data Bank (PDB) [18] from the Research Collaboratory for Structural Bioinformatics (RCSB). The application can display the 3D macromolecular structures from the PDB in any of our virtual environments. Using the program ImmersivePDB, the viewer can move through and around a structure projected in VR. Structures can be compared to one another, they can be automatically aligned, and a variety of visualization modes can be selected from. The software has an interface that makes a connection to the RCSB PDB Web site to download and display files. Both single user and collaborative modes are supported.

To our knowledge, ImmersivePDB is the most fully featured protein browser for virtual environments, which is fully controllable from within the 3D world. In other approaches, for instance, PyMOL's [19] CAVE module, the virtual environment is only used to view and navigate the protein structures, but all other interaction like selecting the visualization mode, etc. is done at the head node in a 2D mouse/keyboard-controlled application.

3.1.1   Data Bank Access

The PDB currently contains over 60,000 protein structures, each of which has a unique, four-letter identifier. For hemoglobin, for instance, the identifier is 4HHB. The user can specify the protein ID in one of two ways: either during a VR session with the Loader window, or in the COVISE configuration file to add a preset menu item for the structure (Fig. 9).

Once the user selects a PDB ID, the system first checks the local cache for the PDB file. If the file is already in the cache, it will not be downloaded or converted to VRML again. If the file is not in the cache, it will be downloaded from the PDB server to the local visualization system with the following command line for hemoglobin:

```
wget www.pdb.org/pdb/files/4HHB.pdb
```

After the download, the file will automatically be converted to three visual representations: cartoon view, stick view, and surface view. All three representations will be stored on disk as VRML files. The conversion happens using a Python script which calls functions of the molecular visualization toolkit PyMOL [19]. The script is called with the following command:

```
pymol.exe -qcr batch.py -- 4HHB.pdb
```

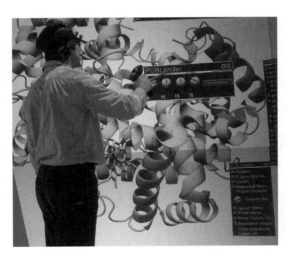

Fig. 9. A StarCAVE user dialing the PDB ID for hemoglobin into the ImmersivePDB loader window.

This command calls the following Python script to create three VRML files for the three supported visual representations.

```
from pymol import cmd
from pymol import preset
from pymol import util
from glob import glob
import sys
import os
path = ""
params = []
basepath = os. getcwd ()
try:
index = sys. argv. index ("--")
params = sys. argv [index:]
if (len(params) == 2):
path = params [1]
cmd. cd (path)
else:
print "No Path specified"
except ValueError:
print "No Path specified"
for file in glob ("*.pdb"):
listname = file. split (".")
name = listname[0];
cmd. load(file, name)
cmd. hide ("all")
cmd. show("sticks")
cmd. save (name + "stix.wrl")
cmd. hide ("all")
preset. pretty(name)
cmd. save (name + "cart. wrl")
cmd. hide ("all")
cmd. show ("surface")
cmd. save (name +"surf. wrl")
cmd. delete ("all")
cmd. system ("rm -f"+ file)
print "Created " + name + " models"
cmd. cd(basepath)
```

3.1.2   Protein Morphs

In addition to proteins from the PDB, our system can visualize protein morphs from the Morph Server of the Database of Macromolecular Movements (Molmovdb) at Yale University. For instance, the calcium pump will be downloaded with the following command line:

```
wget -np www.molmovdb.org/tmp/396506-12995.tar.gz
```

Once the tar file has been downloaded, the time steps will be extracted as PDB files. The PDB files will be processed by the same PyMOL script as individual structures. The resulting VRML files will be loaded into an OpenSceneGraph Switch node, so that by switching through the time step models, the system can animate the morph.

3.1.3   Visualization Modes

Our PDB viewer supports three visualization modes for protein structures: cartoon, stick and surface. These can be selected from a VR menu which comes up when the user right clicks on a protein.

Our system is not limited to displaying one protein at a time. Instead, whenever the user loads a protein, it will be loaded in addition to what has already been loaded and displayed. Each protein can be moved around in 3D space independently, so the user can arrange many proteins around him to compare them or explore their differences.

When it comes to selecting a protein with the input device, we use a special selection mode for the proteins. Normally, in our VR system, users select objects with a virtual laser pointer or stick, by intersecting the pointer with an object. However, in the case of proteins, this is more difficult because the proteins are not solid objects, but they have rather large open areas in between the carbon chains. Hence, the user will often point at the protein without actually intersecting its geometry. We solved this problem by not intersecting with the geometry, but instead intersect with the protein's bounding box. We call the data structure, we use for this selection, the PickBox. Every protein is loaded into its own PickBox, so that the user can select individual proteins when multiple are loaded.

Once multiple proteins are loaded into the system, the user can choose to either lay them out manually by moving them to where the user wants them, or an automatic layout manager can be selected from a VR menu. We offer two different layouts: grid layout, which arranges the proteins in an array, or cylinder layout, where the proteins are arranged around the user on a virtual cylinder (e.g., Fig. 10). Radius and density of proteins on the cylinder are configurable.

3.1.4   Gradual Fading Between Visualization Modes

In some situations, the user wants to switch between two or all three protein visualization modes we support (cartoon, surface, stick). This can either be done manually, but checking selecting the respective boxes in the property sheet of the protein. Or, this can be done automatically as follows. If automatic mode is selected, the software will switch automatically between the selected visualization modes, based on the user's distance from the protein. Switches between modes do not occur suddenly, but the modes are faded in and out gradually, as the user moves. This, for instance, will allow the user to select surface and cartoon mode, and then gradually fade between them by moving closer to the protein, in which case it fades to cartoon mode, or farther away, and it will fade to surface mode. The parameters for this mode, for instance, the starting distance for the fade and the distance by which the visualization mode has fully switched to the next, are user configurable.

FIG. 10. Cylinder layout mode: all proteins are equally spaced on the surface of an invisible cylinder around the user.

3.1.5   Collaborative Mode

The software framework we use for the development of our application proto-types, COVISE, natively supports collaboration between multiple sites. Custom applications written for COVISE can utilize the collaboration API to support collaborative modes within the application. We used this API to make our ImmersivePDB application collaborative, which means that we can run instances of it at multiple sites (there is no theoretical limit to the number of supported sites) and collaboratively view protein structures.

COVISE will automatically offer three collaboration modes: loose, tight, and master/slave mode. In loose mode, the collaborators can view a data set independently, which means that they all look at the same data set, but their camera positions are independent from one another. In tight mode, all users share the same camera view. In master/slave mode, they also share the same camera view, but one user's camera motion dominates over the others. This is useful in training situations where the trainees should not be able to modify the instructor's view. In loose coupling mode, each user can see the other user positions indicated by a set of 3D glasses, a checkerboard pattern with an optional institutional logo where the user's feet are, and a 3D model of a hand with a pointer. This simple indication of an avatar for the collaborators shows what they look at and point to, which is useful when an audio connection is available to the collaborators as well.

Collaborative mode does not require particularly fast network connections. Even standard internet is normally fast enough for smooth collaboration. The bandwidth requirements are minimal, because only the user locations are sent over the network. Protein data sets need to be stored locally in each collaborator's cache, or downloaded from the PDB when a protein is selected.

Figure 11 shows a collaborative session between our booth at the International Supercomputer Conference (ISC) 2010 in Hamburg, Germany and our collaborators at King Abdullah University of Science and Technology (KAUST) in Saudi Arabia.

3.1.6   Amino Acid Sequence Browser

The amino acid browser is a dialog window in the virtual world, which lists all the amino acid chains of the selected protein structure in textual form. The user can interact with it in two ways: one is that the user can select a specific amino acid in the dialog window, and upon selection see where in the protein, the corresponding molecule is located, indicated by a cone-shaped marker. This also works the other way around: the user can move the marker to a place in the protein to find the place in the amino acid sequence it corresponds to.

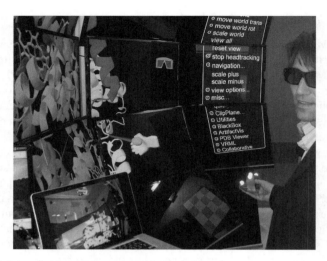

F<small>IG</small>. 11. Collaboration between two sites. Monitor in front shows video of collaborator's virtual environment at KAUST University. Stereo goggles, hand with pointer, and checkerboard pattern indicate collaborator's location in virtual world.

3.1.7 Alignment

The alignment of protein structures helps scientists understand the differences between them and is an important tool for them. The VR environment is very useful for the presentation of aligned proteins because it is easier to see the differences between two aligned proteins in 3D than in 2D, since the aligned offsets between the proteins generally occur in all three dimensions.

We integrated the multiple structural alignment program MAMMOTH-mult algorithm [20] into ImmersivePDB. In order to align two proteins, the user first selects Alignment Mode and loads the two proteins he wants to align. Their IDs will then be listed in a window, and copies of them are created and put on the alignment point interactor, a small cube the user can move to a convenient place to put the aligned proteins. The proteins copied to the alignment point are being colored in solid colors, with different colors for each protein, so that it is easy to distinguish them. These colors are user selectable. The alignment itself happens almost instantaneously and, in our experience, never takes longer than a few seconds.

3.1.8 TOPSAN Integration

The Open Protein Structure Annotation Network (TOPSAN) is an open annotation platform, created to provide a way for scientists to share their knowledge about functions and roles of proteins in their respective organisms. Researchers can add comments to the data bank through a Deki Wiki interface.

Whenever a structure is loaded by the user, ImmersivePDB connects to the TOPSAN server to see if information about the structure is available. If so, this information will be downloaded to the VR viewer and displayed in a floating window (see Fig. 12).

3.1.9 Conclusions

The ImmersivePDB application has been our oldest, but also our most "polished" and most used VR application. Researchers from the campus of UCSD, but also from other universities in Southern California, come to our laboratory to explore their protein structures interactively in 3D. They have told us time and again that they often see features of protein structures which they did not see at the desktop, and they develop a better understanding of the way these proteins function than by using monitor and mouse.

Fig. 12. TOPSAN creator Sri Krishna Subramanian with the ImmersivePDB team in the StarCAVE.

4. Real-Time Data Visualization

In this section, we are going to present an application which is based on real-time sensor input. Real-time sensor data is more and more available globally over the internet, so that monitoring and data processing tools based on these sensors do not have to be colocated with the sensors, but can be located where the users are.

4.1 The Virtual Data Center

In project GreenLight [21], which has been funded by the National Science Foundation (NSF) with $2 million over 3 years, researchers at Calit2 purchased and then populated a Sun Modular Datacenter (Sun MD [22]) with computing, storage, and networking hardware to measure the energy usage of computing systems under real-world conditions. The container can accommodate up to 280 servers, with an eco-friendly design that can reduce cooling costs by up to 40% when compared to traditional server rooms. The Sun MD's closed-loop water-cooling system uses built-in heat exchanges between equipment racks to channel air flow. This allows the unit to cool 25 kW per rack, roughly five times the cooling capacity of typical data centers.

The power consumption of each component in the Sun MD container is constantly being measured by networked Avocent power strips, and the data is sent to a central server. The measurements include data from temperature sensors in 40 locations around the container, to study the energy flow through the system. The goal of project GreenLight is to learn how computer hardware and software can be made more energy efficient. Early results for computer graphics hardware and software are already available [23]. In the following sections, we are going to report on the technical details of the implementation of our virtual reality monitoring application in greater detail.

4.1.1 3D Model

To help researchers understand power consumption and temperature distribution in the Sun MD container, we developed a 3D model of the Sun MD to visualize these measurements spatially. The 3D model, which is depicted in Fig. 13, is based on a CAD model of the data center from Sun Microsystems. To this, we added 3D models of the installed computer systems, such as servers, network switches, and storage systems. The model of the data center is a complete replica of the container, which allows the user to open the doors, enter the container, and pull out the computer racks, all by directly interacting with the 3D objects in VR. We even included a few

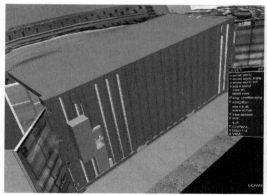

Fɪɢ. 13. Our 3D model of the Sun Mobile Data Center. Left: Bird's eye view. Right: View from the front in the StarCAVE.

dynamic elements like spinning fans and conduits which move with the racks when they get pulled out, to make the model as realistic as possible. We embedded the 3D model of the container in an aerial image of the campus of UCSD, where we placed it in the location it was physically installed. Around the container, we display a cylindrical view of the surrounding area, so that when the user is located at the container, the view around resembles what it is in reality. This is similar to the panoramic view "bubbles" Google Earth's Streetview mode uses.

We created the 3D model of the container and its content with Autodesk 3ds Max, which we also used for many of the interactive components. 3ds Max allows to connect VRML TouchSensors to geometry, which provide a way to trigger Java-Script code when the user clicks on them. JavaScript controls all interactions which cause geometry displacement in the model, such as doors which open or racks which get pulled out. Other interactions, such as the selection of individual components, were implemented in C++, referencing geometry in the container. In order to reference this geometry correctly, we use a common scheme of unique names for the geometry of the scene between the 3ds Max model and the VR application.

The VR application was created as a plugin for the VR software framework COVISE [4], which we use for the development of most of our VR applications. COVISE uses the OpenSceneGraph library [8] for its graphics subsystem. We exported the 3ds Max model with COVISE's own VRML exporter to a .wrl file. Our COVISE plugin loads that VRML file and adds its geometry to the scene graph. In addition to the static model of the container, this file also contains the touch sensor nodes with their associated JavaScript functions to control animation.

Our VR application connects via Web services to the central data server [24], which collects and stores the real-time information from the different types of sensors in the container and retrieves the status of the container in real time. Once received, this data is stored in XML files on our visualization server. We then parse these files to extract the sensor data to display in the VR model. Figure 14 shows two examples of how the instrumented components in the container are displayed using different colors depending on the type of measurement selected. For instance, when looking at temperature data, the components in the container may be depicted in red to indicate a high temperature, and green when they are running cool. This gives the user a quick overview of the state of the devices in the container. We implemented this functionality with an OpenSceneGraph node visitor, which traverses only the part of the scene graph with the computer components and changes their material properties depending on the measured data values. The connection between the data values and the geometry is established by the unique naming scheme mentioned above.

Our 3D application allows a user to visit the data center in VR, without having to physically go to the container. This saves on transportation cost and time but also has further reaching consequences—by allowing technicians and researchers to view the status of the container without having to go there, open it and thus allowing the cool air to escape from it, the measurements will not be interrupted. Many routine maintenance jobs, such as checks for available space, the status of a component, or repairs, can be avoided or at least optimized this way.

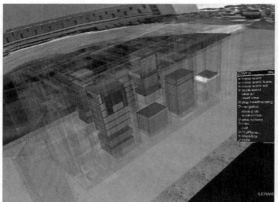

Fig. 14. Left: Bird's eye view of the container with translucent walls, using the same camera perspective as in Fig. 13. Right: The container displayed in the StarCAVE.

The main purpose of the virtual container is to allow scientists who measure the power consumption and performance of their algorithms, to view these measurements spatially. The virtual environment can give clues on whether one hardware component affects another by, for instance, blowing warm air into the other machine's air intake, in which case that machine might run warmer than it would without the hot machine. These side effects can be much more easily detected in a spatial model of the hardware components than in the Web interface. The 3D visualization application can also be used for educational purposes or to reduce maintenance times, by indicating to technicians, the hardware that exhibits problems.

4.1.2 Data Visualization

One result of our research on how to effectively display the data from the GreenLight instrument is about the display of this data in the 3D model. Whereas we first implemented a method to display the data as 2D graphs, which we displayed in the 3D environment, we found that this method made it hard to associate the graph with a certain component in the container, even if the component was highlighted. Also, only a limited number of graphs can be displayed at the same time. Therefore, we decided to put the information about the devices directly on their visual representation by coloring their surface with an appropriate color scheme. This approach makes it harder to see small differences in the data because it is hard to distinguish small differences in color; however, it allows the state of all the hardware to be displayed in the container at once.

Our visualization method of coloring the components in the container led to implementation of the "X-ray mode." Originally, all of the geometry of the container and its components was opaque, so the user had to pull out the computer racks to see the components; this was cumbersome and did not allow simultaneous viewing of all devices. Making the noninstrumented geometry in the container translucent, allowed for simultaneous viewing of all the instrumented geometry, without the need for moving racks. The user is allowed to switch between opaque and X-ray mode because it is sometimes useful to see the container the way it looks in reality, for example, technicians can train for where to find defective components and how to get to them. The user of the interactive system can choose which types of IT components should be selected: all components in the container; or only a subset: switches, storage systems, rack PCs; PC towers; or other components.

During our research and development of the virtual data center, we found that the configuration of the components in the container changes quite frequently, mostly when new components are added and old ones get replaced. Previously, our human 3D modeler updated the 3D model with a CAD tool to represent the new configuration of devices, and in addition, the sensor data was remapped to reflect these changes. To allow a system administrator without 3D modeling skills to make these changes, and to make them much faster, a database was implemented to describe the configuration of the devices in the container. This approach allows devices to be added, moved, and removed quickly and easily without the need for a 3D modeling tool. The 3D modeling tool is still needed when new types of devices are added to the container for which a 3D model has not yet been created.

4.1.3 Conclusions

We presented a visualization tool to view live data from a Web server, mapped onto geometry in a virtual 3D replica of Calit2's mobile data center. This approach allows users to easily view the data acquired by the power consumption sensors in the data center, and it shows clearly where exactly the hardware is installed. This can reduce the amount of in-person visits to the data center, which can play an important role if the data center is located far away from the scientists and engineers using it.

The current version of the interactive software application leaves various things to be desired. In the future, we plan to use the virtual environment not only to view the state of our data center, but also to actively control it. This will require the addition of a data path back to the data center, along with access control mechanisms, but it will be a very intuitive, yet powerful way to administer a data center. We also plan to install additional sensors to be able to obtain a more accurate spatial map of the temperature distribution in the Sun MD. This will help optimize the spatial arrangement of the IT devices in the container to minimize the HVAC requirements.

5. Information Visualization

This section showcases an application designed to display data in VR which does not have inherent 2D or 3D structure. This type of data visualization is often called "information visualization." The challenge of this type of data is to find effective mappings from the multidimensional data domain to the three spatial dimensions in VR systems, as well as time which can sometimes be used as a fourth, independent dimension. We also utilize the unique features of VR, such as 3D stereo, immersion, surround, high-resolution screens, head tracking, and 3D input, to make the higher-dimensional data set more accessible.

5.1   How Much Information

Data is being created at exponentially increasing rates, driven in part by the decreasing costs and increasing number of embedded processors sold each year. Stories abound of scientific data streams are not analyzed due to lack of time. Commercial enterprises have for decades collected operating data in manufacturing, sales, and elsewhere that they were unable to analyze further.

In an attempt to exploit this profusion of data, enterprises now invest in "Business Intelligence" (BI) capability. This typically includes a data warehouse with the ability to retrieve data very flexibly, and software to search for patterns and trends, both by machine learning and by assisting human analysts. This "data analytics" software, however, is primarily still based on old models of information presentation, such as spreadsheets.

The plunging cost of digital hardware now enables alternative ways of presenting and interacting with information. Office workers have access to hardware more powerful than engineering workstations a decade ago; megapixel color displays driven by powerful 3D graphics cards (hundreds of parallel processors running at speeds > 1 GHz [25]) and attached to terabyte storage now add less than \$1000 to the cost of an office computer.

Our research project looks beyond the current desktop environment, to what will be available in a few years. Falling costs should enable dramatically new interfaces. However, application-level analytic software is moving only slowly to take advantage of these interfaces. We therefore built prototypes of an application for visual analytics for the StarCAVE, building on the following key features of it: 3d graphics, stereo vision, 360° surround projection, and user head tracking. Our hypothesis is that immersive VR systems can display complex nonspatial data more effectively than 2D monitors. While we have yet to do a formal user study on this hypothesis, others did similar studies [26] and found that 3D visualization can have measurable benefits over 2D visualization.

The StarCAVE costs approximately \$1 million when it was built in 2007. Commercial off-the-shelf versions of most of its components, albeit with significantly lower resolution and less immersion, are now accessible for a few thousand dollars per screen. An example of such a system is the NexCAVE.

5.1.1   Nonspatial Data

The StarCAVE and other VR systems have generally been used for scientific data, and particularly data with a natural spatial layout. Examples include the data sets used in the rest of this chapter, as well as architectural models, machine parts, medical CT and MRI data, or simulation results of blood flow in arteries. It is natural to show such data in 3D space, because the mapping from data values to 3D coordinates is inherent in the underlying problem.

However, with other kinds of scientific problems, and for most enterprise problems, the data does not have a natural arrangement in a 2D or 3D pattern. For example, each observation could be an individual in a company, a unit on a production line, or a different product. Each observation has multiple columns of quantitative data, again with no natural spatial organization. The question is then how to take advantage of enhanced spatial visualization in the StarCAVE to better understand the data.

5.1.2   Data Set

We analyzed a large data set with over 60,000 top-level and 5 billion low-level observations. It provided the hard drive structure of employees' computers at Microsoft over 5 years [27]. This data set gives the topology of the file systems of each computer, including number of files in each directory, parent directory, and children directories if any. For each file, it includes the file type, file size, and various time-stamp information, including creation date, last modification date, and last access date. This data set allowed us to analyze how employees organized, and to a limited extent how they used, their computers.

5.1.3   Related Work

Ware and Mitchell [28] showed that on interactive 3D displays, graphs can be an order of magnitude larger than in 2D and still be read with the same accuracy by users. We employ this idea by displaying the file system hierarchy as a 3D graph and add 6° of freedom navigational interaction and head tracking, far exceeding the rotational effect they used. Our system is based on the idea that large multidimensional databases are best queried by using an interactive visualization tool, as previously discovered by Stolte et al. [29].

A similar approach to our graph layout algorithm was published by Robertson et al., who created cone trees [30] for a similar purpose. Our approach differs in that our graphs are centered around a selected node and grow around it in all directions, more like Lamping et al.'s hyperbolic tree browser [31], but in 3D. Cone trees grow in a linear direction, not utilizing 3D space as equally balanced as our graphs. Our general idea of mapping nonspatial data into a 3D space, however, is not new. Russo Dos Santos et al. [32] did this for cone trees and other visualization metaphors, but their approach does not involve 3D interaction beyond navigation, whereas we support direct interaction with the data as well.

Parker et al. [33] suggested that using direct 3D interaction and 3D widgets can have benefits over more traditional visualization methods. Our system was built with the same motivation, but for a different type of data, and with a very different implementation of visualization methods.

We also implemented box graphs, which map multidimensional data into a lower dimensional space. In this case, we map 6D data into 3D space. This general idea is not new, a good overview of such mappings for 2D was given by Ward [34] in his XmdvTool. Our approach differs in that we map into 3D space instead of 2D. Our box graph is similar to an interactive 3D scatterplot [35,36], but it uses box glyphs instead of points, allowing six dimensions to be displayed for each observation.

5.1.4   Our Visualization System

Queries over more than 60,000 data records are best done by a database. We use a MySQL database with custom indices to allow for real-time queries from the StarCAVE. For the visualization of the directory trees, and their analysis, we created three novel visualization methods: a hyperbolic node graph, a stat box, and a box graph.

5.1.4.1   Hyperbolic Node Graph.   Similar to Lamping et al.'s hyperbolic tree browser [31], we created a 3D tree which at the beginning is centered around the root directory of the selected user's hard disk. Directories are displayed as spheres, with lines connecting parent and children directories. The user can then choose to add another user's directory tree, whose directories will be displayed in a different color than the first user's. Common directories will be displayed in a third color. Even though the data set we had was anonymized, it used consistent hash codes so that we were able to identify common directories and file extensions.

As opposed to a hyperbolic tree, we map our directory nodes onto invisible, concentric, and evenly spaced spheres around the root directory. Since we use a surround visualization system, there is no need to limit the virtual width, as opposed to 2D graphs which cannot extend beyond the edge of the screen or paper they are displayed on.

When the user clicks on a directory node, the graph automatically recenters on this directory. This allows the user to study a particular part of the tree, even one that is deep down in the tree, while still taking advantage of the 3D space around the user to spread out the nodes of interest.

As shown on the screenshot in Fig. 15, a click on a directory node with a different button brings up four wheel graphs, showing information about the file types in the selected directory, as well as in the entire subtree including and below the selected

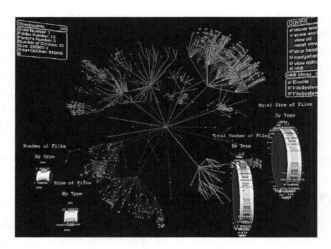

FIG. 15. Screenshot of our 3D hyperbolic graph with node and edge highlighting, as well as wheel graphs and menus.

directory. For each of the above, there is one graph showing the number of files, and one showing the accumulated file size. The wheel graphs are cylinders with bars extending out from the center, the length of the bars indicating file size or number of files of a certain type. We distinguish 11 different file types, based on file extensions: audio, binary, library, text, code, compressed, internet, office, image, video, and other. The user can select between a linear scale and a logarithmic scale for the length of the bars. We find that the wheel graphs occlude less of the scene than traditional bar graphs would, while still conveying the data similarly well. In addition to the wheel graphs, we display a text box which lists file sizes and other information about the selected directory in numeric form. Figure 16 shows what our hyperbolic graph looks like in the StarCAVE.

5.1.4.2 Stat Box.

In order to answer questions about how many of the files on disk were accessed more recently, we created a novel visualization widget, which we call the stat box. The stat box consists of a height field where the last file access date is mapped to the x-axis (starting on left with date of directory scan, older files to the right), the user's directories mapped to the y-axis, and the number of files per directory mapped to the z-axis (height). File age can be selected to be one of the three dates associated with each file: creation date, last modification date, or last access date.

FIG. 16. Hyperbolic graph with wheel graphs in the StarCAVE.

In addition to viewing the stat box as it is, the user can choose to select a certain position on the x-axis to set a boundary for file age. Once the user selects this value, it is visually shown as a translucent plane parallel to the y/z-plane. This plane can be moved along the x-axis with the analog joystick on the 3D input device. Whenever this plane is displayed, all those directories containing files with less than the selected value will be highlighted in the corresponding hyperbolic graph; files with greater values will be dimmed.

5.1.4.3 Box Graph.   The box graph (see Fig. 17) is similar to a scatter plot, but with rectangular boxes instead of points. The boxes are large enough for the user to distinguish differences in shape and color. This graph type allows us to visualize seven dimensions of data records in one graph: three dimensions for the location of the box; three for width, height, and depth of the box; and one for the color. We designed our box graph to map data dimensions to visual parameters as follows. x-axis = file type, y-axis = user bin, z-axis = average file age, width = average number of files per directory, height = number of directories, depth = average file size, color = file type. We map file type both to the x-axis coordinate and box color, so that it is easier to distinguish different rows in the graph from one another. We choose the depth of the boxes to be the average file size, so that the box volume indicates the total number of bytes a user has of the respective

Fɪɢ. 17. Box graph in the StarCAVE.

file type. (Total bytes = number of directories × average number of files per directory × average number of bytes per file.)

Note that we do not draw a box for the file types of individual users, but groups of users. For example, we sort the users of each year's survey by the total number of bytes they store on their hard disk. We then bin a number of users together and map them to one unit on the y-axis. This way we can view the data of an entire year in one graph.

We find that when looking at the box graph in the StarCAVE, we can visualize a much larger amount of data than we can at the desktop. We believe that this is because of the surround nature of the StarCAVE, which allows us to get close to one part of the graph, but still see all the rest of it in the distance. Also, head tracking allows us to "look around" boxes which would otherwise occlude other boxes behind them.

In the menu, the user can interactively scale the box size, or any of the grid coordinate axes to find a good balance between size of the graph and its density. In addition, the user can choose to use a logarithmic scale for these values. The user can also choose to display a striped grid at the bottom of the graph, which helps estimate distance from the viewer. Another option are base lines, which are vertical lines connecting each box to the bottom of the graph. Rulers can be selected to help judge the size of the boxes in each dimension. However, they also considerably impact the frame rate because every box gets a set of lines attached to it.

5.1.5 Conclusions

We created an interactive visualization system for file systems, with the ability to compare many users' file systems to one another and to display up to 6.5 variables simultaneously for each observation. Through a combination of direct interaction with data points and menus for more abstract functionality, we are able to use the system entirely from within our virtual environment, without the need to resort to keyboard and mouse. Our visualization system makes good use of the immersive quality of surround VR systems, as well as direct 3D interaction.

6. Cultural Heritage Visualization

In this section, we describe a project we did with Calit2's cultural heritage researcher Maurizio Seracini. It exemplifies how this science can benefit from modern visualization technology, even if the objects studied are hundreds of years old.

6.1 Walking into a da Vinci Masterpiece

The Adoration of the Magi is an early painting by Leonardo da Vinci 18. Leonardo was given the commission by the Augustinian monks of San Donato a Scopeto in Florence, but departed for Milan the following year, leaving the painting unfinished. It has been in the Uffizi Gallery in Florence since 1670. Three hundred and thirty three years later, in 2003, cultural heritage researcher Maurizio Seracini, sponsored by the Kalpa Group of Loel Guinness, got exclusive access to this masterpiece and took very high-resolution photographs of it under different wave lengths. Under each wave length, he took hundreds of overlapping close-up pictures of the artwork and carefully stitched them together to high-resolution image files with up to $25{,}267 \times 11{,}581$ pixels (~ 292 megapixels; Fig. 18).

In order to display them in our VR environments, we use OpenSceneGraph's terrain rendering engine VirtualPlanetBuilder [37] and treat the images as if they were terrains with an elevation of zero. VirtualPlanetBuilder uses the GDAL [38] library to subdivide the large image into smaller sections, called tiles, and stores these at a number of different resolutions, so that the rendering engine can use mipmapping to render them. This engine is designed to dynamically load the tiles in as needed and automatically select an appropriate mipmap level, while strictly sustaining an interactive frame rate of at least 20 frames per second. The tiled and mipmapped images are created with OpenSceneGraph's osgdem tool [37], which creates .osga files as its output, which encapsulate all tiles and mipmap levels in one

Fig. 18. Leonardo da Vinci: Adoration of the Magi. As seen at Uffizi Gallery, Florence, Italy.

file. The osgdem application is a command line program. A sample call to convert TIFF file Adoration-IR.tif looks like this:

```
osgdem -t Adoration-IR.tif -16
-o Adoration-IR.ive -a Adoration-IR.osga
```

6.1.1 The Application in a 3D Virtual Environment

Our COVISE plugin can load and display multiple such high-resolution spectral image at the same time and still operate at interactive frame rates. Each image can be separately positioned in the 3D world, and the user can click on them to move them around, as seen in Fig. 19A. Alternatively, the user can choose to display the images as a set, which means they will be stacked up and aligned with one another (Fig. 19B). The distance between the images can be adjusted with a dial and can be reduced to practically zero (exactly zero would introduce z-buffer fighting).

If in stack mode the images do not align well, the user can get into manual alignment mode. In this mode, one can place a cone-shaped marker on a feature point which occurs in each spectral image, as seen in Fig. 20. Once all cones are

FIG. 19. Philip Weber at Calit2's stereo display wall, viewing four spectral versions of da Vinci's "The Adoration of the Magi" (visible light, ultraviolet, infrared, X-ray). On the left (A), they are being viewed individually, on the right (B), as a set.

FIG. 20. Philip Weber placing alignment markers on "The Adoration of the Magi."

placed, the images are shifted so that the selected feature points align. With this method, we can only compensate for translational misalignment. Scale, rotation, and potential intraimage warping cannot be compensated for with our system but would be feasible to implement; we simply did not encounter such misalignment with our images.

When the images are all in one plane, the user can switch to a mode in which they can be made translucent, depending on the viewer position, in the following way: the physical space the viewer operates in is subdivided into as many zones as there are images. Each zone corresponds to one of the spectral images and is characterized by its distance from the screen. The software then dynamically adjusts the opacity of the images such that the images which corresponds to the zone the user is in will be displayed fully opaque when the user is in the center of the zone, and it will be more translucent the further the user is away from the center. At the edge of the zone, the image will be at 50% of its opacity, and in the next zone's center, the image will be entirely transparent, making it invisible. This allows the user to select one of the images by adjusting their distance from the screen, while the transitions in between are smooth. In many demonstrations where we let the visitors try out the application, this showed to be a very intuitive way to explore the various spectral images. Figure 21 shows a detail view of the Adoration of the Magi in visible light and infrared.

6.1.2 The Application on a 2D Display with 3D Input

We first created this application for 3D display systems, which make it an immersive experience, especially in free-floating image mode where all spectral images can be moved separately, so that the user can put them side by side to compare them with one another, or even arrange them around the user. However, in stack mode when the user looks at the stack perpendicularly, 3D plays no longer a role, a 2D display system would do just as well at displaying the images.

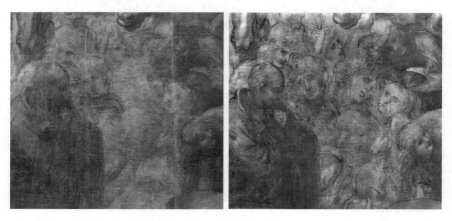

FIG. 21. Detail view of the "Adoration of the Magi" under different spectra of light. Left: visible light. Right: infrared. Images provided by Maurizio Seracini, copyright by Loel Guinness.

This led us to install the application in our auditorium, where it runs on a high-end graphics PC with dual Nvidia Quadro 4500 graphics cards. A 10,000 lumen Sony SRX-R110 projector displays the image on the 32 × 18 ft screen at full 4K resolution of 3840 × 2160 pixels. On the stage, we installed a tethered Ascension Flock of Birds tracking system with a Wanda input device to allow the presenter to interact with the high-resolution painting in real time, using the same 3D input method as in the initially used 3D VR environment. Only now, user and audience do not need to wear glasses, which helps given that the auditorium can hold up to 200 people. Because the auditorium environment requires us to use a fixed viewpoint when rendering the image, given the size of the audience, we do not use head tracking in it. Therefore, the user position cannot be derived from the head position. Instead, we use the wand position as the user position for our fading effect. We adjusted the width of the viewing zones to match the size of the stage, so that the user can "walk into the da Vinci masterpiece." The user can also use the 3D input device to pan the images left/right and up/down by clicking on a point in the painting with the virtual stick, and dragging it into the desired direction. Scaling is implemented by twisting one's hand. Clockwise rotation scales the image up, anticlockwise scales it down. Figure 22 shows a typical demonstration situation with a narrator and a separate system operator.

Fig. 22. "Walking into a da Vinci masterpiece" demonstration on the 4K screen in Calit2's auditorium.

This combination of a 2D display and 3D input has shown to be very effective in demonstrations and motivated us to consider it again for future applications. The main benefit is that the software can be shown to a much larger audience than in, say, the StarCAVE. The 3D input device with its six degrees of freedom allows for a much greater variety of input than a traditional mouse.

7. Conclusion

We presented five software applications developed at Calit2 over the past 5 years, which we consider best practice within five application categories. Each of these applications utilizes the unique features of VR and could not be used equally well at the desktop with keyboard and mouse. We believe that, especially with dropping cost for VR hardware, software will more and more be developed specifically for VR environments, as opposed to first for desktop systems, and then adapted to VR at a later point. This development is going to give researchers, engineers, and consumers powerful software applications to solve their day-to-day problems in new, more intuitive, and more efficient ways. We are excited to be part of this development at this important time when VR is no longer cost prohibitive.

ACKNOWLEDGMENTS

This publication is based in part on work supported by Award No. US 2008-107, made by King Abdullah University of Science and Technology, in particular, the development and construction of the NexCAVE. UCSD, through Calit2, receives major funding from the State of California for the StarCAVE and 4K facilities. UCSD also receives major funding from the National Science Foundation (NSF), award CNS-0821155, which supported the construction of the Calit2 AESOP display, part of the GreenLight Instrument. Other parts of this work have been supported by the National Center for Microscopy and Imaging Research (NCMIR).

REFERENCES

[1] S. Fisher, M. McGreevy, J. Humphries, W. Robinett, Virtual environment display system, in: Proceedings of ACM Workshop on Interactive 3D Graphics, 1986, Chapel Hill, NC.
[2] T. DeFanti, G. Dawe, D. Sandin, J. Schulze, P. Otto, J. Girado, et al., The StarCAVE, a third-generation CAVE and virtual reality OptIPortal, Future Gener. Comput. Syst. 25 (2) (2009) 169–178.
[3] T. DeFanti, D. Acevedo, R. Ainsworth, M. Brown, S. Cutchin, G. Dawe, et al., The Future of the CAVE, Cent. Eur. J. Eng. 1(1), 2011.

[4] D. Rantzau, U. Lang, R. Rühle, Collaborative and interactive visualization in a distributed high performance software environment, in: Proceedings of International Workshop on High Performance Computing for Graphics and Visualization, Swansea, Wales, '96, 1996.

[5] D. Rantzau, K. Frank, U. Lang, D. Rainer, U. Wössner, COVISE in the CUBE: an environment for analyzing large and complex simulation data, in: Proceedings of Second Workshop on Immersive Projection Technology (IPTW '98), Ames, Iowa, 1998.

[6] L. Williams, Pyramidal parametrics, in: ACM SIGGRAPH '83 Proceedings, 1983.

[7] C. Tanner, C. Migdal, M. Jones, The clipmap: a virtual mipmap, in: ACM SIGGRAPH '98 Proceedings, 1998, pp. 151–158.

[8] OpenSceneGraph, Scenegraph based graphics library. http://www.openscenegraph.org, 2004.

[9] E. LaMar, B. Hamann, K. Joy, Multiresolution techniques for interactive texture-based volume visualization, in: IEEE Visualization '99 Proceedings, 1999, pp. 355–361.

[10] P. Bhaniramka, Y. Demange, OpenGL volumizer: a toolkit for high quality volume rendering of large data sets, in: Proceedings of the 2002 IEEE symposium on Volume Visualization and Graphics, 2002.

[11] S. Guthe, M. Wand, J. Gonser, W. Straßer, Interactive rendering of large volume data sets, in: IEEE Visualization '02 Proceedings, 2002, pp. 53–60.

[12] M. Weiler, R. Westermann, C. Hansen, K. Zimmermann, T. Ertl, Level-of-detail volume rendering via 3D textures, in: IEEE Volume Visualization 2000 Proceedings, 2000.

[13] I. Boada, I. Navazo, R. Scopigno, Multiresolution volume visualization with a texture-based octree, Vis. Comput. 3 (17) (2001) 185–197.

[14] S. Prohaska, A. Hutanu, R. Kahler, H.-C. Hege, Interactive exploration of large remote micro-CT scans, in: Proceedings of IEEE Visualization, 2004, pp. 345–352.

[15] Lawrence Livermore National Laboratory, Blockbuster, high-resolution movie player. https://computing.llnl.gov/vis/blockbuster.shtml, 2009.

[16] R. Stockli, E. Vermote, N. Saleous, R. Simmon, D. Herring, The Blue Marble Next Generation—a true color Earth dataset including seasonal dynamics from MODIS, Technical Report, NASA Earth Observatory, October 2005.

[17] R. Sutton, A. Barto, Reinforcement Learning: An Introduction, MIT Press, Cambridge, MA, 1998.

[18] PDB, Protein Data Bank. http://www.pdb.org, 2010.

[19] W. DeLano, The PyMol Molecular Graphics System, DeLano Scientific, San Carlos, CA, 2002. http://www.pymol.org.

[20] D. Lupyan, A. Leo-Macias, A. Ortiz, A new progressive-iterative algorithm for multiple structure alignment, Bioinformatics 21 (15) (2005) 3255–3263, Oxford University Press.

[21] P. Greenlight, Home Page. http://greenlight.calit2.net, 2010.

[22] Oracle, Sun Modular Data Center. http://www.sun.com/service/sunmd/, 2010.

[23] J. Schulze, Advanced monitoring techniques for data centers using virtual reality. SMPTE Motion Imaging Journal, ISSN 0036-1682, July/August, 2010.

[24] C. Farcas, F. Seracini, GLIMPSE Home Page. http://glimpse.calit2.net.

[25] N. G. 480, High-end graphics card. URL: http://www.nvidia.com/object/product_geforce_gtx_480_us.html, 2010.

[26] M. Tavanti, M. Lind, 2D vs. 3D, implications on spatial memory, in: Proceedings of IEEE Symposium on Information Visualization, 2001, pp. 139–145.

[27] N. Agrawal, W. Bolosky, J. Douceur, J. Lorch, A five-year study of file-system metadata, ACM Trans. Storage 3 (3) (2007) 9:1–9:32. http://research.microsoft.com/apps/pubs/?id=72885.

[28] C. Ware, P. Mitchell, Reevaluating stereo and motion cues for visualizing graphs in three dimensions, in: Proceedings of Applied Perception in Graphics and Visualization, 2005, pp. 51–58, Vol. 95.

[29] C. Stolte, D. Tang, P. Hanrahan, Polaris: a system for query, analysis, and visualization of multidimensional relational databases, IEEE Trans. Vis. Comput. Graph. 8 (1) (2002) 52–65.

[30] G. Robertson, J. Mackinlay, S. Card, Cone trees: animated 3D visualizations of hierarchical information, in: Proceedings of the SIGCHI Conference CHI'91, 1991, pp. 189–194.

[31] J. Lamping, R. Rao, P. Pirolli, A focus+context technique based on hyperbolic geometry for visualizing large hierarchies, in: ACM SIGCHI Proceedings, 1995, pp. 401–408.

[32] C.R.D. Santos, P. Gros, P. Abel, D. Loisel, N. Trichaud, J. Paris, Mapping Information onto 3D Virtual Worlds, in: International Conference on Information Visualisation, 2000, pp. 379–386.

[33] G. Parker, G. Franck, C. Ware, Visualization of large nested graphs in 3D: navigation and interaction, J. Vis. Lang. Comput. 9 (1998) 299–317.

[34] M. Ward, XmdvTool: integrating multiple methods for visualizing multivariate data, in: IEEE Visualization Proceedings, 1994, pp. 326–333.

[35] B. Becker, Volume rendering for relational data, in: IEEE Symposium on Information Visualization, 1997, pp. 87–90.

[36] R. Kosara, G. Sahling, H. Hauser, Linking scientific and information visualization with interactive 3D scatterplots, in: Proceedings of WSCG, Plzen, Czech Republic, 2004.

[37] VirtualPlanetBuilder, Terrain Database Creation Tool. http://www.openscenegraph.org/projects/VirtualPlanetBuilder, 2010.

[38] GDAL, Geospatial Data Abstraction Library. http://www.gdal.org, 2010.

[39] osgdem, OpenSceneGraph's utility program for reading geospatial imagery and digital elevation maps. http://www.openscenegraph.org/projects/osg/wiki/Support/UserGuides/osgdem, 2010.

Author Index

Subject Index

A

Advanced configuration and power interface (ACPI), 69–70
AESOP wall, 219–220, 222
Agent migration itinerary plan
  dynamic MA itinerary, 129–130
  gateway/autonomously, WSN, 128
  hybrid MA itinerary, 129–130
  static MA itinerary, 129
Amino acid sequence browser, 239

B

Broadcast camera image characteristics.
  See also TV production system
  black and white levels, 178
  chrominance sampling, 177–178
  gamma, 178–180
  integration time, 175
  sampling and aspect ratio, 175–177
Business intelligence (BI). *See also*
  Information markets
  capability, 247
  information markets, 2–3

C

Camera and lens, 171–174
Camera tracking system, 181–184, 209–211
Chroma-key background, 192–196
Cloud computing systems
  data center level (*see* Data center level)
  hardware and firmware level

    dynamic component deactivation, 65–67
    dynamic performance scaling, 67–69
    high energy consumption, 60–61
    high power consumption problems, 58–60
    operating system level, 70–77
    power and energy models, 52–57
    power/energy management taxonomy, 61–65
    virtualization level, 77–81
Code-centric RFID system
  design issues, CRS, 154–155
  system architecture, 152–153
  system rationale, 151–152
  updating mobile codes, 153–154
Code updating methods, 153–154
COVISE, 239
Cultural heritage visualization, da Vinci masterpiece
  2D display with 3D input, 256–258
  3D virtual environment, 254–256

D

Data center level, power management
  characteristics, 81, 83–84
  cloud computing, implications of, 82, 85
  GreenCloud, 99–100
  multitiered on-demand resource scheduling, 95–96
  non-virtualized systems
    clusters, power and performance, 85–86
    energy-aware consolidation, 88–89

Contents of Volumes in This Series

277